The Trustee Act, 1893 : and other recent statutes relating to trustees : with notes.

F. G. Champernowne

The Making of Modern Law collection of legal archives constitutes a genuine revolution in historical legal research because it opens up a wealth of rare and previously inaccessible sources in legal, constitutional, administrative, political, cultural, intellectual, and social history. This unique collection consists of three extensive archives that provide insight into more than 300 years of American and British history. These collections include:

Legal Treatises, 1800-1926: over 20,000 legal treatises provide a comprehensive collection in legal history, business and economics, politics and government.

Trials, 1600-1926: nearly 10,000 titles reveal the drama of famous, infamous, and obscure courtroom cases in America and the British Empire across three centuries.

Primary Sources, 1620-1926: includes reports, statutes and regulations in American history, including early state codes, municipal ordinances, constitutional conventions and compilations, and law dictionaries.

These archives provide a unique research tool for tracking the development of our modern legal system and how it has affected our culture, government, business – nearly every aspect of our everyday life. For the first time, these high-quality digital scans of original works are available via print-on-demand, making them readily accessible to libraries, students, independent scholars, and readers of all ages.

old books. new life.

The BiblioLife Network

This project was made possible in part by the BiblioLife Network (BLN), a project aimed at addressing some of the huge challenges facing book preservationists around the world. The BLN includes libraries, library networks, archives, subject matter experts, online communities and library service providers. We believe every book ever published should be available as a high-quality print reproduction; printed on-demand anywhere in the world. This insures the ongoing accessibility of the content and helps generate sustainable revenue for the libraries and organizations that work to preserve these important materials.

The following book is in the "public domain" and represents an authentic reproduction of the text as printed by the original publisher. While we have attempted to accurately maintain the integrity of the original work, there are sometimes problems with the original work or the micro-film from which the books were digitized. This can result in minor errors in reproduction. Possible imperfections include missing and blurred pages, poor pictures, markings and other reproduction issues beyond our control. Because this work is culturally important, we have made it available as part of our commitment to protecting, preserving, and promoting the world's literature.

GUIDE TO FOLD-OUTS MAPS and OVERSIZED IMAGES

The book you are reading was digitized from microfilm captured over the past thirty to forty years. Years after the creation of the original microfilm, the book was converted to digital files and made available in an online database.

In an online database, page images do not need to conform to the size restrictions found in a printed book. When converting these images back into a printed bound book, the page sizes are standardized in ways that maintain the detail of the original. For large images, such as fold-out maps, the original page image is split into two or more pages

Guidelines used to determine how to split the page image follows:

• Some images are split vertically; large images require vertical and horizontal splits.
• For horizontal splits, the content is split left to right.
• For vertical splits, the content is split from top to bottom.
• For both vertical and horizontal splits, the image is processed from top left to bottom right.

THE TRUSTEE ACT, 1893.

THE TRUSTEE ACT, 1893,

AND OTHER

RECENT STATUTES RELATING TO TRUSTEES.

WITH NOTES.

BY

F. G. CHAMPERNOWNE, B.A.,

OF LINCOLN'S INN, BARRISTER-AT-LAW,

AND

HENRY JOHNSTON,

OF LINCOLN'S INN, BARRISTER-AT-LAW.

LONDON:

WILLIAM CLOWES AND SONS, LIMITED,

7, FLEET STREET.

1904.

PRINTED BY
WILLIAM CLOWES AND SONS, LIMITED,
LONDON AND BECCLES

PREFACE.

It is to be regretted that the Trustee Act, 1893, should be so framed that, in construing its provisions, only those already well acquainted with its contents, and with the general law of trusts, can safely dispense with the assistance of elaborate annotation.

Many of the difficulties discussed in the present volume arose under the earlier Acts replaced by the Act of 1893, and have been the subject of much judicial comment. For the existence of others the present Act is alone responsible.

Of difficulties not yet covered by authority the following are instances: the use of the word "trustee" (pp. 19, 50, and 77), and of the expressions "leased in perpetuity" (p. 24) and "municipal borough" (p. 26); the tangled enactments as to investments in Isle of Man and Local Loans Stocks (pp. 31 and 39); and the questions how far section 22 affects the old doctrines as to survivorship of powers (pp. 87, 88) and how far a beneficiary's interest may be impounded under section 45 (p. 154).

In the notes to section 16 (p. 72) recent legislation and decisions on the capacity of a married woman trustee to convey land are discussed. It is to be hoped that during the present Session a Bill, already prepared, may become law, and render all such discussion obsolete.

Some general rules for the guidance of trustees in selecting mortgage securities will be found on pp. 20 and 21. The authorities upon which those rules are based are discussed in Appendix A, pp. 225–234.

The jurisdiction to make vesting orders became of diminished importance on the passing of section 30 of the Conveyancing and Law of Property Act, 1881, but is still far from obsolete. Great pains have been taken to classify the decisions dealing with this subject.

Included in the volume are the Trustee Act, 1888, the Amending Act of 1894, the Judicial Trustees Act, 1896, the Colonial Stock Act, 1900, the Trustee Act Rules, 1893 (O. 54A), and the Judicial Trustee Rules.

The authors originally intended to add an appendix containing a complete list of the securities authorised as investments by section 1 of the Trustee Act, 1893. They found, however, that besides entailing much additional labour, the adoption of such a course would unduly increase the size of the volume. They were glad, therefore, to avail themselves of the offer of their friend, Mr. Herbert Ellissen, of the Inner Temple and of the Stock Exchange, to publish such a list, uniform with and supplemental to the present work. Mr. Ellissen's supplemental volume is now in the press, and numerous references to it will be found in the present volume.

For convenience of reference, the text of the Trustee Act, 1893, is printed without notes in Appendix B.

LINCOLN'S INN,
May, 1904.

CONTENTS.

Purchase and Sale.

Various Powers and Liabilities.

PART III.

POWERS OF THE COURT.

Appointment of New Trustees and Vesting Orders.

Payment into Court by Trustees.

Miscellaneous

PART IV,

MISCELLANEOUS AND SUPPLEMENTAL.

TRUSTEE ACT, 1893, AMENDMENT ACT, 1894.

(57 VICT. c. 10)

JUDICIAL TRUSTEES ACT, 1896.

(59 & 60 VICT. c. 35.)

COLONIAL STOCK ACT, 1900.

(63 & 64 VICT. c. 62.)

TABLE OF CASES.

A.

B.

G.

H.

c

TABLE OF STATUTES.

THE TRUSTEE ACT, 1893,

AND OTHER RECENT STATUTES
RELATING TO TRUSTEES.

INTRODUCTION.

THE Trustee Act, 1893, attempts no codification of the law
relating to trustees. The title, "An Act to consolidate Enactments relating to Trustees," is a sufficient indication that
the Act differs widely in extent from such measures as the
Bills of Exchange Act, 1882, the Partnership Act, 1890, and
the Sale of Goods Act, 1893, which are respectively intituled,
"An Act to codify the Law relating to Bills of Exchange"; "An
Act to declare and amend the Law of Partnership"; and "An
Act for codifying the Law relating to the Sale of Goods"

The distinction is one of considerable importance. In construing a statute intended to be a code, the proper course is,
in the first instance, to examine the language of the statute,
and to ask what is its natural meaning, uninfluenced by any
considerations derived from the previous state of the law: *per*
Lord Herschell, in *Bank of England* v. *Vagliano* (1891) A.C. 144.
In the case of a measure which is not a code, but is merely a
consolidating Act, the mode of construction is entirely different.
Knowledge of the previously existing law as established by
statutory enactments and reported decisions is, in this case,
essential, *Mitchell* v. *Simpson*, 25 Q.B.D. 183, *re Budgett* (1894)
2 Ch. 557, and will often make it clear that the true meaning
of the Act is not what otherwise might have been inferred
merely from its wording.*

---

* The following canons for the construction of statutes in general were
laid down in *Heydon's Case* (3 Co. Rep. at p. 7 *b*).—

"For the sure and true interpretation of all statutes in general (be
they penal or beneficial, restrictive or enlarging of the common law) four
things are to be discerned and considered—

"(1) What was the common law before the making of the Act?

"(2) What was the mischief and defect for which the common law
did not provide?

The Act of 1893 contemplates little more than the collection in one statute of provisions relating to trustees, formerly contained in many scattered Acts. Nor is the collection complete, for sections 1 and 8 of the Trustee Act, 1888, have not been incorporated in the Act.

In collecting the various statutory enactments, some attempt at classification has been made, and the Act is divided into four parts, named, "I Investments," "II. Various Powers and Duties of Trustees," "III Powers of the Court," and "IV. Miscellaneous and Supplemental." This classification appears to be due to the accident of the grouping of the various provisions in the earlier Acts rather than to any consideration of logical sequence or practical convenience.

For example, it might be expected that the sections dealing with the powers of trustees to invest upon mortgage, to sell by auction, and to sell mines apart from the surface, would have been found in the same part of the Act. But, in fact, the first is contained in Part I., the second in Part II., and the third in Part III. Section 8 subsection 3, and section 15, each of which makes provision as to the title which a trustee purchasing land should require, are contained, the former in Part I., and the latter in Part II. Section 25, dealing with the appointment of new trustees by the Court, is contained in Part III.; section 10, dealing with appointments by individuals, is contained in Part II.; and section 47, applying those provisions to the case of Settled Land Act trustees, is contained in Part IV. Sections 40 and 49, each of which contains provisions as to the validity of vesting orders, are contained, the former in Part III., and the latter in Part IV. of the Act. Again, the section of the Act of 1893, headed "Liability for loss by reason of improper investments," is contained in Part I. of the Act; the section headed "Implied indemnity of trustees" is contained in Part II.; the section headed "Power to make beneficiary indemnify for breach of trust" is contained in Part III.; and the section headed "Indemnity" is contained in Part IV; while the section of the Trustee Act, 1888, headed "Statute of limitations may be pleaded by trustees," is left unrepealed, and finds no place in the Act of 1893.

Since each section of the Act must be considered in the

"(3) What remedy the Parliament hath resolved and appointed to cure the disease of the commonwealth? and

"(4) The true reason of the remedy?

And then the office of all the judges is always to make such construction as shall suppress the mischief and advance the remedy, and to suppress subtle inventions and evasions for continuance of the mischief and *pro privato commodo*, and to add force and life to the cure and remedy, according to the true intent of the makers of the Act, *pro bono publico*."

See also *Magdalen College Case*, 11 Co. Rep. p. 73 *b*; *re Bethlem Hospital*, 19 Eq. 458; *Cope* v. *Doherty*, 4 K. & J. at p. 374; *Phillips* v. *Rees*, 24 Q.B.D at p. 20; *Pelton* v. *Harrison* (1891) 2 Q.B. 422; *River Wear Commissioners* v. *Adamson*, 2 A.C. 743.

light of previous decisions, and since their capricious grouping obscures the relation of one section to another, the Act has done little to simplify the task of those consulting the statutory provisions relating to trustees. The continued existence of sections 1 and 8 of the Act of 1888, and the passing of the subsequent Acts of 1894, 1896, and 1900, still further add to the difficulty of the subject.

TRUSTEE ACT, 1888.

51 & 52 Vict. c. 59.

An Act to amend the Law relating to the Duties, Powers, and Liability of Trustees.
[24th December, 1888.]

The whole of this Act, except sections 1 and 8, is repealed by the Act of 1893; see section 51 of 1893 Act and Schedule, *post*, pp. 170, 172.

Be it enacted by the Queen's most Excellent Majesty, by and with the advice and consent of the Lords Spiritual and Temporal, and Commons, in this present Parliament assembled, and by the authority of the same, as follows; that is to say—

Sect. 1.
———
Short title, extent, and definition.

Section 1.—(1.) This Act may be cited as the Trustee Act, 1888.

(2.) This Act shall not extend to Scotland.

(3.) For the purposes of this Act the expression "trustee" shall be deemed to include an executor or administrator and a trustee whose trust arises by construction or implication of law as well as an express trustee, but not the official trustee of charitable funds.

(4.) The provisions of this Act relating to a trustee shall apply as well to several joint trustees as to a sole trustee.

Subsection 2.—See the notes to section 52 of the Trustee Act, 1893, *post*, p. 171; and see also notes at pp. 21, 178, 190.

Subsection 3.—Cf. section 50 of the Trustee Act, 1893, *post*, p. 163; and see notes on the definition in that section of "trustee." On the question who is a trustee within the meaning of section 8 of this Act, see *infra*, p. 6.

Subsection 4.—See *post*, pp. 7, 10.

Section 8.—(1.) In any action or other proceeding against a trustee or any person claiming through him, except where the claim is founded upon any fraud or fraudulent breach of trust to which the trustee was party or privy, or is to recover trust property, or the proceeds thereof still retained by the trustee, or previously received by the trustee and converted to his use, the following provisions shall apply :—

> (*a*) All rights and privileges conferred by any statute of limitations shall be enjoyed in the like manner and to the like extent as they would have been enjoyed in such action or other proceeding if the trustee or person claiming through him had not been a trustee or person claiming through him.

> (*b*) If the action or other proceeding is brought to recover money or other property, and is one to which no existing statute of limitations applies, the trustee or person claiming through him shall be entitled to the benefit of and be at liberty to plead the lapse of time as a bar to such action or other proceeding in the like manner and to the like extent as if the claim had been against him in an action of debt for money had and received, but so nevertheless that the statute shall run against a married woman entitled in possession for her separate use, whether with or without a restraint upon anticipation, but shall not begin to run against any beneficiary unless and until the interest of such beneficiary shall be an interest in possession.

(2.) No beneficiary, as against whom there would be a good defence by virtue of this section, shall derive any greater or other benefit from a judgment or order obtained by another beneficiary than he could have obtained if he had brought such action or other proceeding and this section had been pleaded.

(3.) This section shall apply only to actions or other proceedings commenced after the first day of January one thousand eight hundred and ninety, and shall not deprive any executor or administrator of any right or defence to which he is entitled under any existing statute of limitations.

"Action or other Proceeding against a Trustee."—It has been said (re *Chapman* (1896) 1 Ch. at p. 326) that a summons by one trustee to ascertain the liability of the trustees in respect of a breach of trust is not a proceeding "against a trustee." It is submitted that any proceeding in which the liability of the trustee could be declared or enforced is a proceeding against the trustee for the purposes of the section.

In the case of *re Cornish* (1896) 1 Q. B. 99, there is a *dictum* of Esher, M.R., to the effect that the section only applies when a claim is made upon a trustee for the payment of money, and not to a claim for an account for the purpose of showing whether any further claim can be made upon him. The point was not necessary for decision, and the *dictum* is inconsistent with *re Page* (1893) 1 Ch. 304, in which North, J., held that the Act applied to a summons asking for the usual accounts in an administration action, dissenting from the argument addressed to him, that the Act was not intended to relieve trustees from the necessity of accounting to their *cestuis que trust*, and that it could only be used as a bar to an application for payment. See also *How* v. *Earl Winterton* (1896) 2 Ch. 626.

"Trustee."—See definition in section 1, *supra*. Directors of a company are trustees for the company of assets which have come into their hands, or which are under their control *Kingston Cotton Mill Co.* (1896) 1 Ch 331, at p. 347; *Forest of Dean Coal Co*, 10 C.D. 450; *Percival* v. *Wright* (1902) 2 Ch. 421. In respect of dealings with such assets they are trustees within the meaning of this section. *Lands Allotment Co.* (1894) 1 Ch 616 (*ultra vires* investment); *National Bank of Wales, Ltd.* (1899) 2 Ch. 629, at p. 663 (dividends paid out of capital); S.C. sub. nom. *Dovey* v. *Cory* (1901) A. C. 477, at p. 489; *Whitwam* v. *Watkin*, 78 L.T. 188 (*ultra vires* purchase).

A husband who takes possession of his wife's separate estate is a trustee for her, *Wassell* v. *Leggatt* (1896) 1 Ch. 554, in the absence of clear evidence of a gift, *re Flamank*, 40 C.D. 461.

The section does not apply to a trustee in bankruptcy called on to render accounts to the Board of Trade. *Re Cornish* (1896) 1 Q.B. 99.

Mortgagees who have sold under a power of sale are trustees within the section, of the surplus proceeds. *Thorne* v. *Heard* (1894) 1 Ch. 599; see p. 607; S.C. (1895) A.C. 498.

As to executors, see *infra*, p. 10, 11.

"Any Person claiming through him."—These words mean,

not his *cestuis que trust*, but his executors, administrators, or assigns. *Leahy* v. *de Moleyns* (1896) 1 I.R. 206.

"**Except where the Claim is founded upon any Fraud**," etc. —The fraud must be that of, or be in some way imputable to, the person who invokes the aid of the statute, *Thorne* v. *Heard* (1895) A.C. 495.

In order to charge any person with a fraud which has not been personally committed by him, the agent who has committed the fraud must have committed it while acting within the scope of his authority, while doing something and purporting to do something on behalf of the principal. *Thorne* v. *Heard, supra.*

"**To which the Trustee was Party or Privy.**"—It is only by a misuse of language that a person who, in fact, knows nothing of the fraudulent conduct of another, and who in no way benefits by it or ratifies it, can be said to be party or privy to it. One person may be, and often is, liable in law for frauds which he has not committed, but to say that he is party or privy to them is quite another matter, and is only true when he has personally participated in them : *per* Lindley, L.J., *Thorne* v. *Heard* (1894) 1 Ch., at p. 606. The words indicate moral complicity: *per* Kay, L.J., *ibid.,* at p. 608. See also S.C. (1895) A.C. 495.

"**Or is to recover Trust Property . . . still retained.**"—The word "still" refers to the commencement of the action or other proceeding in which the question arises. *Thorne* v. *Heard* (1894) 1 Ch. 599; (1895) A.C. 495.

A trustee may be liable to make good trust money as if it were still in his hands, although he has, in fact, parted with it. (Cf. cases referred to in notes to section 9 of the Trustee Act, 1893, *post*, p. 47.) But in construing this statute the exception is confined to cases in which, at the commencement of the action or other proceeding, the trustee actually has in his hands or under his control the trust property or the proceeds thereof sought to be recovered. *Thorne* v. *Heard, supra.* If it is lost either by the trustee's negligence or unauthorised dealing with it, the exception does not apply. *Ibid., How* v. *Lord Winterton* (1896) 2 Ch. 626; *re Timmis* (1902) 1 Ch. 176.

The exception does not apply to a case where a trustee retains a share of the trust estate, other than the share in respect of which a breach of trust has been committed. *Re Timmis* (1902) 1 Ch. 176.

"**Previously received . . . and converted to his Use.**"—This exception probably applies to the case of money entrusted to a firm as trustees and converted to the use of the firm, although the member of the firm sued had neither received the money nor converted it to his own use; for under section 1 the provisions of the Act apply as well to several joint trustees as to a sole trustee. See *Moore* v. *Knight* (1891) 1 Ch. 547, at p 553. These words mean money which the trustee can be called upon to refund. Thus, where trustees lend trust money on improper security to a person who is indebted to one of the trustees, and out of the money so raised on mortgage the debt to the trustee is discharged, the transaction, if honest, is not a conversion to his own use by the trustee. *Re Gurney* (1893) 1 Ch. 590.

Subsection 1 (a).—The meaning of this subsection has been the subject of much discussion. In *re Bowden*, 45 C D. 444, Fry, L.J. (sitting as an additional judge of first instance), said, with reference to this clause, "If a person had not been a trustee, he could not be sued for a breach of trust; and there is no right or privilege that I am aware of conferred by any statute of limitations in respect of a breach of trust." With reference to this remark, Lindley, L J., in *How* v. *Earl Winterton* (1896) 2 Ch. 626, observed, that to exclude the operation of clause (a) in all cases on the short ground stated by Fry, L J., would be to deprive clause (a) of all meaning whatever.

Rigby, L.J, explained clause (a) as follows.—The clause assumes there is a right of action against the trustee. That must be founded upon some act or omission of his which would be, from the fact of his being a trustee, a breach of trust. Clause (a) has to do with remedies only, not with causes of action. A trustee who undertakes a trust agrees to perform that trust, discard the idea of breach of trust, he is still guilty of breach of duty, and for the purposes of clause (a) he is to be treated as though the breach of trust were nothing more or less than a breach of duty by reason of some act or omission of his. The duty may be thrown on him by virtue of his simple contract to undertake the trust, or by reason of his covenant to undertake it, as where the duty is thrown on him by a deed. Then you must look to the appropriate Act of Limitations to ascertain the period for the running of the statute. *How* v. *Earl Winterton, supra.* No covenant by a trustee is implied merely from his executing a deed containing an appointment of him as trustee, and a declaration by him that he accepts the office. *Holland* v. *Holland*, 4 Ch. 449. It is a question of intention of the parties whether a deed should operate as a covenant or not. *Isaacson* v. *Harwood*, 3 Ch. 225.

Where the trustee has not covenanted to perform the trust, the period of limitation for an action on an implied promise, or an action on the case for breach of duty, or an action for an account, is six years. See *per* Lindley, L.J., *How* v. *Earl Winterton, supra*, at p. 639 If the form of trust instrument is a covenant by the trustee to hold the trust property on specified trusts for specified persons, it is conceived that (if the construction suggested by Rigby, L.J., *supra*, be the correct one) the period of limitation for breach of trust would be twenty years. It would seem, therefore, that unless the trustee have covenanted to perform the trusts, the period of limitation will be the same whether clause (a) or clause (b) apply.

The form of order for an account by trustees entitled to the benefit of the section will be found in *re Davies* (1898) 2 Ch. 142.

Subsection 1 (b). "Brought to recover Money."—These words are satisfied if the action is to make the trustee pay money into a fund against which the applicant has a claim, *How* v. *Earl Winterton* (1896) 2 Ch. 626, at p. 642, or for accounts preliminary to an application for payment of money (*supra*, p. 6).

"And is one to which no Existing Statute applies."—The following cases have been held to fall within this clause, viz. action by newly appointed trustee against old trustees to make good losses from improper investments, *re Bowden*, 45 C.D. 444; the like action by a beneficiary, *re Gurney* (1893) 1 Ch. 590; *re Somerset* (1894) 1 Ch. 231; *Mara* v. *Browne* (1895) 2 Ch. 69; action by beneficiary to make good losses from failure to carry out trust for conversion, *re Swain* (1891) 3 Ch. 233; action by beneficiary for administration where the whole estate had been disposed of upwards of six years previously, *re Page* (1893) 1 Ch. 304; action by reversioners where capital of the trust fund had been paid to the tenant for life, *re Timmis* (1902) 1 Ch. 74, but see the construction put upon the section by Rigby, L J., in *How* v *Earl Winterton*, *supra* (*ante*, p 8), under which some of the above cases would appear to fall under clause (*a*).

"An Action of Debt for Money had and received."—Under section 3 of 21 Jac. 1, c 16 (Limitation Act, 1623), the period of limitation is six years after the cause of action arose. See *How* v. *Earl Winterton* (1896) 2 Ch. 626, *re Somerset* (1894) 1 Ch. 231, at p. 255; *re Timmis* (1902) 1 Ch. 176. This is, however, subject to 9 Geo. IV., c. 121 (the Statute of Frauds Amendment Act, 1828), which provides for cases being taken out of the statute by acknowledgment in writing, part payment of principal, or payment of interest. Payment of interest direct by the mortgagee to the tenant for life (which amounts to payment by the mortgagee to the trustees, and by the trustees to the tenant for life) is not an admission or acknowledgment sufficient to take the case out of the statute. *Re Somerset* (1894) 1 Ch 231; *Mara* v. *Browne* (1895) 2 Ch. 69, at p. 95

"Shall not begin to run . . . unless and until the Interest . . . shall be an Interest in Possession."—Where a beneficiary takes successive interests, *e.g.*, first a life interest to a married woman during the joint lives of herself and her husband, and secondly a life interest on her husband's death, although in respect of her first interest her rights may be barred, in respect of her second interest her rights will only be barred after the expiration of the statutory period commencing from the coming into possession of such second interest. *Mara* v. *Browne* (1895) 2 Ch. 69, at p. 95. The judgment on this point was not reversed on appeal. See S.C. (1896) 1 Ch. 199. The section has in no way altered the principles which determine the time at which a cause of action arises. *Thorne* v. *Heard* (1894) 1 Ch. 599; *Moore* v. *Knight* (1891) 1 Ch 547. In the case of a breach of trust, a cause of action founded upon it accrues to the *cestuis que trust* upon the commission of the breach, and not from its discovery, nor from the time when the loss occurs. *Re Swain* (1891) 3 Ch. 233; *Thorne* v. *Heard, supra; Howell* v. *Young*, 5 B. & C. 259; *Smith* v. *Fox*, 6 Hare 386; see *Thomson* v. *Lord Clanmorris* (1900) 1 Ch. at p. 726. So, where trustees committed an innocent breach of trust by investing on mortgage of property of insufficient value, time ran against the beneficiary entitled in possession from the time when the investment was made. *Re Somerset* (1894) 1 Ch. 231.

Where an annuity was charged upon a fund composed in part of accumulations of rents of certain property during a term preceding the commencement of the annuity, and in breach of trust the trustee neglected to make the accumulations, time ran against the annuitant from the date at which the annuity commenced. *How* v. *Earl Winterton* (1896) 2 Ch. 626, at p. 637

Notwithstanding that an action is not barred under this section, the plaintiff may still be refused relief on the ground of laches; *e g.*, although time does not run against a beneficiary until his interest is in possession, he may be barred, if the circumstances are such as to show that he was guilty of laches in not suing while his interest was in expectancy. *Re Taylor, Atkinson* v. *Lord*, 81 L.T. 812; and see *Roberts* v. *Tunstall*, 4 Hare 257.

It has been suggested that where a fraudulent breach of trust is committed by one of several trustees, time may not run in favour of his innocent co-trustees until discovery of the fraud: *per* Stirling, J., in *Moore* v. *Knight* (1891) 1 Ch. 547, at p. 555. It is submitted, however, that as the claim against the innocent co-trustee is not founded on fraud as against him, time runs from the commission of the breach of trust.

Where one trustee claims contribution from a co-trustee in respect of a liability incurred from loss occasioned by their joint default, time does not begin to run till the date of the judgment establishing the liability of the trustee seeking contribution. *Robinson* v. *Harkin* (1896) 2 Ch. 415.

Subsection 3. "Shall not deprive any Executor or Administrator of any Right or Defence to which he is entitled under any Existing Statute of Limitations."—Under section 8 of the Real Property Limitation Act, 1874, no action or other proceeding can be brought to recover any legacy, but within twelve years next after a present right to receive the same shall have accrued to some person capable of giving a discharge for the same, if no principal or interest shall have been paid or acknowledgment in writing given.

Under that Act, the executor, notwithstanding that he is constructively a trustee, *re Davis* (1891) 3 Ch. 119; *re Lacy* (1899) 2 Ch. 149, has a defence, although the legacy is still retained by the executor, or previously received by him and converted to his use—circumstances which would preclude him from relying on the present section.

On the other hand, it may be necessary for a defendant to show that the present section applies, rather than section 8 of the Act of 1874, so that he may be in a position to rely on subsection 1 (*b*). Thus, where a residue is given to persons who are named both executors and trustees, and a breach of trust is committed, the question arises whether the trustees and executors are liable, *quâ* executors, for not distributing the residue, or as trustees for breach of trust. If the executors and trustees had been different persons, the duties of the executors would have been to pay the debts, legacies, and funeral and testamentary expenses of the testator, and pay the residue to the trustees. Hence, when the executors and trustees are the same person, they cease to hold the assets, *quâ* executors, when they have paid the debts, legacies, and expenses, and thereupon become trustees; and where they wrongfully deal with the residue they are liable as trustees, and an action against them is one "to which no existing statute of limitations applies." They are not to be treated as executors sued for a legacy within section 8 of the Act of 1874. *Re Timms* (1902) 1 Ch. 176; *re Swain* (1891) 3 Ch. 233; *re Page* (1893) 1 Ch. 304.

TRUSTEE ACT, 1893.

56 & 57 VICT. c. 53.

An Act to consolidate Enactments relating to Trustees.
[22nd September, 1893.]

"To consolidate."—As to the distinction between a consolidating Act and a Code, see Introduction, *ante*, p. 1.

BE it enacted by the Queen's most Excellent Majesty, by and with the advice and consent of the Lords Spiritual and Temporal, and Commons, in this present Parliament assembled, and by the authority of the same, as follows :—

PART I.

INVESTMENTS.

Sect. 1.
——————
Authorised
investments.

Section 1.—A trustee may, unless expressly forbidden by the instrument (if any) creating the trust, invest any trust funds in his hands, whether at the time in a state of investment or not, in manner following, that is to say :

(*a*) In any of the parliamentary stocks or public funds or Government securities of the United Kingdom :

(*b*) On real or heritable securities in Great Britain or Ireland :

(*c*) In the stock of the Bank of England or the Bank of Ireland :

(*d*) In India three and a half per cent. stock and India three per cent. stock, or in any other capital stock which may at any time hereafter be issued by the Secretary of

State in Council of India under the authority of Act of Parliament, and charged on the revenues of India:

(e) In any securities the interest of which is for the time being guaranteed by Parliament:

(f) In consolidated stock created by the Metropolitan Board of Works, or by the London County Council, or in debenture stock created by the Receiver for the Metropolitan Police District:

(g) In the debenture or rentcharge, or guaranteed or preference stock of any railway company in Great Britain or Ireland incorporated by special Act of Parliament, and having during each of the ten years last past before the date of investment paid a dividend at the rate of not less than three per centum per annum on its ordinary stock:

(h) In the stock of any railway or canal company in Great Britain or Ireland whose undertaking is leased in perpetuity or for a term of not less than two hundred years at a fixed rental to any such railway company as is mentioned in subsection (g), either alone or jointly with any other railway company:

(i) In the debenture stock of any railway company in India the interest on which is paid or guaranteed by the Secretary of State in Council of India:

(j) In the "B" annuities of the Eastern Bengal, the East Indian, and the Scinde Punjaub and Delhi Railways, and any like annuities which may at any time hereafter be created on the purchase of any other railway by the Secretary of State in Council of India, and charged on the revenues of India, and which may be authorised by Act of Parliament to be accepted by trustees in lieu of any stock held by them in the purchased railway; also in deferred annuities comprised in the register of holders of annuity Class D. and annuities comprised in the register of annuitants Class C. of the East Indian Railway Company:

(*k*) In the stock of any railway company in India upon which a fixed or minimum dividend in sterling is paid or guaranteed by the Secretary of State in Council of India, or upon the capital of which the interest is so guaranteed:

(*l*) In the debenture or guaranteed or preference stock of any company in Great Britain or Ireland, established for the supply of water for profit, and incorporated by special Act of Parliament or by Royal Charter, and having during each of the ten years last past before the date of investment paid a dividend of not less than five pounds per centum on its ordinary stock:

(*m*) In nominal or inscribed stock issued, or to be issued, by the corporation of any municipal borough having, according to the returns of the last census prior to the date of investment, a population exceeding fifty thousand, or by any county council, under the authority of any Act of Parliament or Provisional Order:

(*n*) In nominal or inscribed stock issued or to be issued by any commissioners incorporated by Act of Parliament for the purpose of supplying water, and having a compulsory power of levying rates over an area having, according to the returns of the last census prior to the date of investment, a population exceeding fifty thousand, provided that during each of the ten years last past before the date of investment the rates levied by such commissioners shall not have exceeded eighty

per centum of the amount authorised by
law to be levied :

(o) In any of the stocks, funds, or securities for
the time being authorised for the investment of cash under the control or subject
to the order of the High Court,

and may also from time to time vary any such
investment.

The provisions of this section have been extended to certain
colonial stocks by the Colonial Stock Act, 1900 (*post*, p. 191).

This section replaces, with a few slight alterations, section
3 of the Trust Investment Act, 1889, (52 & 53 Vict. c. 32),
which is repealed by the present Act. (See section 51, and
Schedule, *infra*.)

The Trust Investment Act, 1889, was itself a consolidating
Act. It replaced and extended the provisions of most, but
not all, of the numerous statutes which had, from time to time,
been passed to relieve trustees from the strictness of the rule
of the Court of Chancery. That rule was that trust funds
should be invested in Government Annuities, and Government
Annuities only. Of the Government Annuities, the three per
cent. Consolidated Annuities were adopted by the Court as
holding the balance most fairly between the interests of a
tenant for life and a remainderman. *Howe* v. *Lord Dartmouth*,
7 Ves. at p. 451

Previous Enactments.—The enactments in force before the
Trust Investment Act, 1889, were as follows :—

(1) 4 & 5 William 4 c. 29, enacting that where trustees
were expressly authorised to lend money on real securities in
England, Wales, or Great Britain, they might lend on real
securities in Ireland; but if any minor, unborn child, or person
of unsound mind was interested, such an investment could only
be made with the sanction of the Court of Chancery. This
Act (known as Lynch's Act) was superseded by 22 & 23 Vict.
c. 35, section 32 (*post*), and repealed by the Trust Investment
Act, 1889.

(2) 22 & 23 Vict. c. 35 (Lord St. Leonards's Act), section
32, enacting that a trustee, executor, or administrator, if not
expressly forbidden by some instrument creating his trust to
invest any trust fund on real securities in any part of the
United Kingdom, or on the stock of the Bank of England, or
Ireland, or on East India Stock, might invest such trust fund
on such securities or stock.

The section was repealed by the Trust Investment Act,
1889.

In consequence of decisions refusing to recognise investment on stock created under the India Loan Act (22 & 23 Vict.
c. 39), an Act (30 & 31 Vict c. 132) was passed, extending
the power of investment to any East India Stock charged on

the revenues of India whensoever created. The last-mentioned Act was repealed by the Trust Investment Act, 1889.

Subsequent East India Loan Acts, viz. 32 & 33 Vict. c. 106, 36 Vict. c. 32, 37 Vict. c. 3, 40 & 41 Vict c. 51, 42 & 43 Vict. c. 60, 43 Vict c. 10, and 48 & 49 Vict. c. 28, all provided that any capital stock thereunder created should be deemed to be East India Stock within the Act 22 & 23 Vict. c. 35, section 32, unless and until Parliament should otherwise provide.

(3) 23 & 24 Vict. c. 38, section 10, enacting that the Lord Chancellor might make General Orders, from time to time, as to the investment of cash under the control of the Court, either in the Three per Cent. Consolidated, or Reduced, or New Bank Annuities, or in such other stocks, funds, or securities, as he should think fit; and section 11, enacting that, when any such General Order had been made, trustees, executors, or administrators, having power to invest their trust funds in Government securities, or upon parliamentary stocks, funds, or securities, *or any of them*, might invest such trust funds in any of the stocks, funds, or securities in or upon which, by such General Order, cash under the control of the Court might from time to time be invested.

The latter section was repealed by the Trust Investment Act, 1889.

(4) 23 & 24 Vict. c. 145 (Lord Cranworth's Act), section 25, enacting that trustees under any instrument, dated since 28th August, 1860, might invest in any of the parliamentary stocks, or public funds, or in Government securities, and might vary such investments, subject to a proviso, that no original investment should be made thereunder (except in the Three per Cent. Consolidated Annuities), and that no change of investment should be made, where there was a person, under no disability, entitled in possession to receive the income of the trust fund for his life, or for any greater estate, without the consent in writing of such person.

This section was but little used, and was repealed by the Conveyancing and Law of Property Act, 1881.

(5) 27 & 28 Vict. c. 114 (Improvement of Land Act, 1864), section 60, enacting that trustees authorised to lend money on real securities might invest in any charge, or mortgage of any charge, under that Act; and section 61 providing that no charge under that Act should be deemed such an incumbrance as to preclude a trustee from investing in a purchase or mortgage of the land charged unless expressly prohibited.

These provisions are repealed by the present Act, and re-enacted in section 5. See *post*, p. 34.

(6) 28 & 29 Vict. c. 78 (Mortgage Debenture Act, 1865), section 40, enacting that trustees, having a general power to invest on shares, stock, mortgages, bonds, or debentures, of companies incorporated by or acting under the authority of an Act of Parliament, might invest on mortgage debentures issued under that Act.

This section is repealed by the present Act, and re-enacted
by section 5. See *post*, p. 34.

(7) 30 & 31 Vict. c. 132, section 2, enacting that trustees, executors, and administrators might invest on any securities the interest of which was guaranteed by Parliament, to the same extent and in the same manner as they might invest in East India Stock under 22 & 23 Vict. c. 35, section 32.

This section was repealed by the Trust Investment Act, 1889.

(8) 34 & 35 Vict. c. 27 (Debenture Stock Act, 1871), enacting that a trustee having power to invest in the mortgages or bonds of any railway, or of any other description of company, might, unless forbidden, invest in debenture stock of a railway company or such other company as aforesaid.

This Act is repealed by the present Act, and re-enacted by section 5. See *post*, p. 34.

(9) 34 & 35 Vict c. 47, section 13, enacting that a trustee, executor, or other person empowered to invest money in public stocks or funds or other Government securities, might, unless forbidden by the trust instrument, invest in Consolidated Stock of the Metropolitan Board of Works.

This section was repealed by the Trust Investment Act, 1889.

(10) 38 & 39 Vict. c. 83 (Local Loans Act, 1875), section 27, enacting that trustees having power to invest in the debentures or debenture stock of any railway or other company might, unless forbidden, invest in nominal debentures or nominal debenture stock issued under that Act.

This section is repealed by the present Act, and re-enacted by section 5. See *post*, p. 34.

(11) 43 & 44 Vict c. 8 (Isle of Man Loans Act, 1880), section 7, enacting that trustees having power to invest in securities in the Isle of Man or Colonial securities might, unless forbidden, invest in any securities under that Act.

This section is repealed by the present Act, and re-enacted by section 5. (See *post*, p. 34).

(12) 51 & 52 Vict. c. 41 (Local Government Act, 1888), section 70, making provision for the creation of County Stock, and providing that the Local Government Board might apply for the purposes of that section, with or without modifications, any enactments of any Act relating to stock issued by the Metropolitan Board of Works.

(13) 51 & 52 Vict. c. 59 (Trustee Act, 1888), section 9, enacting that a power to invest in real securities should be deemed to authorise, and to have always authorised, an investment upon mortgage of property held for an unexpired term of not less than two hundred years, and not subject to any reservation of rent greater than one shilling per annum, or to any right of redemption, or to any condition for re-entry, except for non-payment of rent.

This section is repealed by the present Act, and re-enacted by section 5. See *post*, p. 34.

C

(14) Certain Indian Railway Purchase Acts (see *post*, p. 25) enacting, that trustees authorised to invest in guaranteed stock of Indian railways might invest in "B" annuities of those railways.

"A Trustee . . . may invest."—The language of section 3 of the Trust Investment Act, 1889, and of the present section is wide, but it seems reasonably clear that, notwithstanding the definitions of "trustee" contained in section 9 of the Act of 1889 and section 50 of the present Act, this section applies only to trustees who hold funds for investment purposes, and that a trustee who holds funds not for the purpose of investment, but as bare trustee, or for the purpose of specific enjoyment, is not given a power of investment which he did not previously possess.

Before the Act of 1889 came into operation, trustees who held money for investment could only invest on the securities (if any) authorised by the trust instrument, or in Three per Cent. Consolidated Annuities, or in securities authorised by the statutory enactments hereinbefore referred to (*ante*, pp. 15–17). In the absence of express power to vary investments, trustees having once selected an investment, could not vary it. *Re Warde*, 2 J. & H. 191 ; *re Cooper* (1873) W.N. 87, disapproved by Fry and Kay, L.JJ., in *re Dick, Lopes v. Hume-Dick* (1891) 1 Ch. 423, at p. 425.

In *re The National Building Society*, 43 C D. 431, North, J., held that the powers of investment conferred by the Act of 1889 were larger powers given to trustees who already had limited power, and that the Act did not apply to trustees who had no power to invest independently of the Act. It is conceived that the construction adopted by North, J., in that case, must be applied to the present section. See note to section 4, *infra*, p. 34. It may, however, be contended that the decision of North, J. (which was not cited), is impliedly overruled by the case of *re Dick, Lopes v Hume-Dick* (1891) 1 Ch. 423, in H.L. reported as *Hume v. Lopes* (1892) A C. 112. This view, it is submitted, is not correct. In *re Dick (supra)* the Court was dealing with the question whether trust funds, already in a state of investment, could be dealt with under the Act of 1889. It was nowhere suggested that the trustees were not trustees for investment purposes.

These words will not enlarge a power to set apart specified funds to answer by their income a particular purpose. *Re Outhwaite* (1891) 3 Ch. 494.

"Any Trust Funds in his Hands whether at the Time in a State of Investment or not."—The words "whether at the time in a state of investment or not " are taken from the speech of Lord Macnaghten in *Hume v. Lopes* (1892) A.C. 112.

Subsection (a). "Parliamentary Stocks, or Public Funds, or Government Securities of the United Kingdom."—"Parliamentary stocks " and " public funds " appear to be synonymous terms, denoting the annuities which constitute the permanent debt of the country. "Government securities" is a wider term, and formerly included Exchequer bills (Davidson, 2nd edit. vol. iii. p. 23; *Matthews* v. *Brise*, 6 Beav. 239, 244; *Ellis* v. *Eden*, 23 Beav. at p. 548), and would now, it seems, include Exchequer bonds and Treasury bills.

For a list of the public funds or Government securities of the United Kingdom at the present time, see supplementary volume. They consist of (1) perpetual annuities, (2) terminable annuities, and (3) unfunded loans.

The terminable annuities (which are not in the market) could hardly, under any circumstances, form a proper investment for trust money.

Treasury bills carry no interest, but being purchased at a discount, in fact bear income. They are open to the objection that they pass by delivery or delivery and indorsement.

Exchequer bonds carry interest at three per cent. They are transferable by delivery, and being repayable after short periods, are unsuitable for permanent investments, though doubtless a temporary investment in Exchequer bonds or Treasury bills is an admissible mode of dealing with trust money in its passage from one permanent investment to another. See *Matthews* v. *Brise*, 6 Beav. 239, at p. 244; Davidson, 2nd edit. vol. iii. p. 23.

Subsection (b). "Real Securities."—The word "securities" imports a loan. See *Harris* v. *Harris*, 29 Beav. 107. The section does not authorise a purchase of real estate. Trustees frequently make the mistake of buying land, especially "ground rents," when their only authority is, in fact, to *lend* on real security. This leads to some difficulty on a subsequent dealing with the property purchased. The beneficiaries (if *sui juris*) have a right to elect to keep the land. Therefore, to make a good title, the conveyance on the re-sale by the trustee must, if the beneficiaries be all *sui juris*, be executed, not only by the trustee, but also by at least one of the beneficiaries, to show that the beneficiaries have not all elected to keep the land. *Re Patten and Edmonton Guardians*, 52 L.J. Ch. 787; 48 L.T. 870; 31 W.R. 785; *Power* v. *Banks* (1901) 2 Ch. 487, at p. 496. If one or more of the beneficiaries, however, be incapable of electing, the trustees can make a good title without the concurrence of any beneficiary. *Re Jenkins and Randal* (1903) 2 Ch. 362

The phrase "real securities" must mean securities on real property. Real property comprises, besides land and buildings, amongst other things advowsons, profits *à prendre*, free fisheries, fairs and markets, and life estates and reversions. It will thus be seen how very wide in terms is the discretion reposed in trustees. In practice, however, there are but few forms of real property upon which a trustee may properly make an investment.

It is not sufficient for a trustee to show that an investment impeached is an investment on real security. There are various other things to be considered, such as the nature of the property, and the different conditions which may affect its value, *Mant* v. *Leith*, 15 Beav. 524 An investment must be not only "authorised" but "proper." With reference to the duties of trustees in selecting an investment for trust money, the following principles were laid down in *Learoyd* v. *Whiteley*, 12 A.C. 727:—

"As a general rule, the law requires of a trustee no higher degree of diligence in the execution of his office than a man of ordinary prudence would exercise in the management of his own private affairs. Yet he is not allowed the same discretion in investing the moneys of the trust as if he were a person *sui juris* dealing with his own estate. It is the duty of the trustee to confine himself to the class of security authorised, and likewise to avoid all investments of that class which are attended with hazard" (*per* Lord Watson, *Learoyd* v. *Whiteley*, 12 A.C. 727, at p. 733). "They (trustees) must take such care in conducting the business of the trust as a reasonably cautious man would use, having regard, not only to the interests of those who are entitled to the income, but to the interests of those who will take in future, that is to say, . . . trustees are bound to preserve the money for those entitled to the corpus in remainder, and they are bound to invest it in such a way as will produce a reasonable income for those enjoying the income for the present. And in so doing they must use such caution as a reasonably prudent man would with reference to transactions in which he may be engaged of a similar nature" (*per* Cotton, L.J., in *re Whiteley*, 33 C.D. at p. 350). "The duty of the trustee is to take such care as an ordinary prudent man would take if he were minded to make an investment for the benefit of other people for whom he felt morally bound to provide" (*per* Lindley, L J., in *re Whiteley*, *supra*).

The following general rules for the guidance of trustees proposing to lend trust money on real security may be extracted from the authorities.

In making an investment on real security trustees must consider—

1. The nature of the property regarded as a physical object. It should be—

    (a) Permanent in nature and value;

    (b) Income producing;

    (c) Readily marketable.

It is conceived that all incorporeal hereditaments other than permanent rents must fail to comply with one or more of these requirements, the result being that although trustees are *authorised* to invest in any form of real security, in practice they can only properly lend on the security of land (regarded as a physical object), buildings, or permanent rents.

2. The estate or interest of the borrower in the property.

    (a) Its possible duration. It should as a rule be an absolute fee simple.

(b) Its time of enjoyment. It should be in possession. **Sect. 1.**

(c) Its nature. It should be a legal estate and a sole or several interest, and be free from prior incumbrances.

3. The market value of the property and amount of loan. See section 8, and notes thereto, *post*, p. 41.

4. The form of the security. The security should—

    (a) vest in the mortgagee the legal estate;

    (b) vest in the mortgagee sole control over the property;

    (c) be enforceable by sale;

    (d) be enforceable by ejectment and foreclosure;

    (e) not prohibit the mortgagee from calling in the mortgage money,

    (f) contain a covenant for payment;

    (g) secure money, not the return of specific stock;

    (h) in the case of copyholds, be accompanied by a surrender.

The authorities upon which these rules are based are discussed in Appendix A, *post*, p. 225.

"Heritable Securities."—Although section 52 provides that this Act does not extend to Scotland, this express power to invest in "real or heritable securities in Great Britain" clearly authorises trustees subject to English or Irish law to invest on land in Scotland. Under ordinary circumstances a security locally situate out of the jurisdiction would not seem desirable although authorised. Cf. *re Miles's will*, 5 Jur. N.S. 1236.

"In Great Britain or Ireland."—Real security in Ireland is an expressly authorised, but, as a rule, not desirable, investment for English trust funds.

"Great Britain" is defined by the Act of Union (6 Ann. c. 11), and means the kingdoms of England and Scotland. The Isle of Man is no part of the kingdom, but a distinct territory of itself (Co. Litt. 9 (a)). The Channel Islands are "no part of the realm of England," *Calvin's Case*, 7 Rep. 21.

Subsection (c). "Stock of the Bank of England or the Bank of Ireland."—Bank stock is nothing but a share in the capital stock of a company incorporated by Act of Parliament for the purpose of carrying on a banking business. It is merely a share in an incorporated partnership, which has certain statutory privileges, and does the banking business of the State. *Per* James, V.C., *Ogle v. Knipe*, 8 Eq. 434.

For the amount now in existence, see the Supplementary Volume.

Subsection (d). "India . . . Stock."

For list of the present India stocks, see Supplementary Volume.

Subsection (e). "Securities, the Interest of which is guaranteed by Parliament."

"Guaranteed by Parliament."—This does not include

Sect. 1. guaranteed by the Government without the sanction of Parliament, *e.g.* Zanzibar 3 per cent. guaranteed loan.

Virtually, all securities under this subsection are bonds to bearer. As to bonds to bearer, see section 7, *post*, p. 40.

For list of such securities, see Supplementary Volume.

Subsection (f). "Metropolitan Board of Works, or London County Council and Metropolitan Police Debenture Stock."

For the particulars of these stocks, see Supplementary Volume.

Subsection (g). "Debenture, or Rentcharge, or Guaranteed, or Preference Stock of any Railway Company in Great Britain or Ireland, incorporated by Special Act of Parliament, and having during each of the Ten Years last past before the Date of Investment paid a Dividend at the Rate of not less than Three per Centum per Annum on its Ordinary Stock."

As to purchases at a premium under this subsection, see section 2, *post*, p. 30.

"Debenture Stock."—It is conceived that an investment on debentures, as distinct from debenture stock, is not authorised by this subsection.

"Preference."—Many British railways have stocks called "preferred ordinary stock" and "deferred ordinary stock." The question arises whether such preferred ordinary stocks are "preference stocks" within the meaning of this clause.

Section 13 of the Regulation of Railways Act, 1868, enacts that any company which, during the preceding year, has paid dividends at not less than three per cent. on its ordinary stock, may by resolution divide its paid-up ordinary stock into two classes, viz. preferred ordinary stock, and deferred ordinary stock, and issue the same, in substitution for equal amounts of paid-up ordinary stock, on the request of any holder, but not otherwise; the preferred ordinary stock to have a maximum preference of six per cent., and to rank for dividend, *pari passu* with the undivided ordinary stock.

In the case of stocks issued under the Act of 1868, the preferred ordinary stock is not an authorised trust investment under the present subsection. Dividends are declared on the undivided ordinary stock, and for the purposes of this section the splitting of the stock may be disregarded.

In many cases the ordinary stock has been similarly *partially* split at the option of individual holders in pursuance of special Acts. Dividends are declared on the undivided ordinary stock, and for the purposes of this section the preferred ordinary stock are not authorised investments under the present subsection. See *re Brighton and Dyke Railway Co.*, 44 C.D. 28.

In the Great Northern Railway Company *the whole* of the ordinary stock was compulsorily split by special Act, but the Act provides that the converted stocks shall, for the purposes of this subsection, be considered as continuing to be the ordinary stock. The preferred ordinary stock is not, therefore, a "preference stock," and for the purpose of considering whether the necessary dividend has been paid, the preferred ordinary and deferred ordinary must be considered as one stock.

In the cases of the Isle of Wight Railway Company and the Midland Railway Company, the whole of the stock has been, in like manner, split, and the Acts provide that dividends shall continue to be ascertained and declared as if no conversion had taken place.

In the Cardiff Railway Company there is a "preferred ordinary stock of 1896," and "preferred ordinary shares of 1901," which are not the result of "splitting," and appear to be, except in name, simply preference stock or shares respectively. It is conceived that these may be "preference stocks" within this section.

The "ordinary preference stock" of the North British Railway Company also appears to have all the characteristics of a preference stock.

In the cases of the Great Central Railway Company and the Great North of Scotland Railway Company, the whole of the ordinary stock has been split, but there appears to be no express provision in the special Acts. It is conceived, however, that the preferred ordinary stocks are not preference stocks.

"**Stock.**"—See definition, section 50, *post*, p. 163. In some few cases there exist series of "annuities" charged on the undertaking in preference to the ordinary stock. It is conceived that such annuities are "stock" within the meaning of this section, notwithstanding the terms of section 50.

"**Great Britain or Ireland.**"—See *ante*, p. 21.

"**Not less than Three per Cent.**"—The Rule of Court incorporated by paragraph (*o*) (see *post*, p. 28) only requires that a dividend shall have been paid, and specifies no rate. The requirement of a dividend at the rate of three per cent. is thus rendered nugatory.

"**During each of the Ten Years last past before the Date of Investment.**"—As to continuing to hold stock in a company, which, after investment made, fails to pay a dividend on its ordinary stock, see Trustee Act, 1893, Amendment Act, 1894, section 4, *post*, p. 176.

For a list of the stocks under this subsection, see Supplementary Volume.

Subsection (h). "Stock of any Railway or Canal Company in Great Britain or Ireland whose Undertaking is leased in Perpetuity or for a Term of not less than Two Hundred Years at a Fixed Rental to any such Railway Company as is mentioned in Subsection (g), either alone or jointly with any other Railway Company."

"Stock."—See *ante*, p. 23.

This subsection authorises investment in any stock, preference or ordinary.

"Great Britain or Ireland."—See *ante*, p. 21.

"Leased in Perpetuity or for a Term, etc., at a Fixed Rental." It is conceived that these words must be given a popular rather than a technical meaning, and should not be too strictly construed. It is conceived that the distinction intended to be drawn is between the stock of companies, whose undertaking is vested in another company in consideration of an unvarying annual payment (whether actually rent or not), and that of a company whose undertaking is worked and maintained by another company in consideration of a percentage of the profits.

If this be so, the undertaking of a company is "leased at fixed rental," notwithstanding that in fact it has been absolutely conveyed to another company in consideration of the latter paying a fixed dividend or rate of interest on a fixed amount of stock or fixed capital of the former; and although the former company (*e.g.* the Hammersmith and City Railway Company) has been dissolved.

"A Term of not less than Two Hundred Years," *i.e.* unexpired at the time the investment is made. See the Amendment Act, 1894, section 4, *post*, p. 176, as to continuing to hold an investment which has ceased to be authorised.

"Any such Company as is mentioned in Subsection (g)," *i.e.* a company which has paid a dividend of not less than three per cent. on its ordinary stock during each of the ten years prior to investment. So far as this subsection is concerned, the requirement of a minimum dividend of three per cent. is not abrogated by the Rule of Court (*post*, p. 28).

"Any other Railway Company."—Whether such as mentioned in subsection (*g*) or not.

For a list of the stocks under this subsection, see Supplementary Volume.

Subsection (i). "Debenture Stock of any Railway Company in India, the Interest on which is paid or guaranteed by the Secretary of State in Council of India."

As to purchases at a premium under this subsection, see section 2, *post*.

"Debenture Stock."—See *ante*, p 22.

"India."—The Interpretation Act, 1889, section 18, defines "India" as meaning British India, together with any territories of any native prince or chief under the suzerainty of Her Majesty exercised through the Governor-General of India, or through any governor or other officer subordinate to the Governor-General of India.

The same section defines "British India" as meaning all territories and places within Her Majesty's dominions which

are for the time being governed by Her Majesty through the
Governor-General of India or through any governor or other
officer subordinate to the Governor-General of India.

For list of the debenture stocks comprised in this subsection,
see Supplementary Volume.

Subsection (j). "B" Annuities of Eastern Bengal, East
Indian, and the Scinde Punjaub and Delhi Railways, and like
Annuities, and Annuities "D" and "C" of East Indian Railway.

For list of annuities comprised in this subsection, see Supplementary Volume.

Subsection (k). "Stock of any Railway Company in India
upon which a Fixed or Minimum Dividend in Sterling is paid
or guaranteed by the Secretary of State in Council of India,
or upon the Capital of which the Interest is so guaranteed."

As to purchases at a premium under this subsection, see
section 2, *post*.

"Stock."—See definition, section 50, *post*, p. 161.

"India."—Defined by the Interpretation Act, 1889. See
ante, p. 24.

For list of the stocks comprised under this head, see
Supplementary Volume

Subsection (l) "Debenture or Guaranteed or Preference
Stock of any Company in Great Britain or Ireland, established
for the Supply of Water for Profit, and incorporated by Special
Act of Parliament or by Royal Charter, and having during each
of the Ten Years last past before the Date of Investment paid
a Dividend of not less than Five per Centum on its Ordinary
Stock."

As to purchases at a premium under this subsection, see
section 2, *post*.

"Stock."—See *ante*, p. 23.

"Great Britain or Ireland."—See *ante*, p. 21.

"Ordinary Stock."—In many companies the ordinary stock
is divided into different classes, entitled to different rates of
maximum dividend In the application of this subsection to
such companies, it is conceived that it is necessary that a
dividend at the rate of 5 per cent. per annum shall have been
paid for the requisite period on each class of ordinary shares.

For a list of the stocks within this subsection, see Supplementary Volume.

Subsection (m). "Nominal or Inscribed Stock issued or to
be issued by the Corporation of any Municipal Borough, having
according to the Returns of the last Census prior to the Date
of Investment a Population exceeding Fifty Thousand, or by
any County Council, under the Authority of any Act of Parliament or Provisional Order."

As to purchases at a premium under this subsection, see
section 2, *post*.

"**Nominal Stock.**"—This expression appears to be taken from the Local Loans Act, 1875, where a nominal debenture means (see section 5) a debenture in which the principal sum is made payable to a person therein named, and is transferable in writing in manner directed by the local authority. It appears to mean what is more commonly called "registered" stock.

"**Inscribed Stock.**"—This expression would appear to mean stock transferable by inscription in books of stock kept by the corporation issuing the stock, or by bankers as registrars on behalf of the corporation.

"**Stock.**"—See definition, section 50, and cf. *ante*, p. 23.

"**Municipal Borough.**"—This expression was used in the Trust Investment Act, 1889, to which the Interpretation Act, 1889, had no application. As used in that Act it probably meant any urban community incorporated for municipal purposes, and would thus include Scotch cities and burghs. The Interpretation Act, 1889, provides (section 15) that in every Act passed after the commencement of that Act (1) the expression "municipal borough" shall mean "as respects England and Wales, any place for the time being subject to the Municipal Corporations Act, 1882." (2) The expression "municipal borough" shall mean, "as respects Ireland, any place for the time being subject to the Act of the session of the 3rd and 4th years of the reign of her present Majesty, chapter 108, intituled 'An Act for the Regulation of Municipal Corporations in Ireland.'" There is no definition of the expression "municipal borough" as applied to Scotland. This raises the question whether in the present section the expression "municipal borough" includes Scotch municipalities. It is conceived that the only effect of the Interpretation Act is to give a precise meaning to the expression as used in reference to England and Ireland, leaving to the expression, as used with reference to Scotland, the meaning which it had in the Trust Investment Act, 1889, viz. any urban community incorporated for municipal purposes.

"**Census.**"—When the boundaries of the borough of Bournemouth were varied between the date of the census and of the making of the census returns, with the result of bringing the population from below 50,000 to upwards of 50,000, and the alteration in the population was noted in the census return, it was held that trustees could invest in stock issued by the corporation of the borough. *Re Druitt* (1903) 1 Ch. 446.

"**County Council**" means a council established under the Local Government Act, 1888, the Local Government (Scotland) Act, 1889, or the Local Government (Ireland) Act, 1898.

"**Any Act of Parliament.**"—These words cover the Local Loans Act, 1875, as well as special Acts.

For list of stocks comprised in this subsection, see Supplementary Volume.

Subsection (n). "Nominal or Inscribed Stock issued or to be issued by Commissioners incorporated by Act of Parliament for the Purpose of supplying Water, and having a Compulsory Power of levying Rates over an Area having, according to the Returns of the last Census prior to the Date of Investment, a Population exceeding Fifty Thousand, provided that during each of the Ten Years last past before the Date of Investment the Rates levied by such Commissioners shall not have exceeded Eighty per Centum of the Amount authorised by Law to be levied."

"Nominal Stock."—See *ante*, p. 26.

"Inscribed Stock."—See *ante*, p. 26.

"Stock."—See definition, p. 163, and cf. *ante*, p. 23.

"Commissioners."—In the case of the Edinburgh water undertaking, the authority is called "the Edinburgh Water Trustees." It is conceived that they are "commissioners" within this subsection.

The powers of the Glasgow Water Commissioners have been transferred to the Glasgow City Corporation. It is conceived that stock issued by the commissioners before transfer is still an authorised investment under this subsection.

Many municipal corporations issue "water stock." It is conceived such stock is not an authorised investment under this subsection, but if at all, under subsection (*m*), *supra*.

"Incorporated by Act of Parliament."—Incorporation by registration under the Companies Act, 1862, is not incorporation by Act of Parliament, *re Smith, Davidson* v. *Myrtle* (1896) 2 Ch. 590; but incorporation by charter, which derives its force from a preceding Act of Parliament may be, *Elve* v. *Boyton* (1891) 1 Ch. 501.

"Compulsory Power of levying Rates."—Some water commissioners have no power themselves to levy a rate, but have power to call upon certain local authorities to raise any money required by them. It is conceived that stock issued by such trustees is not an authorised investment under this subsection.

"Eighty per Cent. of the Amount authorised"—It is thought there are but four cases of investments authorised under this subsection (see Supplementary Volume); in three of them the amount authorised to be raised is unlimited. It is conceived that in these three cases the proviso in the subsection may be disregarded.

For list of the investments under this subsection, see Supplementary Volume.

Subsection (o). "Stocks, Funds, or Securities for the Time being authorised for the Investment of Cash under the Control or subject to the Order of the High Court."

"**High Court**" is defined by the Interpretation Act, 1889, as meaning, when used with reference to England or Ireland, Her Majesty's High Court of Justice, in England or Ireland, as the case may be.

The present Rule of the High Court in England (Order XXII., Rule 17, as amended by R.S.C., 10th February, 1897; October, 1899; July, 1901; and January, 1904) is as follows:—

17—(1) Rule 1 of the Rules of the Supreme Court, August, 1888, is hereby annulled (except so far as it annulled Order XXII., Rule 17, of the Rules of the Supreme Court, 1883), and the following rule shall stand in lieu thereof: Cash, under the control of, or subject to, the Order of the Court, may be invested in the following stocks, funds, or securities, namely—

(1) Two and three-quarter per Cent. Consolidated Stock (to be called after the 5th of April, 1903, Two-and-a-half per Cent. Consolidated Stock).

(2) Consolidated Three Pounds per Cent. Annuities.

(3) Reduced Three Pounds per Cent. Annuities

(4) Two Pounds Fifteen Shillings per Cent. Annuities.

(5) Two Pounds Ten Shillings per Cent. Annuities.

(6) Local Loans Stock under the National Debt and Local Loans Act, 1887.

(7) Exchequer Bills.

(8) Bank Stock.

(9) India Three-and-a-half per Cent. Stock.

(10) India Three per Cent. Stock.

(11) Indian guaranteed railway stocks or shares, provided in each case that such stocks or shares shall not be liable to be redeemed within a period of fifteen years from the date of investment.

(12) Stocks of Colonial Governments guaranteed by the Imperial Government.

(13) Mortgage of freehold and copyhold estates respectively in England and Wales.

(14) Metropolitan Consolidated Stock, three pounds ten shillings per cent.

(15) Three per Cent. Metropolitan Consolidated Stock.

(16) Two-and-a-half per Cent. Metropolitan Consolidated Stock.

(17) Two-and-a-half per Cent. London County Consolidated Stock.

(18) Three per Cent. London County Consolidated Stock

(19) Inscribed Two-and-a-half per Cent. Debenture Stock issued by the Corporation of London, and secured by a trust deed dated 24th June, 1897.

(20) Debenture, Preference, Guaranteed, or Rentcharge Stocks of railways in Great Britain or Ireland having for ten years next before the date of investment paid a dividend on ordinary stock or shares.

(21) Nominal Debentures or nominal Debenture Stock under Local Loans Act, 1875, or under the Isle of Man Loans Act, 1880, provided in each case that such debentures or stock shall

not be liable to be redeemed within a period of fifteen years from the date of investment.

(22) Debenture, Preference, Guaranteed, or Rentcharge Stocks of railways in Great Britain or Ireland guaranteed by railway companies owning railways in Great Britain or Ireland which have for ten years next before the date of investment paid a dividend on ordinary stock or shares.

Numbers (1), (2), (3), (4), (5), and (6) are also authorised by subsection (a).

(7) Exchequer Bills are not now issued, Treasury Bills having been substituted under the authority of the Treasury Bills Act, 1877.

(8) Bank Stock is also authorised by subsection (c).

(9) and (10) India Stocks are also authorised by subsection (d).

(11) Indian Guaranteed Railway Stocks are also authorised by subsection (k), subject to the qualification in section 2, post, p. 30, which qualification is not identical with that in the Rule of Court. Under the Rule of Court a stock redeemable within fifteen years cannot be bought at all, but under section 2 such a stock may be bought at or under its redemption value. Under the Rule of Court a stock redeemable after more than fifteen years may be purchased at any price; under section 2 the price must not be more than 15 per cent. above the redemption price. See, further, the notes to section 2, post, p. 31.

(12) Guaranteed Colonial Stocks are also authorised by subsection (e).

(13) Mortgages are also authorised by subsection (b).

(14), (15), (16), (17), and (18), Metropolitan and London County Stocks are also authorised by subsection (f).

(19) Inscribed Stock of the City of London. This is not covered by subsection (m); the City of London not being "a municipal borough" as defined (see ante, p. 26), nor a county council, nor was the loan raised under the authority of any Act of Parliament or Provisional Order.

"Inscribed."—See ante, p. 26.

(20) British Railway Stocks are also authorised by subsection (g). It is to be observed that the Rule of Court does not require that the railway company be incorporated by special Act of Parliament. It is conceived that a company registered under the Companies Acts, 1862 to 1900, for working a light railway authorised by the Light Railway Commissioners under the Light Railways Act, 1896, would, on complying with the requirements as to dividends, be within this clause.

As to the requirement that a dividend shall have been paid for ten years, see ante, p. 23.

(21) Nominal debentures or debenture stock under the Local Loans Act, 1875, are also authorised by subsection (m), subject to the provisions of section 2. Under the Rule of Court there is no limit as to the size of the borough or local authority issuing the loan, as in subsection (m), and the proviso

Sect. 1.

as to redemption in the Rule of Court materially differs from section (2). As to the differences, see *ante*, p. 29, in reference to Indian Railway Stocks, where a similar divergence arises, and notes to section 2, *post*, p 31.

Isle of Man Loans.—See *post*, sections 2 and 5, pp. 31, 39.

Ireland.—The present rule of the High Court in Ireland is Order LXII., Rule 70. It is not so extensive as the rule of the English Court. Its most noteworthy feature is that it includes deposit receipt in the Bank of Ireland.

"**And may also from Time to Time vary any such Investment.**"—The subject of varying investments has already been incidentally referred to (see *ante*, p. 18). It has been there pointed out that, in the absence of a power to vary investments, trustees holding a fund already invested could not formerly sell and reinvest, and that one of the mischiefs intended to be remedied by the Trust Investment Act, 1889 (now replaced by the present section), was the absence of power to vary investments already made.

The construction of the power to vary was much discussed in the Court of Appeal in *re Dick, Lopes* v. *Hume-Dick* (1891) 1 Ch. 429.

The power is to "vary any such investment;" *i.e.* any such investment as hereinbefore mentioned. *Per* Fry, L.J., in *re Dick* (1891) 1 Ch. 429. This was held to mean any such investment as hereinbefore mentioned, and to include investments made by a testator during his life, as well as those made by his trustees after his death. Even this construction of the Act of 1889 did not dispose of all difficulty, for it did not go beyond such investments as are mentioned in the section, and "it is quite possible, then, that there might be under the will or settlement investments of descriptions not mentioned in section 3, and, if the will or settlement contained no power to vary, they would not be variable under the power given in this section," *per* Kay, L.J., in *re Dick*, *supra*. The House of Lords, however, placed a wider construction on the Act, under which the difficulty did not arise.

The present section refers to funds in a state of investment in the hands of the trustee, hence the power to vary "any such investment as hereinbefore mentioned" applies to any investment in the hands of the trustee, whether of the description mentioned in subsections (*a*) to (*o*) or not.

For definition of "trust," "trustee," "instrument," "stock," and "securities," see section 50, *infra*.

Sect. 2.

Purchase at a premium of redeemable stocks.

Section 2.—(1.) A trustee may under the powers of this Act invest in any of the securities mentioned or referred to in section one of this Act, notwithstanding that the same may be redeemable, and that the price exceeds the redemption value.

(2.) Provided that a trustee may not under the powers of this Act purchase at a price exceeding its redemption value any stock mentioned or referred to in subsections (*g*), (*i*), (*k*), (*l*), and (*m*) of section one, which is liable to be redeemed within fifteen years of the date of purchase at par or at some other fixed rate, or purchase any such stock as is mentioned or referred to in the subsections aforesaid, which is liable to be redeemed at par or at some other fixed rate, at a price exceeding fifteen per centum above par or such other fixed rate.

(3.) A trustee may retain until redemption any redeemable stock, fund, or security which may have been purchased in accordance with the powers of this Act.

This section replaces section 4 of the Trust Investment Act, 1889, which section is repealed by the present Act. See section 51, and Schedule, *infra*. Subsection 2 has been extended to the Colonial Stocks authorised as trust investments by the Colonial Stock Act, 1900, see *post*, p. 191.

"A Trustee."—See definition, section 50, *post*, p. 161, and note to section 1, *ante*, p. 18.

"Securities mentioned or referred to in Section 1."— Section 1, subsection (*o*), authorises investment in any securities for the time being authorised for the investment of cash under the control of the High Court. The Rule of Court authorises investment in Indian Guaranteed Railway Stocks, debenture stock under the Local Loans Act, 1875, or under the Isle of Man Loans Act, 1880, with a proviso in each case that such stocks shall not be liable to be redeemed within a period of fifteen years from the date of investment.

Isle of Man Debenture Stock is not expressly mentioned or referred to in section 1; and since only such Isle of Man Debenture Stock as is not redeemable within fifteen years is (as being authorised for the investment of funds in Court) referred to in section 1, subsection (*o*), the present section (subsection 1) does not authorise the purchase of Isle of Man Debenture Stock when redeemable within fifteen years.

Indian Guaranteed Railway Stock is included in the securities expressly mentioned or referred to in section 1, subsection (*k*), without any proviso as to period of redemption. It is submitted, therefore, that the present section (subsection 1) makes it clear that investment may be made on such stock although redeemable within fifteen years, but subject to the provisions of subsection 2.

Section 1 subsection (*m*) authorises investment in nominal

Sect. 2.

or inscribed stock issued by certain large towns or by county councils. A certain number of stocks, viz. nominal debenture stocks, issued under the Local Loans Act, 1875, by the large towns or by county councils, are included in subsection (*m*) and the Rule of Court. As to such the above note on Indian Railway Stock applies. Some securities, however, such as debenture stock issued by a small town or a district council, are included in the rule but not in subsection (*m*). As to such the note above on Isle of Man Debenture Stock applies.

"**At some other Fixed Rate.**"—Stocks liable to be paid off on average market price during a stated period preceding redemption (such as some of the Indian Railway Stocks) are not liable to be redeemed "at a fixed rate;" nor, it is conceived, are stocks which are liable to be paid off at a given number of years' purchase of a given percentage (*e g.* 50 per cent.) of the gross earnings of the company.

In the case of several Indian Guaranteed Railways, the Secretary of State has power to purchase the undertaking of the company at a fixed price to be paid to the company. Although stock in such companies would not appear to be technically within this section, yet as under the terms of the contracts with the Secretary of State the rights and interests of the stockholders are in substance those of holders of redeemable stocks, trustees would be well advised to consider themselves bound by the requirements of this section when investing in the purchase of such stocks.

"**A Trustee may retain.**"—Cf. the Amendment Act, 1894, section 4, *post*, p. 176.

For definition of "trustee" and "securities," see section 50, *infra*.

Sect. 3.

Discretion of trustees

Section 3.—Every power conferred by the preceding sections shall be exercised according to the discretion of the trustee, but subject to any consent required by the instrument, if any, creating the trust with respect to the investment of the trust funds.

This section replaces section 5 of the Trust Investment Act, 1889, which section is repealed by the present Act. See section 51, and Schedule, *infra*.

"**Discretion of the Trustee.**"—In order properly to exercise his discretion, the trustee must have regard to the rights and interests of all parties concerned. This is particularly important where there are beneficiaries entitled in succession. For if it appear that the trustee has made an investment at the instance and for the benefit of one or more of the *cestuis que trust* without having regard to the interests of the others, and loss result from the investment, that is a breach of trust for which the trustee is responsible. *Raby* v. *Ridehalgh*, 7 De G.M. & G. 104; *Stuart* v. *Stuart*, 3 Beav. 430; *re Dick*, *Hume* v. *Lopes* (1891) 1 Ch. at p. 431. So also, a discretionary power to postpone conversion must not be exercised with intent to produce an unequal effect as between tenant for life and remainderman. *Rowlls* v. *Bebb* (1900) 2 Ch. 107.

On the same principle, it would be an improper exercise of the power of varying investments to exercise it simply for the purpose of securing to a beneficiary the advantage of the rule laid down in the cases of *Scholefield* v. *Redfern*, 2 Dr. & Sm. 173; *Freeman* v. *Whitbread*, 1 Eq. 266; *re Clarke*, 18 C.D. 160; *Bulkeley* v. *Stephens* (1896) 2 Ch. 241; viz. that, as between tenant for life and reversioner, no apportionment will be made with reference to the increase or decrease of price of stock, arising out of the nearness or remoteness of a period of investment to or from the day when dividends are payable.

The commencement of an action for administration does not deprive trustees of their discretionary powers, even though they be plaintiffs, *Cafe* v. *Bent*, 3 Hare, 245; but after judgment, powers, whether as to investment, *Widdowson* v. *Duck*, 2 Mer. 498; 16 R.R. 206; *Bethell* v. *Abraham*, 17 Eq. 24, or otherwise, *re Gadd*, 23 C.D. 134, can only be exercised subject to the direction of the Court.

"Subject to any Consent required."—The power of consenting, or withholding consent, is given to the donee (usually the tenant for life) for his own benefit, and he is not in a fiduciary position as to it, *Dicconson* v. *Talbot*, 6 Ch. 32, at p. 37. Hence, trustees would not be precluded from lending on mortgage to a person whose consent to a change of investment is requisite, *re Laing* (1899) 1 Ch 593.

It was held in *Harrison* v. *Thexton*, 5 Jur. N.S. 550, that, notwithstanding a tenant for life, whose consent to changes of investment was requisite, withheld consent, yet having due regard to the ulterior interests created under the settlement, the trustees were bound to insist on a change being made in the investment of a fund not invested on proper security, and a decree was made ordering such change to be effected. *De Manneville* v. *Crompton*, 1 V. & B. 354, was decided on the same principle.

Consent to the exercise of a power means previous or contemporaneous consent where (as in the case of consent to a power of investing or changing investments) the nature and object of the power, and the circumstances of the case, point to a previous consent. *Greenham* v. *Gibbeson*, 10 Bing. 363, 38 R.R. 458; *Bateman* v. *Davis*, 3 Mad. 98; 18 R.R. 200. *Stevens* v. *Robertson*, 37 L.J. Ch 499, is a decision of Stuart, V.C., to the contrary, but it is material to observe that the case of *Greenham* v. *Gibbeson* (*supra*) was not cited, and it is submitted the case cannot be relied on.

Consent cannot be given prospectively, *Child* v. *Child*, 20 Beav. 50. To prove consent it is necessary that there should

D

be knowledge of the nature of the proposed investment, *re Massingberd*, 63 L.T. 296.

For definition of "trustee" and "instrument," see section 50, *infra*.

Section 4.—The preceding sections shall apply as well to trusts created before as to trusts created after the passing of this Act, and the powers thereby conferred shall be in addition to the powers conferred by the instrument, if any, creating the trust.

This section replaces section 6 of the Trust Investment Act, 1889, which section is repealed by the present Act. See section 51, and Schedule, *infra*.

"**The Powers thereby conferred.**"—The true mode of construing the powers is to read them into the will *Re Dick* (1891) 1 Ch at p. 421; and see *re Moody, Woodroffe v Moody* (1895) 1 Ch. 101

"**In addition to the Powers conferred by the Instrument.**"—This appears to indicate that the powers of investment given by section 1 are given only to trustees who already have a power of investment, either expressly, or by implication, under the declaration of trust. See note, "A trustee ... may invest," *ante*, p. 18.

For definition of "trust" and "instrument," see section 50, *infra*.

Section 5.—(1.) A trustee having power to invest in real securities, unless expressly forbidden by the instrument creating the trust, may invest and shall be deemed to have always had power to invest—

> (*a*) on mortgage of property held for an unexpired term of not less than two hundred years, and not subject to a reservation of rent greater than a shilling a year, or to any right of redemption or to any condition for re-entry, except for non-payment of rent; and
>
> (*b*) on any charge, or upon mortgage of any charge, made under the Improvement of Land Act, 1864.

(2.) A trustee having power to invest in the mortgages or bonds of any railway company or of any other description of company may, unless the

contrary is expressed in the instrument authorising
the investment, invest in the debenture stock of a
railway company or such other company as aforesaid.

(3.) A trustee having power to invest money in
the debentures or debenture stock of any railway
or other company may, unless the contrary is
expressed in the instrument authorising the investment, invest in any nominal debentures or nominal
debenture stock issued under the Local Loans Act,
1875.

(4.) A trustee having power to invest money in
securities in the Isle of Man, or in securities of the
government of a colony, may, unless the contrary is
expressed in the instrument authorising the investment, invest in any securities of the Government of
the Isle of Man, under the Isle of Man Loans Act,
1880.

(5.) A trustee having a general power to invest
trust moneys in or upon the security of shares,
stock, mortgages, bonds, or debentures of companies
incorporated by or acting under the authority of an
Act of Parliament, may invest in, or upon the
security of, mortgage debentures duly issued under
and in accordance with the provisions of the
Mortgage Debenture Act, 1865.

Subsection 1 (a) replaces section 9 of the Trustee Act,
1888. Subsection 1 (b) replaces section 60 of the Improvement
of Land Act, 1864. Subsection 2 replaces section 1 of the
Debenture Stock Act, 1871. Subsection 3 replaces section 27
of the Local Loans Act, 1875. Subsection 4 replaces section 7
of the Isle of Man Stock Act, 1880. Subsection 5 replaces
section 40 of the Mortgage Debenture Act, 1865. All the
above-mentioned sections are repealed by the present Act.
See section 51, and Schedule, *infra*.

The wording of the marginal note should be observed.
The marginal note, however, forms no part of the Act. *Sutton
v. Sutton,* 22 C.D. 511; *Claydon v. Green,* L.R. 3 C.P. 511;
re Venour, Venour v. Sellon, 2 Ch. D. 522; *A.-G. v. G.E. Ry. Co.,*
11 C.D. at p. 465.

It has been pointed out in the Introduction (*ante,* p. 1)
that this Act is not a code to be interpreted without reference
to previous enactments or decisions. A knowledge of such
enactments and decisions is peculiarly necessary in construing
the present section.

Subsection 1 (*a*).—Subsection 1 (*a*) first appeared on the statute book as section 9 of the Trustee Act, 1888, which was as follows : "A power to invest trust money in real securities shall authorise, and shall be deemed to have always authorised, an investment upon mortgage of property held for an unexpired term of not less than two hundred years, and not subject to any reservation, etc."

At the date of the passing of that Act, Lord St. Leonards's Act (see *ante*, p. 15) was in force, and it is conceived that section 9 of the 1888 Act operated to extend not only express powers, but also the power conferred by section 32 of Lord St. Leonards's Act (*ante*, p. 15). Eight months later section 32 of Lord St. Leonards's Act was repealed by the Trust Investment Act, 1889, and the power to invest on real securities re-enacted by section 3 of that Act, no reference being made in the Act of 1889 to section 9 of the Act of 1888 It seems clear that the combined effect of section 9 of the 1888 Act and the Act of 1889 was to authorise any trustee, not expressly forbidden, to invest on leasehold securities of the nature mentioned in the 1888 Act. It is conceived, therefore, that there is no ground for the suggestion which has been made (Wolstenholme on the Conveyancing and Settled Land Acts, 8th edit., p. 206), that it may be a question whether section 5 (1) (*a*) extends section 1 so as to authorise an investment on leaseholds.

"**Mortgage.**"—See definition "including equitable charge," section 50, *post*, p. 161. Notwithstanding the definition, trustees cannot safely dispense with the legal estate. See *ante*, p. 21, and Appendix A.

It will be observed that the terms specified are not necessarily capable of enlargement under section 65 of the Conveyancing and Law of Property Act, 1881, and section 11 of the Conveyancing Act, 1882.

Subsection 1 (*b*).—Subsection 1 (*b*) first appeared in the statute book as part of section 60 of the Improvement of Land Act, 1864 (27 & 28 Vict. c. 114), as follows : "All trustees, directors, and other persons who may be authorised to invest any money on real security shall (unless the contrary be provided by the instrument directing or authorising such investment) have power at their discretion to invest money on such charges, or on mortgages thereof." It is conceived that a trustee, whose only authority for an investment on real security was Lord St. Leonards's Act, could not make an investment under the 1864 Act, for since "instrument" was not defined (as it is in section 50 of this Act) as including an Act of Parliament, there was no "instrument" authorising the investment on real security. It is conceived that the reason why subsections 1 (*a*) and (*b*) are not included in section 1 is to be found in the insertion of the words, "and shall be deemed to have always had power." As the expression "may be authorised" in the Act of 1864 appeared to refer to authority not given at the date of the Act, trustees under an instrument coming into operation before the 29th July, 1864, the date when the statute was passed, could not safely assume that the Act applied to their case (Lewin, 9th edit., p. 364). Subsection 1 may, therefore, have been separately enacted so as to introduce the words above referred to, and thus cure any breaches of trust which might have been committed in the past.

Subsection 2.—This subsection replaces section 1 of the Debenture Stock Act, 1871 (34 & 35 Vict. c. 27). The preamble of that Act recited that by divers Acts of Parliament, and more particularly the Companies Act, 1863 (*sic.* the proper title is "The Companies Clauses Consolidation Act, 1863"), companies authorised to issue debenture stock were empowered to raise, by means of such stock, all moneys which they might for the time being be authorised to raise on mortgage or bond; and that doubts were entertained whether it was lawful for trustees, authorised to invest trust funds in the mortgages or bonds of companies, to invest such funds in debenture stock.

The preamble makes it clear that the Legislature, in speaking of companies, mortgages, bonds, and debenture stock, was dealing only with companies incorporated by special Act of Parliament or expressly authorised by statute to issue debenture stock, with mortgages, bonds, and debenture stock such as are issued under the Companies Clauses Consolidation Act, 1845, and with debenture stock such as is issued under the Companies Clauses Consolidation Act, 1863.

It is conceived that, having regard to its history, the same limitation must be placed on the present subsection. It is dealing with companies regulated by the Companies Clauses Acts or similar special enactments, and has no bearing on the securities issued by companies incorporated by registration under the Companies Acts 1862 to 1900. "Mortgages or bonds" is an expression used in the Companies Clauses Acts, but seldom, if ever, used in speaking of borrowed capital of registered companies, where the term "debenture" is almost universal. In construing the words "railway or other companies," it is conceived that, since the special words do not exhaust the *genus*, *Fenwick* v. *Schmalz*, L.R. 3 C.P. 313; *re Stockport Ragged Schools* (1898) 2 Ch. 687, the *ejusdem generis* rule should be applied. See, however, *re Sharp*, 45 C.D. 286.

Debenture stock of a company under the Companies Acts 1862 to 1900 is essentially different from debenture stock issued by railway and other companies under the Companies Clauses Act, 1863. Debenture stock issued under the Act of 1863 is a security of an anomalous character, and more closely resembles preference stock, with a right to a receiver in certain events, than a mortgage debt. It is irredeemable, unless Parliament in the particular case, otherwise enacts; the interest is payable only out of profits; and though the debenture stockholders can obtain the appointment of a receiver if the interest be in arrear, they can take only "the fruit of the tree;" they cannot realise their security by foreclosure or sale (Palmer's Company Precedents, vol. iii., 8th edit, pp. 6, 7).

Debenture stock of a company under the Companies Acts 1862 to 1900 is merely borrowed capital consolidated for the sake of convenience (Lindley on Companies, p. 195). Apart from its history, there seems no particular reason why this sub-section should not empower trustees, expressly authorised to invest on the debentures of a registered company, to invest on debenture stock of such a company. Having regard, however, to its history, it is submitted that trustees cannot safely act on this view. Contributory mortgages are an improper investment (see *post*, p 231). Many of the objections to a contributory mortgage also attach to a share in debenture stock issued by registered companies.

There is no statutory enactment (except section 21 of the Settled Land Act, 1882) authorising trustees to invest on mortgages or bonds of a railway or other company.

Subsection 3.—This subsection replaces section 27 of the Local Loans Act, 1875 (38 & 39 Vict. c. 83). Though the point is probably of very little importance, the question again arises whether, in using in the Act of 1875, the expression, "debentures or debenture stock of any railway or other company," the Legislature contemplated securities of a company registered under the Companies Act, 1862.

A consideration of section 1 (*m*) (*ante*, p. 14), the Rule of of Court (*ante*, p. 28), and the present subsection, leads to the following conclusions:—

1. Under the present subsection a trustee authorised by the trust instrument to invest in debentures or debenture stock of any railway or other company may, unless the contrary is expressed in the instrument authorising the investment, invest in *any* nominal debentures or nominal debenture stock issued by any local authority under the Local Loans Act, 1875 (without any limit as to population), although such debentures or debenture stock are redeemable within fifteen years, and may do so free from the statutory limitation as to price contained in section 2.

2. The Trustee Act, 1893, is (see definition, section 50) an instrument, and section 1 authorises investment on debenture stock of a railway company, but it imposes limits on the investments which it authorises trustees to make on nominal debentures or debenture stock under the Local Loans Act, 1875. Such limitations, as constituting an "expression of the contrary," are not, it is to be assumed, dispensed with by the present subsection.

3. The express powers conferred by section 1 (*m*) to invest on nominal or inscribed stock of large towns and county councils, and by section 1 (*o*) to invest in nominal debentures or nominal debenture stock under the Local Loans Act, 1875, remain unaffected by the present section. See notes to section 2, *ante*, p. 32.

In *re Maberly*, 33 C.D. 455, it was held that trustees with power to invest in railway debenture stock, on which a dividend had been paid for ten years, could not invest on debentures or debenture stock under the Local Loans Act, unless the local authority had paid a dividend for ten years   That case was decided on section 27 of the Act of 1875, which gave trustees "the same" power of investing in local loan debentures as they had of investing on railway debentures or debenture stock.   The present subsection cannot be so construed.

Subsection 4.—This subsection replaces section 7 of the Isle of Man Loans Act, 1880. A consideration of the Rule of Court (*ante*, p. 28), of the Colonial Stock Act, 1900 (*post* p. 191), and of this subsection, leads to the following conclusions :—

1. Under the present subsection a trustee who is authorised by the trust instrument to invest in securities in the Isle of Man or of a colony, may, unless the contrary is expressed in the instrument, invest in *any* securities of the Isle of Man under the 1880 Act, whether redeemable within fifteen years or not.

2. The Trustee Act, 1893, is, by virtue of the definition in section 50, an instrument, and section 1 incorporating the Rule of Court authorises investment on securities in the Isle of Man and certain Colonial Guaranteed Stocks (see *ante*, p. 28); but by providing that Isle of Man Debentures or Debenture Stock on which an investment is made must not be redeemable within fifteen years, it expresses a contrary intention, which will have the effect of excluding for the purposes of the present section securities under the Act of 1880 redeemable within fifteen years.

3. Section 1 (*o*) of this Act incorporating the Rule of Court is not affected by this subsection (see *ante*, p 28).

4. The Colonial Stock Act, 1900 (*post*, p 191), is, by virtue of the definition in section 50 of the present Act, an instrument authorising trustees to invest in certain Colonial Stocks.   The effect of the present subsection since the passing of that Act would appear to be to authorise trustees to invest in Isle of Man Stock, whether redeemable within fifteen years or not.

Subsection 5 —This replaces section 40 of the Mortgage Debenture Act, 1865, which is an Act enabling certain companies, whose objects are limited to making advances on lands, etc., and to borrowing money on mortgage debentures, to issue mortgage debentures founded on securities upon or affecting land.

For definitions of "trustee," "trust," "instrument," "mortgage," "property," "securities," and "stock," see section 50, *infra.*

Section 6.

Section 6.—A trustee having power to invest in the purchase of land or on mortgage of land may invest in the purchase, or on mortgage of any land, notwithstanding the same is charged with a rent

Power to invest, notwithstanding drainage charges

Sect. 6.

under the powers of the Public Money Drainage Acts, 1846 to 1856, or the Landed Property Improvement (Ireland) Act, 1847, or by an absolute order made under the Improvement of Land Act, 1864, unless the terms of the trust expressly provide that the land to be purchased or taken in mortgage shall not be subject to any such prior charge.

This section replaces section 27 of the Public Money Drainage Act, 1846; section 53 of the Landed Property Improvement (Ireland) Act, 1847, and section 61 of the Improvement of Land Act, 1864.

"Mortgage of Land."—See notes to section 1, *ante*, p. 19, and Appendix A as to investment on mortgage under this Act.

For definitions of "trustee," "land," and "mortgage," see section 50, *infra*.

Sect. 7.

Trustees not to convert inscribed stock into certificates to bearer.

Section 7.—(1.) A trustee, unless authorised by the terms of his trust, shall not apply for or hold any certificate to bearer issued under the authority of any of the following Acts; that is to say—

(*a*) The India Stock Certificate Act, 1863 ;
(*b*) The National Debt Act, 1870 ;
(*c*) The Local Loans Act, 1875 ;
(*d*) The Colonial Stock Act, 1877.

(2.) Nothing in this section shall impose on the Bank of England or of Ireland, or on any person authorised to issue any such certificates, any obligation to inquire whether a person applying for such a certificate is or is not a trustee, or subject them to any liability in the event of their granting any such certificate to a trustee, nor invalidate any such certificate if granted.

This section replaces section 4 of the India Stock Certificate Act, 1863 (26 & 27 Vict c. 73); section 29 of the National Debt Act, 1870 (33 & 34 Vict. c. 71); section 21 of the Local Loans Act, 1875 (38 & 39 Vict. c. 83); and section 12 of the Colonial Stock Act, 1877 (40 & 41 Vict. c. 59).

The wording of the marginal note should be observed. As to the effect of marginal notes, see *ante*, p 35.

"Certificate to Bearer."—A direction to invest "in the names" of trustees precludes investment in bearer securities.

Re Roth, Goldberger v. *Roth* (1896) W.N. 16; 74 L.T. 50; cf. *Webb* v. *Jonas*, 39 C.D. at pp. 664, 666; *Field* v. *Field* (1894) 1 Ch. at p. 429.

It has been held that bearer securities may, without breach of trust, be deposited in a box at a banker's on account of all the trustees, one being allowed by the rest to keep the key of the box in order to obtain the coupons, the bankers seeing that only coupons are taken out. *Mendes* v. *Guedalla*, 2 J. & H. 259, at p. 278. Another course (which the authors believe is generally followed) is to deposit the securities in the joint names of the trustees with the bankers to the trust, for safe custody and for the collection of coupons. *Re de Pothonier, Dent* v. *de Pothonier* (1900) 2 Ch. 529.

Bearer securities must not be left in the custody of one of several trustees, *Lewis* v. *Nobbs*, 8 C.D. 591; nor of the solicitor or any other agent other than the bankers of the trustees. *Field* v. *Field* (1894) 1 Ch. 425; *re de Pothonier, supra.*

As to custody of title deeds and non negotiable securities, see *re Sisson's Settlement, Jones* v. *Trappes* (1903) 1 Ch. 262.

For definitions of "trust" and "trustee," see section 50, *infra.*

Section 8.—(1.) A trustee lending money on the security of any property on which he can lawfully lend shall not be chargeable with breach of trust by reason only of the proportion borne by the amount of the loan to the value of the property at the time when the loan was made, provided that it appears to the court that in making the loan the trustee was acting upon a report as to the value of the property made by a person whom he reasonably believed to be an able practical surveyor or valuer instructed and employed independently of any owner of the property, whether such surveyor or valuer carried on business in the locality where the property is situate or elsewhere, and that the amount of the loan does not exceed two equal third parts of the value of the property as stated in the report, and that the loan was made under the advice of the surveyor or valuer expressed in the report.

Sect. 8.

Loans and investments by trustees not chargeable as breaches of trust.

(2.) A trustee lending money on the security of any leasehold property shall not be chargeable with breach of trust only upon the ground that in making such loan he dispensed either wholly or partly with the production or investigation of the lessor's title.

(3.) A trustee shall not be chargeable with breach of trust only upon the ground that in effecting the purchase of or in lending money upon the security of any property he has accepted a shorter title than the title which a purchaser is, in the absence of a special contract, entitled to require, if in the opinion of the court the title accepted be such as a person acting with prudence and caution would have accepted.

(4.) This section applies to transfers of existing securities as well as to new securities, and to investments made as well before as after the commencement of this Act, except where an action or other proceeding was pending with reference thereto on the twenty-fourth day of December one thousand eight hundred and eighty-eight.

This section replaces, with slight verbal alterations, section 4 of the Trustee Act, 1888 (51 & 52 Vict. c. 59), which section is repealed by the present Act. See section 51, and Schedule, *infra*.

In subsection 1 of the repealed section the words "on which he can lawfully lend" did not appear; but at the end of the subsection there was the following sentence: "And this section shall apply to a loan upon any property of any tenure, whether agricultural or house or other property, on which the trustee can lawfully lend." This alteration does not appear to affect the scope of the enactment, for the references in subsection 1 to the local situation of the property, and in subsection 2 to the title which a purchaser may require, appear to indicate sufficiently that the wide meaning given by section 50 (see p. 161, *infra*) to the word "property" cannot here be applied.

Subsection 1.—Before the Act of 1888 the Courts of Equity had indicated and given effect to certain general principles for the guidance of trustees in lending money on the security of real estate. Thus it had been laid down that in the case of ordinary agricultural land the margin ought not to be less than one-third of its value; whereas in cases where the subject of the security derived its value from buildings erected upon the land, or its use for trade purposes, the margin ought not to be less than one-half. These were not laid down as hard-and-fast limits up to which trustees would be invariably safe, and beyond which they could never be in safety to lend, but rather as indicating the lowest margins which in ordinary circumstances a careful investor of trust funds ought to accept. *Per* Lord Watson in *Learoyd* v. *Whiteley*, 12 A.C. 727.

Trustees are not bound to take the precautions stated in the subsection. The Act merely says if they do so they shall not be liable by reason *only* of the proportion borne by the amount of the loan to the value of the property. The subsection only deals with the question of value. The trustee must show that the loan is not improper independently of value, *Blyth* v *Fladgate* (1891) 1 Ch. 737; *re Walker*, 59 L.J. Ch. 386. See *ante*, p. 20, and Appendix.

To obtain the protection afforded by the enactment, it must be shown to the Court—

1. That in making the loan the trustee was acting upon a report as to the value of the property;
2. That the report was made by a person whom the trustee reasonably believed to be an able practical surveyor or valuer;
3. That the surveyor or valuer was instructed and employed independently of any owner of the property;
4. That the amount of the loan does not exceed two equal third parts of the value of the property as stated in the report; and
5. That the loan was made under the advice of the surveyor or valuer expressed in the report.

It is not essential that the surveyor or valuer should carry on business in the locality where the property is situate. Before the Act of 1888 trustees could not safely act on the opinion of a surveyor who did not carry on business in the locality, *Budge* v. *Gummow*, 7 Ch. 719, *Fry* v *Tapson*, 28 C D. 268. It would seem from the wording of the section that the surveyor or valuer must be actually engaged in business at the time of the report; the report of a surveyor or valuer who has retired from business would not suffice. It would also seem that the report must be in writing.

The report must state the value of the property. It is not sufficient only to state the amount which the surveyor or valuer thinks may be safely advanced upon the security of the property. *Re Stuart* (1897) 2 Ch. 583.

The surveyor or valuer must be a person whom the trustee himself believes to be an able practical surveyor or valuer. He must exercise his own judgment, and not leave the selection of the surveyor or valuer to his solicitor *Fry* v. *Tapson*, 28 C.D. 268. It is not the solicitor's business to select the surveyor or valuer. If a solicitor be asked to name a valuer, he should submit a name or names to the trustees, and tell them everything which he knows to guide their choice, but leave the choice to them. *Per* Kay, J., in *Fry* v. *Tapson*, *supra*, at p. 281.

The surveyor or valuer must be paid by the mortgagee. He can, however, charge the fee to the mortgagor. *Smith* v. *Stoneham* (1886) W.N 178. The surveyor or valuer must not be employed on the terms that if the mortgage be carried into effect he shall receive a higher fee. *Smith* v. *Stoneham*, *supra*.

The words in subsection 1, "believed to be," do not refer to the words "instructed and employed." The surveyor or valuer

Sect. 8. must *in fact* be so instructed and employed. *Re Somerset* (1894) 1 Ch. 231; *re Walker*, 59 L.J. Ch. 386; cf. *re Stuart* (1897) 2 Ch. 583.

Although trustees are not bound to take the precautions, or limit the amount of a loan to the proportion prescribed by the section, under ordinary circumstances they run grave risks in omitting such precautions or in making an advance of more than two-thirds of the value of the security. The rules in the section constitute a standard by which the conduct of trustees will be judged, and in any case where they feel justified in advancing more than two-thirds of the value, they should at least comply with all the other provisions of the subsection. *Re Stuart* (1897) 2 Ch. 583 As to obtaining relief under section 3 of the Judicial Trustees Act, 1896, where the provisions of this section have not been complied with, see *post*, p. 186.

In the case of a mortgage of a ground rent, small as compared with the rack rent of the property, payable under a lease having sixty or more years to run, the market value of the security is practically free from all causes of depreciation other than fluctuations of the money market; and the income cannot decrease, for if the ground rent be not paid, the right of re-entry can be exercised and the rack rent received instead of the ground rent (see *Vickery* v *Evans*, 32 Beav. 376). Trustees, therefore, can lend a somewhat larger sum on such a security than the sum authorised by this section (see *Vickery* v. *Evans*, 32 Beav. 376), provided, of course, that the ground rent suffices to pay the interest on the mortgage (see *post*, p. 227), and that the ground rents could be readily sold for a sum sufficient to pay the principal sum advanced (see as to market value, *post*, p. 228). Probably a loan of three-fourths of the market value instead of merely two-thirds would be justifiable, *i.e.* a ground rent of £4 worth twenty-five years' purchase would be a good trustee security for £75 to £80 at 4 per cent., although the amount authorised by this section would only be £66 13*s.* 4*d.* The amount lent in *Vickery* v. *Evans*, *supra*, was just over twenty years' purchase of the ground rents.

"Property on which he can lawfully lend."—See note, *supra*, p. 42.

Subsection 2.—Section 15 (*post*, p. 70) deals with the subject of a trustee purchasing leaseholds without calling for the title to the freehold.

This subsection is not an absolute protection to a trustee, it merely enacts that he shall not be chargeable by reason *only* that in making the loan he dispensed with the investigation of the lessor's title.

Subsection 3.—Cf. section 15 (*post*, p. 70). This subsection deals only with length of title, it does not authorise the waiver of other defects in title.

It is conceived that in the application of this section greater latitude will be allowed to trustees purchasing than to trustees investigating the title with a view to a loan. The sole object of a mortgagee is to obtain a thoroughly safe security, and it is conceived that the circumstances under which a trustee mortgagee can accept anything short of a perfect title must be very special. In the case of a purchase, however, the acquisition of the property in the interests of the trust estate may be so desirable that, given a reasonably probable assurance of a good holding title, trustees might be justified in waiving slight defects. But even in making a purchase trustees cannot waive serious defects of title. *Eastern Counties Railway Co.* v. *Hawkes*, 5 H.L.C. 363; *ex parte Governors of Christ's Hospital*, 2 H. & M. 168. And if conditions of sale or the terms of a contract are very special, trustees ought not to bind themselves by signing the contract. See *ex parte Governors of Christ's Hospital, supra.*

"The Title which a Purchaser is . . . entitled to require."—A purchaser under an open contract is entitled to call for the title mentioned below in the following cases of sale —

1. Of freeholds of inheritance, or for lives or copyholds, title for forty years next before the contract. In the case of freeholds for lives, the lease for the lives must be produced though more than forty years old.

2. Of freeholds, formerly copyhold but enfranchised within forty years of the sale, the freehold title back to and including the enfranchisement, and beyond that, the copyhold title back to forty years before the contract, but not the title to make the enfranchisement.

3. Of leaseholds, production of the lease under which the property is held in all cases; and, if the lease be more than forty years old, the title under the lease for the forty years before the contract, otherwise the whole title subsequent to the lease; but not in any case the title to the freehold, nor in the case of the sale of property held by underlease, the title to any leasehold reversion.

4. Of an advowson, title for at least a hundred years before the contract.

5. Of titles or other property held under a grant from the Crown, production of the original grant in all cases, and title thereunder for the forty years next before the contract.

6. Of a reversionary interest, production of the instrument which created it, in all cases; and, in addition, proof that possession of the land has been in accordance with the instrument so produced. See Williams on Vendor and Purchaser, pp. 77–83.

There is no rule relating to the length of title a mortgagee may require. Trustees lending on mortgage are impliedly by this section authorised to accept the same length of title as a purchaser under an open contract could insist on; and in either buying or lending on mortgage to accept an even shorter title,

Sect. 8.

subject to the risk of the Court at some subsequent date saying they have accepted a shorter title than a person acting with prudence and caution would have accepted.

"**If in the Opinion of the Court, etc.**"--These words impose a very large qualification on the generality of the enactment in the subsection. Trustees are not protected for accepting a short title, unless the title actually accepted be not only of such length, but be in *all* respects such, as a prudent and cautious person would have accepted

It would seem that if a trustee failed to escape liability under the provisions of this subsection, he could not get relief under section 3 of the Judicial Trustees Act, 1896.

Subsection 4. "Transfers."—A transfer of a mortgage cannot be safely taken from the mortgagee alone without first inquiring of the mortgagor as to the state of the mortgage debt, and the interest thereon, and obtaining a favourable reply, and without giving notice of the transfer to the mortgagor. *Turner* v. *Smith* (1901) 1 Ch. 213. In practice, the mortgagor is made a party to the transfer, whenever his concurrence can be procured. Williams on Vendor and Purchaser, p. 437.

"**24th day of December, 1888.**"—This is the date when the Trustee Act, 1888, came into operation.

For definitions of "trustee" and "property," see section 50, *infra*.

Sect. 9.

Liability for loss by reason of improper investments

Section 9.—(1.) Where a trustee improperly advances trust money on a mortgage security which would at the time of the investment be a proper investment in all respects for a smaller sum than is actually advanced thereon, the security shall be deemed an authorised investment for the smaller sum, and the trustee shall only be liable to make good the sum advanced in excess thereof with interest.

(2.) This section applies to investments made as well before as after the commencement of this Act, except where an action or other proceeding was pending with reference thereto on the twenty-fourth day of December one thousand eight hundred and eighty-eight.

This section replaces section 5 of the Trustee Act, 1888, which section is repealed by the present Act. See section 51, and Schedule, *infra*.

A mortgage investment by a trustee may be wrongful either as being wholly unauthorised or authorised but improper.

This section deals only with the single instance of an authorised investment improper by reason of the amount of the advance.

First, as to unauthorised investments. If a trustee admit that he has received a trust fund, and state that he afterwards applied it in a way not authorised by the trust, the Court will fasten upon the receipt, and not allow him to discharge himself by pleading a breach of duty; as, if a trustee admit that he once had a fund in his hands, but that he afterwards lent it on personal security not within the terms of the trust. Lewin, 10th edit., p. 1195; *Vigrass* v. *Binfield*, 3 Mad. 62; *Wyatt* v. *Sherratt*, 3 Beav. 498; *Roy* v. *Gibbon*, 4 Hare 65. It follows that where a trustee has made an unauthorised investment, the case must be treated as if the investment had not been made, or had been made for the trustee's own benefit, out of his own moneys, and he had at the same time retained trust moneys in his hands. *Knott* v. *Cottee*, 16 Beav. 77, *re Salmon*, 42 C.D. 351, *per* Kekewich, J.

The *cestuis que trust*, if *sui juris*, may, however, elect to waive the breach of trust, and take to the unauthorised investment. *Re Jenkins and Randall's Contract* (1903) 2 Ch. 362. Such election is a complete waiver of the breach of trust (see *Thornton* v. *Stokill*, 1 Jur., N.S. 751); they could not, for instance, elect to take to a house wrongly purchased, and then sue the trustee for damages for breach of trust for accepting a defective title.

If they cannot, or do not, elect to take to the unauthorised investment, they yet have the right to follow their trust funds, and have a lien on the property for the payment thereof. *Knott* v. *Cottee*, *supra*; *re Salmon*, *supra*, *per* Kekewich, J. A lien is not, strictly speaking, enforceable by sale until established by a decree of a Court of Equity, binding the persons affected by the lien. *Fisher on Mortgage*, 484; *A.-G.* v. *Sittingbourne Railway*, 1 Eq. 636. Obviously in most cases a title could not be made without the order of the Court. An action to enforce a lien of necessity gives the person whose property is charged an opportunity of redeeming. It sometimes happens that the *cestuis que trust* are in a position to sell, and do sell, the property subject to lien, without the assistance of the Court. See *re Salmon*, 42 C.D. 351; *re Lake, ex parte Howe* (1903) 1 K.B. 439. In such a case it is essential that the trustee should be given an opportunity of redeeming. *Re Salmon*, *supra*; *re Lake*, *supra*. Where no such opportunity be given, then if the *cestuis que trust* be capable of electing, they will be deemed to have elected to take to the property, and thus to have waived the breach of trust. See *re Salmon*, *supra*; *re Lake*, *supra*. Though if the *cestuis que trust* be incapable of electing, the trustee has been held to remain liable for his breach of trust. *Head* v. *Gould* (1898) 2 Ch. 250.

Secondly, as to authorised but improper investments. Such an investment is, from the first, part of the trust estate. The trustee is only liable for the loss, and that liability is to

Sect. 9. be enforced when the investment is realised. *Re Salmon*, 42 C.D. 351, *per* Cotton, L.J.; *re Turner* (1897) 1 Ch. 536.

In such a case as that described in the present section, the trustee would, before the Act of 1888, have been liable for the entire loss. *Budge* v. *Gummow*, 7 Ch. 719; *Bell* v. *Turner* (1874) W.N. 113.

"**Proper Investment in all Respects.**"—The section only applies where the breach consists solely of making too large an advance. *Re Walker*, 59 L.J. Ch. 386; *Waite* v *Parkinson*, 85 L.T. 456. The onus of proving that the investment was in all other respects proper is on the trustee. *Jones* v. *Julian*, 25 L.R. Ir. 45; *Want* v. *Campain*, 9 T.L.R. 254.

"**Authorised Investment.**"—This means "authorised and proper," if those terms have the meaning attributed to them in this note.

"**24th day of December, 1888.**"—This is the date when the Act of 1888 came into operation.

For definitions of "trust," "trustee," and "mortgage," see section 50, *infra*.

PART II.

VARIOUS POWERS AND DUTIES OF TRUSTEES.

Appointment of New Trustees.

Sect. 10.

Power of appointing new trustees

Section 10.—(1.) Where a trustee, either original or substituted, and whether appointed by a court or otherwise, is dead, or remains out of the United Kingdom for more than twelve months, or desires to be discharged from all or any of the trusts or powers reposed in or conferred on him, or refuses or is unfit to act therein, or is incapable of acting therein, then the person or persons nominated for the purpose of appointing new trustees by the instrument, if any, creating the trust, or if there is no such person, or no such person able and willing to act, then the surviving or continuing trustees or trustee for the time being, or the personal representatives of the last surviving or continuing trustee, may, by writing, appoint another person or other persons to be a trustee or trustees in the place of the trustee dead, remaining out of the United

Kingdom, desiring to be discharged, refusing, or being unfit or being incapable, as aforesaid.

(2.) On the appointment of a new trustee for the whole or any part of trust property—

(*a*) the number of trustees may be increased; and

(*b*) a separate set of trustees may be appointed for any part of the trust property held on trusts distinct from those relating to any other part or parts of the trust property, notwithstanding that no new trustees or trustee are or is to be appointed for other parts of the trust property, and any existing trustee may be appointed or remain one of such separate set of trustees; or, if only one trustee was originally appointed, then one separate trustee may be so appointed for the first-mentioned part; and

(*c*) it shall not be obligatory to appoint more than one new trustee where only one trustee was originally appointed, or to fill up the original number of trustees where more than two trustees were originally appointed; but, except where only one trustee was originally appointed, a trustee shall not be discharged under this section from his trust unless there will be at least two trustees to perform the trust; and

(*d*) any assurance or thing requisite for vesting the trust property, or any part thereof, jointly in the persons who are the trustees, shall be executed or done.

(3.) Every new trustee so appointed, as well before as after all the trust property becomes by law, or by assurance, or otherwise, vested in him, shall have the same powers, authorities, and discretions, and may in all respects act, as if he had been originally appointed a trustee by the instrument, if any, creating the trust.

E

Sect. 10.

(4.) The provisions of this section relative to a trustee who is dead include the case of a person nominated trustee in a will but dying before the testator, and those relative to a continuing trustee include a refusing or retiring trustee, if willing to act in the execution of the provisions of this section.

(5.) This section applies only if and as far as a contrary intention is not expressed in the instrument, if any, creating the trust, and shall have effect subject to the terms of that instrument and to any provisions therein contained.

(6.) This section applies to trusts created either before or after the commencement of this Act.

This section replaces section 31 of the Conveyancing and Law of Property Act, 1881 (44 & 45 Vict. c. 41), section 5 of the Conveyancing Act, 1882 (45 & 46 Vict. c 39), and section 6 of the Conveyancing and Law of Property Act, 1892 (55 & 56 Vict. c. 13), which sections are repealed by the present Act (see section 51, and Schedule, *infra*) Section 31 of the Conveyancing and Law of Property Act, 1881, was itself a re-enactment, with slight alterations and additions, of sections 27 and 28 of Lord Cranworth's Act (23 & 24 Vict. c. 145).

"A Trustee."—By virtue of section 50, "the expressions 'trust' and 'trustee' include implied and constructive trusts . . . and the duties incident to the office of personal representative of a deceased person." This definition is taken from the Trustee Act, 1850 (13 & 14 Vict. c. 60, s. 2). No such definition was contained in the Conveyancing and Law of Property Act, 1881, nor in Lord Cranworth's Act. The preamble to Lord Cranworth's Act clearly indicates that the power of appointment given by that Act was only intended to apply to trustees appointed under instruments. Accordingly, in spite of the reference in the later Acts, to "the instrument, *if any*, creating the trust; " and, in spite of the definition of trustee in the present Act, it is submitted that the present section can only apply to express trustees, and not to constructive trustees. The language of subsections 1, 2, and 3 appears to assume that the trustees referred to have had trusts or powers "reposed in or conferred on" them, and that they have been "appointed."

There seems no reason for limiting the section to the case of trustees with active duties to perform, thus excluding bare trustees, see note "To perform any trust," *infra*, p. 64, and the judgment of North, J., there cited.

The further question arises whether the section applies to executors and administrators. Under the Trustee Act, 1850, it was held by Kay, J., in *In re Moore*, 21 C.D. 778, that, by virtue of the definition of "trustee" above referred to, the

Court, although it could not remove an executor, could appoint trustees to perform the duties of an executor. In *In re Wittey* (1890) W.N. 1, the Court of Appeal intimated an inclination of opinion that *In re Moore* went too far, and that the Court could not, under the Trustee Act, 1850, appoint a person to discharge duties which belonged only to the office of executor, and not to that of trustee. In *Eaton v. Daines* (1894) W.N. 32, Kekewich, J., suggested that, in *In re Moore*, Kay, J., had not gone so far as to hold that the Act gave power to appoint a trustee to perform the duties of an executor. It would, however, appear from the judgment of Kay, J , in *Brown v. Burdett,* 40 C D. 253, that in his view the Court had this power, though the new trustee appointed to perform such duties would not be able to exercise the power of sale given to executors by Lord St. Leonards's Act. As to appointments by the Court, the question seems to be set at rest by section 25, subsection 3 of the present Act (which appears not to have been referred to in *Eaton v. Daines*). It is now, however, raised as to the present section, in consequence of the inclusion of that section in an Act containing the above definition of trustee, and the absence of any provision such as that contained in subsection 3 of section 25. It is submitted that the correct view is that no power is given by this section to appoint a new executor, or a trustee to perform the duties of an executor, but that when the duties of an executor are performed, and the property remains vested in him, as express trustee of the will, the section gives power to appoint a new trustee in his place. This appears to be the view acted upon by Stirling, J., in *In re Earl of Stamford, Payne v. Stamford* (1896) 1 Ch 288, 297. In cases, however, in which the executor is not named a trustee in the will, it is suggested that, after performing his duties as executor, he will be merely a constructive trustee of any property remaining under his control, and that the present section will not apply to him. In such a case, application will have to be made to the Court for the appointment of a trustee under section 25 (cf. *In re Davis's Trusts*, 12 Eq 214). The case of *re Ratcliff* (1898) 2 Ch. 352, would seem to be an authority for such an application, though it is not clear whether in that case the new trustee was not to be appointed to act as co-trustee with the executrix. If so, the case suggests that the executrix was a trustee for the general purposes of the will, although not named as trustee by the will

As to the power of the Court to appoint a judicial trustee to be an executor, see Judicial Trustees Act, 1896, section 1 (2), p. 181, *infra.*

Express provision is made by section 3 of the Trustees Appointment Act, 1890 (53 & 54 Vict. c. 19), making the provisions of this section apply to the charitable trusts therein mentioned. The language of the present section is wide enough to include charitable trusts in general. *Re Coates and Parsons*, 34 C.D. 370.

Express provision is made by section 47 of the present Act,

Sect. 10. making this section applicable to trustees for the purposes of the Settled Land Acts, 1882 to 1890 (see p. 156, *infra*).

"**Is dead.**"—That this includes the case of death in the lifetime of the testator, see subsection 4. Where, therefore, a person is nominated by the will to exercise the statutory power, such person may appoint in the event of the death of one or all of the trustees in the lifetime of the testator. Where there is no such person nominated, the power can be exercised by a trustee who survives the testator, or by the personal representatives of such trustee; but if no person nominated as trustee survives the testator, the power cannot be exercised, for there has never been any "last surviving or continuing trustee" whose personal representative could claim to act. *Nicholson* v. *Field* (1893) 2 Ch. 511. As to the power of the Court to appoint in such a case, see notes, "Whenever it is expedient to appoint a new trustee (6)," and "Or although there is no existing trustee," to section 25, *infra*, pp 97, 102. As to when death is to be presumed, see notes to section 26, subsection 4, *infra*, p. 109.

"**Remains out of the United Kingdom for more than Twelve Months.**"—Lord Cranworth's Act made no provision for this event, which was first provided for by section 31 of the Conveyancing and Law of Property Act, 1881. *Re Walker and Hughes Contract*, 24 C D 698; *re Coates and Parsons*, 34 C D. 370. The present section was held not to apply in a case in which during the twelve months the trustee was in England during one week, and transacted business of the trust. *In re Walker, Summers* v. *Barrow* (1901) 1 Ch. 259 As to when the Court will appoint a new trustee in place of a trustee who is abroad, see notes to section 25, *infra*, p. 98; and as to vesting orders when a trustee is out of the jurisdiction, see sections 26 and 35, *infra*, pp. 103, 129.

"**Desires to be discharged.**"—As to the retirement of a trustee without the appointment of a new trustee, see section 11, *infra*; and as to the general right of a trustee to be discharged from the trusts, see *Forshaw* v. *Higginson*, 20 B 485; *Greenwood* v. *Wakeford*, 1 B 576, 581; *Courtenay* v. *Courtenay*, 3 Jo. and Lat. 519, 533; *re Chetwynd* (1902) 1 Ch. 692.

"**From all or any of the Trusts or Powers.**"—The words "all or any of" were not in section 31 of the Conveyancing and Law of Property Act, 1881, and are here inserted in view of the difficulty raised in *Savile* v. *Couper*, 36 C.D. 520, and in *re Moss's Trusts*, 37 C.D. 513, that there was no power to appoint, under that section and section 5 of the Conveyancing Act, 1882, trustees of a part of the trust property, unless there was a vacancy as to the whole.

"**Refuses . . . to act.**"—A doubt has been suggested whether a "refusing" includes a "disclaiming" trustee (Lewin, 10th edit, p. 767, but see p 777). There is, however, authority against the proposition, "a disclaiming trustee never was a trustee," advanced as the ground for this doubt. *Re Hadley*, 5 D.G. and Sm. 67; *Noble* v. *Meymott*, 14 Beav. 471. The cases last cited show that the expression, "a trustee declining to act," includes a trustee disclaiming. In several cases it seems to be suggested that refusing and declining have not identical meanings. *Mitchell* v. *Nixon*, 1 Ir. Eq. Rep. 155; *Crook* v. *Ingoldsby*, 2 Ir. Eq Rep. 375; *re Woodgate*, 5 W.R. 448, *contra; Travis* v. *Illingworth*, 2 Dr. and Sm. 344; 34 L.J. Ch. 481. Although there is no direct authority on the point, it is submitted that the expression "a refusing trustee," as well as "a declining trustee," includes a disclaiming trustee. That disclaimer by a person nominated trustee by a will dates back to the death of a testator, see *Peppercorn* v. *Wayman*, 5 De G. and Sm. 230. That conduct may amount to a disclaimer, see *re Birchall, Birchall* v. *Ashton*, 40 C.D. 436. As to renunciation of probate being evidence of disclaimer of trusts of a mixed fund, see *re Gordon*, 6 C D 531. That a trustee cannot disclaim part of a trust, see *re Lord and Fullerton's Contract* (1896) 1 Ch. 228. As to disclaimer of powers, see notes to section 22, *infra*.

Refusal to act clearly includes refusal by a trustee who has accepted the trust, and presumably means, not refusal to act on a particular occasion, but general refusal to act. Such a case will generally come under the provision for the event of a trustee desiring to be discharged, but will also include, *e g.*, the payment of the trust fund into Court under section 42 *re William's Settlement*, 4 K. & J. 87, and possibly such constant disagreement between trustees as to make action impossible, cf. *Dodson* v. *Powell*, 18 L.J Ch. 237.

"Unfit to act."—An absconding bankrupt trustee is unfit (though not incapable) within the section. *Re Wheeler and De Rochow* (1896) 1 Ch. 315. As a rule, the Court will remove a bankrupt trustee as unfit to act. *Re Barker*, 1 C.D. 43; *r Adams*, 12 C.D. 634. In such cases it is submitted that the donee or continuing trustees could appoint under the present power. But where the bankrupt objects, it will usually be better (and more especially when a vesting order is required) to apply to the Court under section 25. An infant is not "unfit" to act within the meaning of the section, *re Tallatire*, (1885) W N. 191, although an infant trustee will be replaced by the Court.

The power to appoint a new trustee on the ground of the unfitness of the old trustee is obviously one to be exercised with extreme caution where there is any possibility of the unfitness being disputed. In such cases (apart from the case of bankruptcy referred to above) it may be better to commence an action for the removal of the existing trustee. That the Court will not as a rule remove a trustee against his will under section 25, see notes, p 96, *infra*. See also note, "In the place of a trustee dead, &c.," p. 57, *infra*

"Incapable of acting.'—This includes the case of unsoundness

Sect. 10. of mind, *In re Blake* (1887) W N. 173, and generally personal incapacity as contrasted with legal incapacity, *In re Watts*, 9 Hare, 106; but not the case of infancy, *In re Tallatire* (1885) W.N. 191. As to the jurisdiction of the Court to appoint in cases of incapacity, see notes to section 25, *infra*, p. 98.

"**Persons nominated for the Purpose of appointing New Trustees.**"—Where the instrument nominates persons to appoint new trustees, without specifying the events in which the power is to arise, *re Walker and Hughes*, 24 C.D. 698, or when the instrument specifies the events, and includes amongst them the event which has occurred, the section gives power to such person to appoint. But when the instrument specifies the events in which the power is to arise, and does not include amongst them the particular event that has occurred, the section gives the power, not to such persons, but to the surviving or continuing trustees, or the representatives of the last trustee. *In re Wheeler and De Rochow* (1896) 1 Ch. 315. Where the instrument authorises the appointment of a new trustee in the place of a trustee who is desirous of retiring, it is submitted that the donee will not be a "person nominated for the purpose of appointing," in the event of a trustee desiring to retire from part only of the trusts, and will have no power under this section to appoint a new trustee of part only of the trust property. See note "For the whole or any part of the trust property," *infra*, p. 58.

Where the power is given by express reference to an earlier Act, e.g. Lord Cranworth's Act (23 & 24 Vict. c. 145), the donee will be the person to exercise the statutory power for the time being, *re Blake* (1887) W.N 173, unless perhaps where the event giving rise to the power was not one contemplated in the earlier Act. See judgment of North, J., in *re Walker and Hughes*, *supra*.

"**No such Person able and willing to act.**"—This includes the case of a person nominated for the purpose being a lunatic, *re Blake* (1887) W.N. 173, and the case of two nominated to jointly appoint being unable to agree, *re Sheppard's Settlement Trusts* (1888) W.N. 234, and possibly also the case where the person nominated cannot be found, *Cradock* v. *Witham* (1895) W.N. 75.

In the case of the person nominated for the purpose of appointing being unwilling to appoint, on the ground that an appointment was unnecessary or inexpedient, it would be undesirable for the trustees to override the decision of the person so nominated, except when such decision is clearly erroneous or improper.

As to the jurisdiction in lunacy to appoint new trustees where the donee of a power to appoint is a lunatic, see Lunacy Act, 1890 (53 Vict. c. 5), sections 128, 129; and *re Shortridge* (1895) 1 Ch. 278.

A power of appointing new trustees given to a tenant for

life may be exercised after he has alienated his interest. *Hardaker* v. *Moorhouse*, 26 C.D. 417. Where the trusts are being administered by the Court, the persons nominated to appoint new trustees may appoint, but the Court will see that they do not appoint improper persons, *per* Jessel, M.R., *Tempest* v. *Lord Camoys*, 21 C.D. 571, 578; *In re Norris, Allen* v. *Norris*, 27 C.D. 333; *In re Gadd, Eastwood* v. *Clark*, 23 C.D. 134.

"**Then the Surviving or Continuing Trustees or Trustee.**"— By virtue of subsection 4 (see notes, *infra*, p. 60), the expression "a continuing trustee" includes a refusing or retiring trustee, if willing to act in the execution of the provisions of this section. But unless it be shown that he is willing and competent to join in making the appointment, the concurrence of such a trustee is not necessary. *Re Coates and Parsons*, 34 C D. 370; *re Norris, Allen* v. *Norris*, 27 C.D. 333.

"**Or the Personal Representatives of the Last Surviving or Continuing Trustee.**"—The question who are the "personal representatives" of a last trustee was fully discussed in *In re Parker's Trusts* (1894) 1 Ch. 707, a case in which a last trustee of a will by his will appointed "general executors," and also purported to appoint special executors for the purpose of executing, in continuation to himself, the trusts of the will of the original testator. The general executors obtained probate, and appointed new trustees of the earlier will It was held that the appointment was good, and that the concurrence of the special executors was not required. As to the rights of general and special executors respectively, see also *In re Cohen's Executors and London County Council* (1902) 1 Ch. 187.

The executor of a sole trustee is the personal representative of "the last surviving" trustee. *Re Shafto's Trusts*, 29 C.D. 247. The personal representative of the survivor of two persons nominated trustees in a will, both of whom died before the testator, is not by virtue of subsection 4 a personal representative of a "last surviving trustee" *Nicholson* v. *Field*, (1893) 2 Ch. 511. It is submitted that where one of two persons named as trustees of a will survives the testator and dies, and the other person named as trustee subsequently disclaims, the executor of the deceased trustee will be the personal representative of "the last surviving trustee" within the language of the section (for the disclaimer dates back to the death of the testator. *Peppercorn* v. *Wayman*, 5 D.G. and Sm 230).

The question whether the personal representatives of a last trustee are themselves trustees will sometimes arise. In so far as the property or the power of dealing with the property is vested in them, they are, of course, constructive trustees. Whether they are the trustees of the instrument for all purposes depends on the language of the instrument (see Underhill, Law of Trusts, 5th edit., pp. 288, 289). It would appear that only if the instrument mentions the heirs or personal representatives of the trustees generally, or of the last surviving trustee, will the personal representatives be trustees for all purposes. *Mortimor* v. *Ireland*, 11 Jur. 721; *re Osborne and Rowlett*, 13 C.D. 774; *re Morton and Hallett*, 15 C.D. 143; *re Cunningham and Frayling* (1891) 2 Ch. 567; *re Pixton and Tong's Contract* (1897) W N. 178, 46 W.R. 187; *Ingleby and Norwich Union Insurance Co*, 13 L.R. Ir. 326; and cf. section 38 (2) of Settled Land Act, 1882, set out p. 157, *infra*.

"**May by Writing appoint.**"—No obligation is imposed on the personal representatives of a last surviving trustee to exercise the power. *Re Sarah Knight's Will*, 26 C.D. 82

Before exercising the power, the donee should communicate with tenant for life and remainderman, if they are *sui juris*. *O'Reilly* v. *Alderson*, 8 Hare 101.

It has been argued that since the power is given to appoint "by writing," the appointment may be made by will. *Re Parker's Trusts* (1894) 1 Ch. 707. Although in that case the language of the section was held to be "inapplicable to an appointment by the last surviving trustee in place of himself, and to take effect at his own death," it seems still open to argument that an appointment by will by a donee, other than a last surviving trustee, might be a valid (though doubtless an improper) exercise of the power. It is obviously desirable in all cases that appointments should be made by deed; and where a vesting declaration is required, this is essential. See section 12, *infra*.

"**Another Person or Persons to be a Trustee or Trustees.**"— It has been held under similar powers contained in a settlement that, on the double grounds that the power is fiduciary, and that "other person" means person other than the donee of the power, the donees cannot appoint one of themselves to be a trustee *In re Skeats's Settlement, Skeats v. Evans*, 42 C.D. 522 (referred to with approval in *re Shortridge* (1895) 2 Ch. 278); *re Newen, Newen* v. *Barnes* (1894) 2 Ch. 297. In the recent case of *Montefiore* v *Guedalla* (1903) 2 Ch. 723, it was held by Buckley, J., that a power to appoint trustees (not expressly limited to "other" persons) authorises the donees of the power of appointment to appoint one of themselves, although "it is a most salutary rule that they should do so only in special circumstances." The result, therefore, appears to be that an appointment by any persons to whom the statutory power is given, of one of themselves, would be invalid under the section, if the same construction is to be placed on the expression "another person" therein as was given to "other person" in *re Skeats* and *re Newen* cited above. Apart from those words, such an appointment would, under the general principle laid down in *re Skeats, re Newen, re Shortridge, Tempest* v *Camoys*, 58 L.T. 221, and *Montefiore* v. *Guedalla*, though not absolutely invalid, be improper, unless in most exceptional circumstances. The correctness of the decision in *re Skeats* as to the meaning of "other person" is questioned in Farwell on Powers, 2nd edit, p. 655.

In considering who are proper persons to be appointed trustees, the principles on which the Court acts when appointing trustees should be considered. See notes to sections 25 and 47, *infra*, pp. 99 and 158. It does not, however, follow that an appointment out of Court of a person whom the Court would not itself have appointed is invalid. *Re Earl of Stamford, Payne* v. *Stamford* (1896) 1 Ch. 288; *In re Kemp's Settled Estates*, 24 C D. 485; *Foster* v. *Abraham*, 17 Eq. 351; *In re Norris, Allen* v. *Norris*, 27 C.D. 333.

Section 19 of the Interpretation Act, 1889 (52 & 53 Vict. c. 63), provides that the expression "person," in every Act passed after the 1st of January, 1890, "shall, unless the contrary intention appears, include any body of persons corporate or unincorporate." The present section, which, unlike the section it replaces, is contained in an Act passed after the date mentioned, appears, therefore, to authorise the appointment of a corporation to be a trustee. The practical objection to adopting this course, viz that a corporation could not hold in joint tenancy with an individual, *Law Guarantee Society* v *Bank of England*, 24 Q.B D. 406, has been removed by the Bodies Corporate (Joint Tenancy) Act, 1899 (62 & 63 Vict. c. 20). That the Court had no power under the Trustee Act, 1850, to appoint a corporation trustee, see *Billing* v. *Brogden* (1888) W.N 238.

"**In the Place of the Trustee dead, remaining out of the United Kingdom, etc.**"—The effect of the section is to enable the persons entitled to exercise the power to remove a trustee without his concurrence, *e.g.* in the cases of lunacy, absence, and unfitness, and it is apprehended that this power can be exercised in proper cases even if the trustee is known to be unwilling to retire. It therefore appears that in this respect the power given by the present section to individuals is greater than that given to the Court by section 25. See notes to that section, *infra*, p 96.

Subsection 2. "On the Appointment of a New Trustee."—The question arises whether "the appointment of a new trustee" here referred to is an appointment under the powers of the present section only, or whether the expression includes an appointment, however made. It might have been supposed that the provisions of subsection 2 were only ancillary to those of subsection 1. The opening words of subsection 3, "every new trustee so appointed," appear to indicate that all that has gone before relates to only one method of appointment, namely, an appointment under subsection 1, and the reference in subsection 2 to discharge "under this section" supports this view. On the other hand, in his note on this subsection, Mr. Wolstenholme states that the subsection applies to appointments "under powers in trust deeds as well as under the statutory powers" In re *Paine's Trusts*, 38 Ch. D. 725; re *Moss's Trusts*, 37 Ch. D. 513, re *Hetherington's Trusts*, 34 Ch. D. 211; and re *Nesbitt's Trusts*, 19 L.R. Ir. 509, it seems to have been assumed that

Sect. 10. these words were applicable to appointments by the Court under the Trustee Act, 1850.

"**For the Whole or any Part of Trust Property.**"—These words do not occur in section 31 of the Conveyancing and Law of Property Act, 1881. In *Savile* v. *Couper*, 36 Ch. D. 520, and in *re Moss's Trusts*, 37 Ch. D. 513, it was held that under that section and section 5, subsection 1 of the Conveyancing Act, 1882, there was no power to enable the existing trustees of the whole property to retire from the trusts as to part by means of an appointment of new trustees of that part, although this could be effected under the power of appointing new trustees given to the Court by section 32 of the Trustee Act, 1850. The insertion of the words, "all or any of" in subsection 1 (see note above), and of the words "for the whole or any part of trust property" in subsection 2, appears to remove the difficulty discussed in those cases.

"**The Number of Trustees may be increased.**"—Similar provision was formerly contained in subsection 2 of section 31 of the Conveyancing and Law of Property Act, 1881. It should be noted that the power of appointing an additional trustee under this section only arises when a vacancy exists. When there is no vacancy an additional trustee can only be appointed by the Court *Re Brackenbury's Trusts*, 10 Eq. 45; *re Gregson's Trusts*, 34 C.D. 209; and see note, "In addition to," to section 25, *infra*, p. 101.

"**A Separate Set of Trustees.**"—Similar provision was formerly contained in section 5 of the Conveyancing Act, 1882, as amended by section 6 of the Conveyancing and Law of Property Act, 1892. Independently of these provisions the Court had power to appoint separate sets of trustees for separate parts of the trust property under section 32 of the Trustee Act, 1850, *In re Paine's Trusts*, 28 C.D. 725; *re Hetherington's Trusts*, 34 C.D. 211; *re Moss's Trusts*, 37 C.D. 513; *re Cotterill's Trusts*, (1869) W.N. 183; *re Cunard's Trusts*, 27 W.R. 52; *re Aston's Trusts*, 25 L.R. Ir. 96; and also under its ordinary jurisdiction in an administration action, *re Grange, Cooper* v. *Todd*, 81 W.N. 50. Where there were no trustees the Court appointed new trustees of part only of the trust property, there being no active duties as to the other part, *re Dennis's Trusts*, 12 W.R. 575. But an individual donee of a power of appointment in the usual form had no power to appoint a new trustee of part only of the trust property. *Savile* v. *Couper*, 36 C.D. 520, *re Moss's Trusts*, 37 C.D. 513; *re Nesbitt's Trusts*, 19 L.R. Ir. 509; and see note above, "For the whole or any part of trust property."

"**Held on Trusts distinct from those relating to any other Part.**"—The fact that in certain events the trusts of the different parts of the trust property may coalesce does not prevent the trusts being "distinct trusts" for the purpose of appointment of new trustees. *In re Hetherington's Trusts*,

34 C.D. 211; *In re Moss's Trusts*, 37 C.D. 515. But it would
seem that unless the parts are presently separable, separate
sets of trustees cannot be appointed. For instance, if property
is settled upon trust for A for life, and on the death of A, upon
trust as to one moiety for B and as to the other moiety for C,
it is submitted that separate sets of trustees could not be
appointed in the lifetime of A. On the other hand, if property
is settled as to one moiety upon trust for A for life, and after
the death of A for B, and as to the other moiety upon trust
for A for life, and after the death of A for C, it is submitted
that separate sets of trustees could be appointed even in the
lifetime of A.

"Not be obligatory to appoint more than one New
Trustee, etc."—Similar provision was formerly contained in
section 31 of the Conveyancing and Law of Property Act, 1881,
subsection 2 (c). Before that Act came into force it appears
to have been doubtful whether under Lord Cranworth's Act, or
under instruments which did not contain special provisions
relating to the matter, one trustee could be appointed in place
of two, or two in place of three, *re Mercer*, 38 Sol. J. 388;
Hulme v. *Hulme*, 2 M. & K. 682; *Lonsdale* v. *Beckett*, 4 D.G.
& Sm. 73; *West of England Bank* v. *Murch*, 23 C.D. 138,
but there was no general rule that to make a valid appointment
all the existing vacancies need be filled up, *In re Fagg*, 19 L.J.
Ch. 175; *re Cunningham and Wilson* (1877) W.N. 258.

It must be remembered that this section takes effect only
if and as far as a contrary intention is not expressed in the
trust instrument (see subsection 5). An indication of an
intention that the original number of trustees should always
be kept up (cf. *Emmet* v. *Clark*, 3 Gif 32; *re Cunningham and
Wilson*, *supra*) would probably be held to be an expression of a
contrary intention as to this provision.

It must also be remembered that the section imposes no
obligation to appoint, and thus now, as formerly (see *Peacock* v.
Colling, 33 W.R. 528), the mere fact that he is the sole survivor
does not oblige a trustee to appoint a co-trustee, in cases in
which the instrument contemplates a single trustee acting.

"Shall not be discharged under this Section."—In the
case of an appointment under this section, therefore, a trustee
cannot be discharged from the trust, unless on the appointment being completed there will be at least two trustees. The
provision does not apply in the case of appointments made
otherwise than under this section. (As to the question whether
this subsection applies to such last-mentioned appointments,
see note, "On the appointment of a new trustee," *supra*) The
result of an attempt to appoint a sole trustee, where two or
more trustees were originally appointed, would appear to be to
make him a co-trustee with the retiring trustees or trustee.
It must be remembered, however, that by virtue of subsection
5 this provision only takes effect subject to the terms of the
instrument creating the trust.

Sect. 10. "Any Assurance or Thing requisite for vesting the Trust Property."—As to vesting declarations, see section 12, *infra*.

"Every New Trustee so appointed . . . shall have the same Powers."—This provision reproduces subsection 5 of section 31 of the Conveyancing and Law of Property Act, 1881, which subsection was a re-enactment of the concluding provisions of section 27 of Lord Cranworth's Act (23 & 24 Vict. c. 145) so far as they related to appointments under that Act. For a similar provision as to trustees appointed by the Court, see section 37, *infra*.

"As well before as after all the Trust Property becomes . . . vested in him."—As to the doubt formerly existing whether a new trustee is actually such until transfer of the estate to him, see Lewin on Trusts, 10th edit., p 770. See also *Mara* v. *Browne* (1896) 1 Ch. 199, 213

Subsection 4. "A Person nominated Trustee in a Will but dying before the Testator."—This provision was formerly contained in subsection 6 of section 31 of the Conveyancing and Law of Property Act, 1881, which subsection replaced section 28 of Lord Cranworth's Act (23 & 24 Vict. c 145). The personal representative of the survivor of two persons nominated trustees in a will, both of whom died before the testator, is not a personal representative of a "last surviving trustee" within subsection 1. *Nicholson* v *Field* (1893) 2 Ch. 511. (See note above, "Or the personal representatives of the last surviving or continuing trustee.")

"A Refusing or Retiring Trustee if willing to act in the Execution of the Provisions of this Section."—This provision was formerly contained in subsection 6 of section 31 of the Conveyancing and Law of Property Act, 1881 (see note, "Then the surviving or continuing trustees or trustee," *supra*). Where the appointment is made not under this section but under a power in the instrument for the "surviving or continuing trustees or trustee" to appoint, a retiring trustee has no power to appoint. *In re Coates and Parsons*, 34 C.D. 370.

Subsection 5. "If and as far as a Contrary Intention is not expressed."—This is a re-enactment of subsection 7 of section 31 of the Conveyancing and Law of Property Act, 1881. Section 32 of Lord Cranworth's Act (23 & 24 Vict. c 145) was as follows: "None of the powers or incidents hereby conferred or annexed to particular offices, estates, or circumstances shall take effect or be exerciseable if it is declared in the deed, will, or other instrument creating such offices, estates, or circumstances that they shall not take effect; and where there is no such declaration, then if any variations or limitations of any of the powers or incidents hereby conferred or annexed are contained in such deed, will or other instrument, such powers or incidents shall be exerciseable or shall take effect only subject to such variations or limitations."

The insertion in the trust instrument of an express power

to appoint new trustees is not, in itself, an expression of an intention to exclude the present section. *Re Coates and Parsons,* 34 C.D. 370; *re Wheeler and De Rochow* (1896) 1 Ch. 315 (in each of which cases the express power provided for some, not all, of the events on which the statutory power arises); *Cecil* v. *Langdon,* 28 C.D. 1 (in which case the express power, which was subject to the consent of the tenant for life, only applied to filling up vacancies amongst the original trustees); *In re Llvyd's Trusts* (1888), W.N. 20 (in which case the instrument expressly adopted the provisions of Lord Cranworth's Act, section 27); and *re Sheppard's Settlement Trusts* (1888) W.N. 234 (in which case the donees of the express power refused to exercise it). In the above cases none of the trusts were created after 1881, but since in the cases *re Coates and Parsons* and *re Wheeler and De Rochow* the trusts were created when section 27 of Lord Cranworth's Act was in force, it is submitted that, even in the case of trust instruments dated since 1881, the same rule would apply. See also note above, "Not be obligatory to appoint more than one new trustee, etc."

"**Shall have Effect subject to the Terms of that Instrument.**"—Where the instrument imposes a fetter on the exercise of a power to appoint new trustees contained therein, *e.g.* if it makes the consent of a beneficiary necessary to its exercise, such fetter will not, by virtue of this subsection, apply to the exercise of the statutory power, in circumstances in which the power in the instrument is inapplicable. See judgment of Fry, L.J., in *Cecil* v. *Langdon,* 28 Ch. D. at p. 6. So, too, where a private Estate Act provided that section 27 of Lord Cranworth's Act (23 & 24 Vict. c. 145) should apply to a certain will "provided that every new trustee of the estate should be appointed with the approbation of the Court of Chancery," it was held that the obligation to obtain the approbation of the Court did not apply to or affect the power given by section 31 of the Conveyancing and Law of Property Act, 1881. *Re Lloyd* (1888) W.N. 20.

"**Trusts created before or after the Commencement of the Act.**"—This subsection (6) replaces subsection 8 of section 31 of the Conveyancing and Law of Property Act, 1881. The power of appointment given by section 27 of Lord Cranworth's Act (23 & 24 Vict. c. 145) was not applicable in the case of trusts created before that Act. The power given by the present section, however, is applicable in the case of such trusts.

For definitions of "trust,' "trustee," "instrument," and "property," see section 50, *infra.*

Section 11.—(1.) Where there are more than two trustees, if one of them by deed declares that he is desirous of being discharged from the trust, and if his co-trustees and such other person, if any, as is

Sect. 11.

empowered to appoint trustees, by deed consent to the discharge of the trustee, and to the vesting in the co-trustees alone of the trust property, then the trustee desirous of being discharged shall be deemed to have retired from the trust, and shall, by the deed, be discharged therefrom under this Act, without any new trustee being appointed in his place.

(2.) Any assurance or thing requisite for vesting the trust property in the continuing trustees alone shall be executed or done.

(3.) This section applies only if and as far as a contrary intention is not expressed in the instrument, if any, creating the trust, and shall have effect subject to the terms of that instrument and to any provisions therein contained.

(4.) This section applies to trusts created either before or after the commencement of this Act.

This section is a re-enactment of section 32 of the Conveyancing and Law of Property Act, 1881 (44 & 45 Vict. c. 41), which section is repealed by the present Act. See section 51, and Schedule, *infra.*

"Trustees."—See note "A trustee," to section 10, *supra*, p. 50. For the reasons there discussed, it is submitted that the term "trustee" is only here applicable to express trustees, and does not include executors or administrators.

"Where there are more than Two Trustees."—The section does not enable a trustee to retire so as to leave a sole trustee; and cf. section 10, subsection 2 (c), *supra*, p. 49.

"By Deed."—An appointment under section 10 may be made "by writing."

"Desirous of being discharged."—Apart from this section, a trustee may, before acting, disclaim the trust; and in that case, of course, no discharge is required. Such disclaimer, to be valid, must be of the whole of the trust, and not of part only. *Re Lord and Fullerton's Contract* (1896) 1 Ch. 228. As to disclaimer of powers, see Conveyancing Act, 1882 (45 & 46 Vict. c. 39), section 6; *re Eyre* (1883) W.N. 153; and notes to section 22, *infra*, p 85. After accepting the trusts, a trustee may be discharged by the appointment of a new trustee in his place, either by an individual, under a power in the instrument or under section 10 of the present Act, or by the Court, under section 25, or under its inherent jurisdiction. Except on the appointment of a new trustee in his place, the trustee can only be discharged under this section or under a special power in the instrument, or by the consent of all the beneficiaries, or

by the Court acting under its inherent jurisdiction in an action. **Sect. 11.**
Under section 25 the Court has no jurisdiction to discharge a
trustee without appointing another in his place, and will not
now, for the sake of discharging one trustee, adopt the plan
of reappointing two trustees, in place of themselves and their
co-trustee desirous of retiring. See notes to section 25, *infra*,
p. 100. As to the general right of a trustee to be discharged
from the trusts, see *Forshaw* v. *Higginson*, 20 B. 485; *Greenwood* v. *Wakeford*, 1 B. 576, 581; *Courtenay* v. *Courtenay*, 3 Jo.
& Lat. 519, 533; *re Chetwynd* (1902) 1 Ch. 692.

"**Discharged from the Trust.**"—The section does not
authorise the discharge of a trustee from part only of the trust,
though under section 10 a trustee may be discharged from the
trusts of part of the trust property upon the appointment of a
new trustee of such part.

"**Shall be deemed to have retired from the Trust and shall
by the Deed be discharged therefrom.**"—The result of the
retirement of one trustee is, presumably, to vest in the co-
trustees all powers and discretions which would have become
vested in them were the retiring trustee dead, or had he
disclaimed (As to survivorship of powers, see section 22, *infra* ;
and as to the effect of disclaimer in vesting powers in the other
trustees, see *Cafe* v. *Bent*, 5 Hare 37.)

"**Any Assurance or Thing requisite for vesting the Trust
Property.**"—The mere discharge of the trustee does not, as in
the case of disclaimer or death, itself vest the property in the
co-trustees. (As to vesting by vesting declaration, see section
12, subsection 2, *infra*.)

"**A Contrary Intention.**"—Cf. section 10, subsection 5,
supra, p. 60.

For definitions of "trust," "trustee," "instrument," and
"property," see section 50, *infra*.

Section 12.—(1.) Where a deed by which a **Sect. 12.**
new trustee is appointed to perform any trust
contains a declaration by the appointor to the effect {Vesting of
trust property
that any estate or interest in any land subject to {in new or
the trust, or in any chattel so subject, or the right {continuing
trustees.
to recover and receive any debt or other thing in
action so subject, shall vest in the persons who by
virtue of the deed become and are the trustees for
performing the trust, that declaration shall, without
any conveyance or assignment, operate to vest in
those persons, as joint tenants, and for the purposes
of the trust, that estate, interest, or right.

(2.) Where a deed by which a retiring trustee

Sect. 12. is discharged under this Act contains such a declaration as is in this section mentioned by the retiring and continuing trustees, and by the other person, if any, empowered to appoint trustees, that declaration shall, without any conveyance or assignment, operate to vest in the continuing trustees alone, as joint tenants, and for the purposes of the trust, the estate, interest, or right to which the declaration relates.

(3.) This section does not extend to any legal estate or interest in copyhold or customary land, or to land conveyed by way of mortgage for securing money subject to the trust, or to any such share, stock, annuity, or property as is only transferable in books kept by a company or other body, or in manner directed by or under Act of Parliament.

(4.) For purposes of registration of the deed in any registry, the person or persons making the declaration shall be deemed the conveying party or parties, and the conveyance shall be deemed to be made by him or them under a power conferred by this Act.

(5.) This section applies only to deeds executed after the thirty-first of December one thousand eight hundred and eighty-one.

This section replaces section 34 of the Conveyancing and Law of Property Act, 1881, which section is repealed by the present Act. See section 51, and Schedule, *infra*.

"Where a Deed by which a New Trustee is appointed to perform any Trust contains a Declaration."—The vesting declaration authorised by the present section can only be made by deed, and only by the deed appointing a new trustee. The appointment may be one made either under section 10 or under a power in the trust instrument.

The deed will require a 10*s.* stamp as an appointment of new trustees, and a further 10*s.* stamp as a conveyance. *Hadgett* v. *Commissioners of Inland Revenue*, 3 Ex. Div. 46; section 62 of Stamp Act, 1891.

"To perform any Trust."—These words do not imply that the trustee must have some substantial duty to perform, but include a bare trustee. *Per* North, J., *London and County Banking Co.* v. *Goddard* (1897) 1 Ch. 642.

" That any Estate or Interest in any Land subject to the Trust."—The estate and interest need not, at the time of the declaration, remain vested in the old trustees. Thus where a mortgagor of land by deposit of deeds declared himself trustee of the legal estate for the mortgagee, and later conveyed the legal estate to a subsequent incumbrancer with notice of the prior mortgage, it was held that a vesting declaration, in a deed appointing new trustees of the legal estate, operated to divest the estate from the second mortgagee. *London and County Banking Co.* v. *Goddard* (1897) 1 Ch. 642 ; and see especially the judgment of North, J., S.C., pp 650, 651. It is submitted that, had the second mortgagee in that case had no notice of the prior mortgage, the land vested in him would not have been "land subject to the trust," and that the vesting declaration would not have operated to divest it. It is conceived that the doubt suggested by the learned editor of Lewin on Trusts (10th edit., pp. 773, 774), whether the decision in the last-mentioned case does not go too far, is not well founded.

It is further submitted that the vesting declaration will not operate to vest a legal estate which has never been in the trustees, and, *e.g.*, could not operate to get in a bare legal estate outstanding in a stranger at the date of the declaration of the trusts.

" Any Land subject to the Trust "—It is submitted that this can only apply to land in England or Ireland. By virtue of section 41 of the present Act, and section 2 of the amending Act of 1894, the High Court in England, and the High Court in Ireland, may make vesting orders of land and personal estate in any part of His Majesty's dominions except Scotland.

" The Persons who by virtue of the Deed become and are the Trustees for performing the Trusts."—These are the new trustees, together with the continuing trustees (if any).

" That Declaration shall, without any Conveyance or Assignment, operate to vest."—It is submitted that the appointment of new trustees in itself vests all equitable interests in the persons who upon such appointment are the trustees, and that a conveyance, assignment, or vesting declaration is, strictly, only necessary for vesting the legal estate. Cf. *Warburton* v. *Sandys*, 14 Sim. 622 ; *Dodson* v. *Powell*, 18 L J. Ch. 237 ; see also Wolstenholme, Conveyancing and Settled Land Acts, 8th edit., p. 222, Key and Elphinstone, Precedents, 6th edit, p. 104 ; and for a contrary view, Hood and Challis, Conveyancing and Settled Land Acts, 8th edit., p 370.

That a vesting declaration may operate to vest a legal estate which the outgoing trustee could not himself convey, see note above, " That any estate or interest, etc.," *supra*, p. 64.

" Any Legal Estate or Interest in Copyhold or Customary Land."—These must be conveyed by surrender and admittance in the proper form. Thus the rights of the lord of the manor are preserved intact. In case of difficulty in obtaining the

F

Sect. 12. surrender, application must be made to the Court for a vesting order, under section 26, and, when desired, section 34.

"**Land conveyed by Way of Mortgage.**"—A vesting declaration as to mortgage lands would necessarily bring the trusts upon the title of the mortgage property (see observations of North, J., in *London and Banking Co.* v. *Goddard* (1897) 1 Ch. 642, at p. 649), and accordingly where a transfer could be obtained in the usual form, it would not be desirable, even if possible, to make a vesting declaration. In case of difficulty in obtaining a transfer in the usual form, it was doubtless considered that the mortgagor was entitled to be secured the protection of a vesting order of the Court, and the consequent benefit of section 40 (p. 142, *infra*). Where difficulty is experienced in obtaining a transfer, application must be made to the Court for a vesting order under section 26. *Re Harrison's Settlement* (1883) W.N. 31; *re Keeley's Trusts*, 53 L T. 487.

The exception is not restricted to a legal as distinguished from an equitable estate in the mortgaged land, but it has no application to the right to receive the mortgage moneys, which right accordingly may be dealt with by a vesting declaration The exception does not prevent an equitable mortgagee (under a mortgage deed by which the mortgagor has declared himself a trustee of the legal estate for the mortgagee) from making a vesting declaration on the appointment of a new trustee of the legal estate under a power in the mortgage deed. *London and County Banking Co.* v. *Goddard* (1897) 1 Ch. 642.

"**Transferable in Books kept by a Company.**"—Since it is the universal rule with English companies (whether under the Companies Acts or not) not to recognise trusts on their registers, great inconvenience would be caused if such companies were required to recognise vesting declarations made under this section. Where difficulty is experienced in obtaining a transfer of shares from the registered holder or his personal representatives, application must be made to the Court for a vesting order, under section 35. *Re Harrison's Settlement* (1883) W N. 31.

"**Registration of the Deed in any Registry.**"—Subsection 4 relates to registration of deeds, as in Yorkshire and Middlesex, not to registration of title under the Land Transfer Acts, 1875 and 1897. With regard to registration of title under the Land Transfer Acts, Rule 151 of the Land Transfer Rules, 1903, provides that when the power of disposing of registered land has by virtue of the operation of any statutory power become vested in some person other than the registered proprietor (as, for instance, under this section), and the registered proprietor refuses to execute a transfer, or his execution of a transfer cannot be obtained, or can only be obtained after undue delay or expense, the registrar may, after due notice under the Land Transfer Rules to such proprietor, and on production of the land certificate and such evidence as he may deem sufficient, make such entry in or correction of the register as under the circumstances he shall deem fit. The power conferred on the registrar by Rule 151 is extended by Rule 174 to registered charges.

"The 31st of December, 1881."—This is the date since which the Conveyancing and Law of Property Act, 1881, has been in operation.

For definitions of "trustee," "trust," "land," "conveyance," "mortgage," "stock," and "property," see section 50, *infra*

Purchase and Sale.

Section 13.—(1.) Where a trust for sale or a power of sale of property is vested in a trustee, he may sell or concur with any other person in selling all or any part of the property, either subject to prior charges or not, and either together or in lots, by public auction or by private contract, subject to any such conditions respecting title or evidence of title or other matter as the trustee thinks fit, with power to vary any contract for sale, and to buy in at any auction, or to rescind any contract for sale and to re-sell, without being answerable for any loss.

(2.) This section applies only if and as far as a contrary intention is not expressed in the instrument creating the trust or power, and shall have effect subject to the terms of that instrument and to the provisions therein contained.

(3.) This section applies only to a trust or power created by an instrument coming into operation after the thirty-first of December one thousand eight hundred and eighty-one.

This section replaces section 35 of the Conveyancing and Law of Property Act, 1881, which section is now repealed. See section 51, and Schedule, *infra.*

"**Trust for Sale or Power of Sale.**"—In the absence of context a trust for, or power of, sale, means power to sell for money. *Payne* v. *Cork Co* (1900) 1 Ch. at p. 314. Trustees cannot sell for shares or securities of a company without express authority, or the sanction of the Court, *re Morrison* (1901) 1 Ch. 701 ; *re New* (1901) 2 Ch. 534 , *re Tollemache* (1903) 1 Ch. 457 , nor in consideration of a rent-charge (Sugden on Powers, 8th edit.,

Sect. 13. p. 277; Farwell on Powers, 2nd edit., p. 553); nor, in the case of leaseholds, by sub-demise for the whole term less one day, *re Walker and Oakshott* (1901) 2 Ch 383; neither should trustees sell at a price to be fixed by valuation (Williams on Vendor and Purchaser, p. 280); nor give an option to purchase at a future time, *Clay* v. *Rufford*, 5 De G. & Sm. 768; *Oceanic Steam Co* v. *Sutherbury*, 16 C D. 236.

" Property."—See definition, section 50, *post*, p. 161.

" Trustee."—See subsections 2 and 3, which appear to limit the operation of the section to trusts or powers created by instrument. It is open to question whether an administrator is a trustee within the section. And see definition of " instrument " in section 50, *post*, p 161.

Mortgagees are given similar powers by section 19 of the Conveyancing and Law of Property Act, 1881.

" Concur . . . in selling."—Apart from statutory authority, trustees with a trust for, or power of, sale are justified in concurring with other persons in a joint sale if (1) such a mode of sale is beneficial, (2) the purchase-money is apportioned before completion and the apportioned share of the trustees is duly paid to them, and (3) the apportionment is made by the trustees acting under proper advice. *Re Cooper and Harlech*, 4 C D. 802, at p. 814, and see *re Parker and Beech's Contract* (1887) W.N. p. 27

The proper mode of apportioning the prices of a life estate and a reversion when sold together for a lump sum, is to value each interest separately, not to put a value on one and deduct that from the total price *Re Cooper and Harlech, supra ; Morris* v. *Debenham*, 2 C.D. 540.

" Any Part of the Property."—These words do not authorise a sale of fixtures apart from the land to which they are annexed, *re Yates*, 38 C.D 112 (a case on section 19 of the Conveyancing and Law of Property Act, 1881), nor to sell a house in flats, *re Yates*, at p 121. The words mean that what is sold should be a separable part of the trust property in the state in which it was subjected to the trust (see *re Yates, supra*). As to sale of surface apart from minerals, see section 44, *post*, p. 149.

A conveyance, under this section, of part of the trust property, carries all legal incidents ordinarily accompanying a grant, as, for instance, appurtenances such as ways over the grounds of third persons, and (although the section does not authorise the mere grant of an easement. *Dayrell* v. *Hoare*, 12 A. & E. 356) also apparent continuous easements over the land retained. *Born* v. *Turner* (1900) 2 Ch. 211 Thus on a sale of a house, with windows overlooking vacant land retained by the trustees, there would pass to the purchaser a right to access of light over the land retained. *Born* v. *Turner, supra*.

" Subject to any such Conditions."—As to the conditions which may be inserted on a sale of business as a going concern, cf. *Hawksley* v. *Outram* (1892) 3 Ch. 359.

Sect. 13.

Trustees may act upon the power given by the Sale of Land by Auction Act, 1867, and the Sale of Goods Act, 1893, section 58, respectively, to fix a reserve price, and reserve the right of bidding. *Re Peyton*, 30 Beav. 252 (decided before the passing of either of the above Acts). Indeed it is their duty so to do (see note to *re Peyton, supra*).

Trustees may make all such conditions as a prudent and reasonable owner selling in his own right would impose, *Falkner* v. *Equitable Reversionary Society*, 4 Drew. 352, but notwithstanding section 14, *infra*, it still behoves them not to "damp" the sale by depreciatory conditions; for although under section 14 the purchaser cannot raise any objection, a sale under depreciatory conditions is a breach of trust, for any loss consequent on which the trustees are personally responsible.

"Power to vary or rescind."—Such a power was held not to be unduly depreciatory. *Falkner* v. *Equitable Reversionary Society, supra*

"Without being answerable for any Loss."—These words do not protect from loss arising from undue delay in reselling. *Taylor* v. *Tabrum*, 6 Sim 281.

"Contrary Intention"—Contrast the language of section 1, and of section 17, subsection 5.

"31st of December, 1881."—This is the date since which the Conveyancing and Law of Property Act, 1881, has been in operation.

For definitions of "trust," "trustee," "instrument," and "property," see section 50, *infra*.

Sect. 14.
Power to sell subject to depreciatory conditions.

Section 14.—(1.) No sale made by a trustee shall be impeached by any beneficiary upon the ground that any of the conditions subject to which the sale was made may have been unnecessarily depreciatory, unless it also appears that the consideration for the sale was thereby rendered inadequate.

(2.) No sale made by a trustee shall, after the execution of the conveyance, be impeached as against the purchaser upon the ground that any of the conditions subject to which the sale was made may have been unnecessarily depreciatory, unless it appears that the purchaser was acting in collusion with the trustee at the time when the contract for sale was made.

(3.) No purchaser, upon any sale made by a

Sect. 14.   trustee, shall be at liberty to make any objection
against the title upon the ground aforesaid.

(4.) This section applies only to sales made after
the twenty-fourth day of December one thousand
eight hundred and eighty-eight.

This section replaces section 3 of the Trustee Act, 1888,
which section is repealed by the present Act   See section 51,
and Schedule, *infra*

To sell under conditions unnecessarily depreciatory is a
breach of trust on the part of trustees (see *ante*, p. 69)   In
Dance v. *Goldingham*, 8 Ch. 902, the Court, at the suit of a
cestuis que trust, restrained a purchaser from completing a
purchase under conditions held to be unduly depreciatory.
In *Dunn* v. *Flood*, 28 C.D. 586, the Court held that a purchaser
could refuse to complete on the ground that the conditions
were depreciatory.   The present section in the interests of
vendors and purchasers of real estate curtails the rights of
the *cestuis que trust*, and abolishes that of a purchaser, to
object to the stringency of the conditions under which trustees
sell.

"24th of December, 1888."—The date on which the Trustee
Act, 1888, came into operation.

For definitions of "trustee" and "conveyance," see section
50, *infra*

Sect. 15.

Power to sell
under 37 & 38
Vict. c. 78.

Section 15.—A trustee who is either a vendor
or a purchaser may sell or buy without excluding
the application of section two of the Vendor and
Purchaser Act, 1874.

This section replaces section 3 of the Vendor and Purchaser
Act, 1874, which section is repealed by the present Act.   See
section 51, and Schedule, *infra*.

Section 2 of the Vendor and Purchaser Act is as follows :—
"In the completion of any such contract as aforesaid, and
"subject to any stipulation to the contrary in the contract, the
"obligations and rights of vendor and purchaser shall be
"regulated by the following rules , that is to say—
"First—Under a contract to grant or assign a term of
"years, whether derived or to be derived out of a freehold or
"leasehold estate, the intended lessee or assign shall not be
"entitled to call for the title to the freehold.
"Second—Recitals, statements, and descriptions of facts,
"matters, and parties contained in deeds, instruments, Acts of
"Parliament, or statutory declarations, twenty years old at the
"date of the contract, shall, unless and except so far as they
"shall be proved to be inaccurate, be taken to be sufficient
"evidence of the truth of such facts, matters, and descriptions.

"Third—The inability of the vendor to furnish the "purchaser with a legal covenant to produce and furnish "copies of documents of title shall not be an objection to title "in case the purchaser will, on the completion of the contract, "have an equitable right to the production of such documents.

"Fourth—Such covenants for production as the purchaser "can and shall require shall be furnished at his expense, and "the vendor shall bear the expense of perusal and execution "on behalf of and by himself, and on behalf of and by necessary "parties other than the purchaser.

"Fifth—Where the vendor retains any part of an estate to "which any documents of title relate, he shall be entitled to "retain such documents."

Section 2, Rule 1 of the Vendor and Purchaser Act, subject to any stipulation to the contrary in the contract, precludes an intended lessee or assignee of a lease from calling for the title to the freehold. This rule, however, does not prevent such lessee or assignee having constructive notice of his lessor's title, *Patman* v. *Harland*, 17 Ch D. 353; *Mogridge* v. *Clapp* (1892) 3 Ch 382; *Imray* v. *Oakshette* (1897) 2 Q B 229, and this presumably is not altered by the provisions of section 3 of the Conveyancing Act, 1882, as to constructive notice. See *Holloway Brothers, Ltd* v. *Hill* (1902) 2 Ch. 612.

The effect of section 3 (1), of the Conveyancing and Law of Property Act, 1881, is, in the case of an assignment of an underlease, to preclude the intended assignee from calling for the title to the leasehold interest, out of which the underlease is derived, and the effect of section 13 (1) of the same Act is, in the case of the grant of an underlease to be derived out of an existing underlease, to preclude the intended sub-lessee from calling for the title to the leasehold interest, out of which the existing underlease is derived. *Gosling* v. *Woolf* (1893) 1 Q.B 39 (in the head note to which case the law would appear to be correctly stated, though the judgment, it is submitted, suggests an erroneous construction of section 3 (1)).

Section 66 (3) and (4) of the Conveyancing and Law of Property Act, 1881, protects trustees from liability in respect of any omission to negative the above stipulations contained in that Act.

It is submitted that, in spite of the comprehensive expressions of Rule 1 of section 2 of the Vendor and Purchaser Act, and of section 66 (1), (3), and (4) of the Conveyancing and Law of Property Act, and notwithstanding the omission from the present section of any such express condition as that in section 8 (3) of the present Act, trustees would not be protected in cases in which the omission to negative the stipulations of those Acts amounted to negligence, or to a want of such reasonable care as may be expected of a business man in dealing with his own property. That the omission to exclude in cases in which a substantial premium is to be paid, or substantial sums laid out upon the land to be demised, might be held to amount to such negligence, is suggested by a consideration of the judgments

Sect. 15. in the above cited cases, *Patman* v. *Harland* (see p. 359), and *Imray* v. *Oakshette* (see p. 229). Whether or not the trustees would, under the above sections, be protected from personal liability, it is clear that in such cases the right to call for a proper title should be reserved.

It must further be remembered that there is no statutory provision precluding an intending under-lessee from calling for the title to the existing lease or underlease, out of which the intended underlease is to be derived. In such a case the trustees would clearly be responsible if loss were incurred by the omission to call for an abstract, and production of the existing lease or underlease, and of any instruments by which the same had been dealt with. So, in taking an assignment of a lease or underlease, such lease or underlease and documents of title showing dealings with such lease or underlease should of course be abstracted and produced. The result is that the documents which, in the case of the grant of an underlease, or the assignment of a lease or underlease, can be called for without special conditions, are those which, in the ordinary course, would necessarily be in the hands of the intending lessor, or assignor, or his mortgagees, but not including any relating to the freehold title. This rule, however, must be read subject to section 1 of the Vendor and Purchaser Act, 1874, which provides that, in the case of a sale of land, forty years shall be a sufficient root of title. The effect of that section is that in the case of an existing lease or underlease more than forty years old, which is to be sold, or out of which an underlease is to be granted, the existing lease or underlease and the title thereto for forty years next before the contract, need alone be abstracted and produced under an open contract. The rule must also be read subject to section 8 (3) of the present Act, which contains provisions protecting trustees who, in lending money on leasehold security, dispense with production of the lessor's title, and who, in purchasing or lending money, accept a shorter title than a purchaser is entitled to demand, "if, in the opinion of the Court, the title accepted be such as a person, acting with prudence and caution, would have accepted"

The above sections of the Vendor and Purchaser Act, 1874, and Conveyancing and Law of Property Act, 1881, do not apply to mortgages.

For definition of the word "trustee," see section 50, *infra.*

Sect. 16.

Married woman as bare trustee may convey

Section 16.—When any freehold or copyhold hereditament is vested in a married woman as a bare trustee she may convey or surrender it as if she were a *feme sole*.

This section replaces section 6 of the Vendor and Purchaser Act, 1874 (37 & 38 Vict. c. 78), which section is repealed by the present Act. See section 51, and Schedule, *infra.*

"**Freehold or Copyhold Hereditaments.**"—The section does Sect. 16.
not apply to leaseholds. As to the effect of this omission, see ——————
p. 74, *infra.*

"**Bare Trustee.**"—The expression is somewhat ambiguous.
The better opinion seems to be that a bare trustee means a
trustee to whose office no duties were originally attached, or
who, although such duties were originally attached to his
office, would, on the requisition of his *cestuis que trust*, be
compellable in equity to convey the estate to them, or by their
direction, *Christie* v. *Ovington*, 1 C.D 279. This definition,
though not approved of by Jessel, M.R., in *Morgan* v. *Swansea
Urban Authority*, 9 C.D. 582, was approved by Stirling, J., in
re Cunningham and Frayling (1891) 2 Ch 567. Compare
subsection 2 of section 18, *post*, p. 78.

A title was made under the repealed section in *re Docwra*,
29 C D 693, although the married woman was a trustee for
sale, and had a beneficial interest. The circumstances, however, in that case were peculiar, for a sale had been made
under an order of the Court, and the trustee had therefore
no duty to perform, except to obey the order of the Court.

"**May convey or surrender as if she were feme sole.**"—
The Married Women's Property Act, 1882, does not enable
a married woman, trustee of land, to convey the land as a
feme sole Re Harkness and Allsopp (1896) 2 Ch. 358.

The decision in *re Harkness and Allsopp* appears to be
equally applicable to the case of land vested in a married
woman as mortgagee to secure trust moneys, for, notwithstanding the contention to the contrary raised in argument in
re Howgate v. *Osborn* (1902) 1 Ch 451, it is submitted that
the mortgage land cannot be vested in the married woman as
her separate property. It is submitted, therefore, that the
Married Women's Property Act, 1882, though it enables a
married woman not a trustee (*re Brooke and Fremlin* (1898)
1 Ch. 647), does not enable a married woman trustee to convey
mortgaged lands as a *feme sole* It remains to be considered in
what cases the present section is available for that purpose.

A married woman mortgagee, upon payment of principal,
interest, and costs by any person entitled to redeem, becomes
a bare trustee of the mortgaged property for the mortgagor
or his nominee, and, where that property is a freehold or copyhold hereditament, can convey under this section. This is the
case whether the mortgage moneys belong to the woman for
her separate use, *re Brooke and Fremlin's Contract* (1898) 1
Ch. 647, or upon trust for others, *re Howgate and Osborn's
Contract* (1902) 1 Ch. 451, at p. 456; and whether the
assurance be a reconveyance to the mortgagor, *re Brooke and
Fremlin, supra; re Howgate and Osborn, supra,* or a transfer
to a transferee by his direction, *re West and Hardy* (1904)
1 Ch. 145; also reported in 89 L.T. 579, where it appears that
the mortgagor concurred in the transfer, and whether the

Sect. 16. married woman be sole mortgagee, *re Brooke and Fremlin,*
supra; re Howgate and Osborn, supra, or entitled jointly with
others, *re West and Hardy, supra.* The dates of the mortgage
and of the marriage are, for this purpose, alike immaterial.

A married woman mortgagee, upon payment of principal,
interest, and costs by a person *not* entitled to redeem, does not
necessarily become a bare trustee for such person. It is submitted that she would only so become a bare trustee if she
had contracted to transfer, and that in the case of her being
a trustee of the mortgage moneys, and consequently of the
mortgage security, she would have no power so to contract,
Avery v. G ' ' 6 Eq. 606. In the result, therefore, it is
submitted t | married woman, in whom a mortgage is vested
to secure trust oneys, cannot convey the mortgaged land under
this section upon payment by an intending transferee, except
when acting under the direction of some person entitled to
redeem.

A married woman mortgagee, who has not received payment of principal, interest, and costs, is not a trustee for the
mortgagor, *re Brooke and Fremlin, supra; Warner v. Jacob,* 20
C D. 220, and, in the case of a trust mortgage, can only convey
under this section if it can be shown that she is a bare trustee
for the transferee. It is submitted that she is such a bare
trustee when a new trustee has been appointed, or in any case
in which the right to receive the mortgage money has become
vested in another person, *e g.* in the case of mortgaged freeholds
becoming (under the old law) vested in the heir of a deceased
mortgagee, and the right to the moneys being vested in his
executors. Cf *re Skitter,* 4 W.R 791.

In *re West and Hardy, supra,* Farwell, J., decided that a
purchaser was not entitled to proof that a married woman
mortgagee, who had conveyed the mortgaged freeholds on a
transfer of the mortgage, was not a trustee of the mortgage
moneys. He appears to have so decided on the ground that,
having no notice of any trusts, the purchaser would obtain a
good title. It is submitted, however, that the capacity of the
married woman to convey either a legal or an equitable interest
in land cannot depend on notice or want of notice, and that in
every case where a conveyance by a married woman without
the concurrence of her husband appears on the title, it is
equally necessary for the purchaser to satisfy himself that, in
fact, the land belonged to the woman beneficially, as that her
marriage had taken place, or the land had been acquired by
her, subsequent to 1882.

It will be observed that the present section does not apply
to leaseholds, and accordingly in the case of leaseholds vested
in a married woman trustee—whether by way of mortgage or
otherwise—the assignment must be made by the husband.

For definition of "trustee," see section 50, *infra.*

Various Powers and Liabilities.

Section 17.—(1.) A trustee may appoint a
solicitor to be his agent to receive and give a
discharge for any money or valuable consideration
or property receivable by the trustee under the
trust, by permitting the solicitor to have the
custody of, and to produce, a deed containing any
such receipt as is referred to in section fifty-six of
the Conveyancing and Law of Property Act, 1881;
and a trustee shall not be chargeable with breach
of trust by reason only of his having made or
concurred in making any such appointment; and
the producing of any such deed by the solicitor
shall have the same validity and effect under the
said section as if the person appointing the solicitor
had not been a trustee.

(2.) A trustee may appoint a banker or solicitor
to be his agent to receive and give a discharge for
any money payable to the trustee under or by
virtue of a policy of assurance, by permitting the
banker or solicitor to have the custody of and to
produce the policy of assurance with a receipt
signed by the trustee, and a trustee shall not be
chargeable with a breach of trust by reason only
of his having made or concurred in making any
such appointment.

(3.) Nothing in this section shall exempt a
trustee from any liability which he would have
incurred if this Act had not been passed, in case
he permits any such money, valuable consideration,
or property to remain in the hands or under the
control of the banker or solicitor for a period longer
than is reasonably necessary to enable the banker
or solicitor (as the case may be) to pay or transfer
the same to the trustee.

(4.) This section applies only where the money
or valuable consideration or property is received
after the twenty-fourth day of December one
thousand eight hundred and eighty-eight.

(5.) Nothing in this section shall authorise a

trustee to do anything which he is in express terms forbidden to do, or to omit anything which he is in express terms directed to do, by the instrument creating the trust.

Subsections 1, 2, 3, and 4 re-enact in slightly altered language section 2 of the Trustee Act, 1888, which is repealed by the present Act (see section 51, and Schedule, *infra*). Subsection 5 is taken from section 12 of the same Act.

Subsection 1.—This subsection nullifies the decision in *re Bellamy and the Metropolitan Board of Works*, 24 C D. 387, where it was held that, as trustee vendors could not properly authorise their solicitor to receive purchase-money payable to them, their solicitor could not give a good discharge for it under section 56 of the Conveyancing and Law of Property Act, 1881   That section enacts that, "Where a solicitor produces a deed, having in the body thereof, or endorsed thereon, a receipt for consideration money, or other consideration, the deed being executed, or the indorsed receipt being signed, by the person entitled to give a receipt for that consideration, the deed shall be sufficient authority to the person liable to pay, or give the same for his paying, or giving the same to the solicitor, without the solicitor producing any separate or other direction or authority in that behalf from the person who executed or signed the deed or receipt."

The deed must be actually produced. *Day* v. *Woolwich B S.*, 40 C.D. 491.

The solicitor referred to is the solicitor acting on behalf of the person sought to be charged, *Day* v. *Woolwich B.S*, 40 C.D. 491; *re Hetling and Merton* (1893) 3 Ch 269, and he must be permitted to have the custody of the deed, and to produce it, otherwise the purchaser is not protected, *re Hetling and Merton*, *supra*; see *King* v. *Smith* (1900) 2 Ch. 425. Nevertheless, in ordinary cases, and in the absence of some special reason for so doing, a purchaser is not entitled to require proof that the solicitor has his client's permission to have custody of the deed, and to produce it, *re Hetling and Merton*, *supra*. In most cases the principle of estoppel would apply to prevent the person who executed and parted with possession of the deed disputing the authority of his solicitor to receive the money on production of the deed, *King* v. *Smith* (1900) 2 Ch 425

When a solicitor is authorised to receive money on behalf of a client, a valid tender can be made to a clerk of the solicitor who purports to have his master's authority to accept or reject a tender   *Moffatt* v. *Parsons*, 5 Taunt. 307, 15 R R. 506; *Wilmott* v. *Smith*, 3 Car. & P. 453; 31 R.R. 732; *Bingham* v. *Allport*, 1 N & Manning, 398, 38 R.R 385, *Finch* v. *Boning*, 4 C.P D. 143   So it is conceived a solicitor authorised to receive consideration money under section 56 of the Conveyancing and Law of Property Act, 1881, or this section, can act by a clerk. In subsection 2 the banker authorised to receive policy moneys must in practice always act by deputy. See also *Day* v. *Woolwich B S*, 40 C D. 491

The production of a deed executed by an attorney of a trustee under a general power of attorney is not sufficient. *Re Hetling and Merton* (1893) 3 Ch 269.

One of several trustees, not being a solicitor, cannot be authorised by the others to receive the purchase-money on behalf of all, *re Flower and Metropolitan Board of Works*, 27 C.D 592; but if one of the trustees is a solicitor, it is conceived that the subsection enables payment to be made to him in his capacity of solicitor exercising the statutory authority.

" **A Trustee.**"—See notes to subsection 5, *infra*

Subsection 2.—See notes to subsection 1

Subsection 3.—It is no part of the duty of a solicitor, as such, to receive trust money. *Wyman* v. *Paterson* (1900) A.C. 271. Hart, L C, observed (*exp. Townsend*, 1 Moll 139) that if trustees permitted their solicitor to receive trust money, and he became bankrupt next day, they would be held responsible. This is not in accordance with modern opinion, and the question has been set at rest by this subsection, *per* Lord Macnaghten, *Wyman* v. *Paterson*, *supra*, at p 280. This subsection must be taken to be a statutory declaration of the law in this country, and, by analogy, it must be treated as applicable in the case of Scottish trustees, *Wyman* v. *Paterson*, *supra*, as to Scottish trustees, see notes to section 52, *post* Six months was held to be an unreasonable time in *Wyman* v *Paterson*, *supra*. As an ordinary rule, it is conceived, the money should be put under the control of the trustees at the latest within a day or two following its receipt But it has been said (*per* Lord James of Hereford in *Wyman* v. *Paterson*, *supra*), "if a new security was in sight, or could fairly be anticipated promptly to come into existence, the money might, without breach of trust, remain, with the object of being so transferred, in the hands of the solicitor, that solicitor being employed for a purpose that was not completed at the time when the money was in his hands."

As to the indemnity of a trustee in respect of the acts of agents, see section 24, *post*, p. 91.

Subsection 4.—"24th day of December, 1888," the date upon which the 1888 Act came into operation

Subsection 5 "A Trustee. . . . by the Instrument creating the Trust."—The reference to "instrument creating the trust" appears to show that the section only applies to trusts created by an instrument. It is open to question whether an administrator is a trustee within the section.

The subsection is taken from section 12 of the Trustee Act, 1888.

For definitions of "trust," "trustee," "instrument," "property," and "transfer," see section 50, *infra*.

Section 18 —(1.) A trustee may insure against loss or damage by fire any building or other insurable property to any amount (including the amount of any insurance already on foot) not exceeding three equal fourth parts of the full value of such building or property, and pay the premiums for such insurance out of the income thereof or out of the income of any other property subject to the same trusts, without obtaining the consent of any person who may be entitled wholly or partly to such income.

(2.) This section does not apply to any building or property which a trustee is bound forthwith to convey absolutely to any beneficiary upon being requested to do so.

(3.) This section applies to trusts created either before or after the commencement of this Act, but nothing in this section shall authorise any trustee to do anything which he is in express terms forbidden to do, or to omit to do anything which he is in express terms directed to do, by the instrument creating the trust.

Subsections 1 and 2 replace section 7 of the Trustee Act, 1888, which section is repealed by the present Act (see section 51, and Schedule, *infra*). Subsection 3 is taken from section 12 of the same Act.

Subsection 1.—The enactment is permissive only Apart from the statute, trustees are not bound to insure, or liable for not so doing. *Bailey* v. *Gould*, 4 Y. & C. 221; *Dobson* v. *Land,* 8 Hare 216; *Fry* v. *Fry*, 27 Beav. 144, at p. 146; Lewin on Trusts, 10th edit., p. 684.

" A Trustee "—See note to subsection 3, *infra*

"Including the Amount of any Insurance already on foot."— It is conceived that these words apply to any insurance, by whomsoever effected, to the benefit of which the trust estate is entitled, *e.g* a trustee of a reversion expectant on the determination of a lease under which the lessee is bound to insure for the benefit of the reversioner in three-fourths of the value, is not entitled under this section to insure again So a trustee mortgagee, where the mortgagor has duly insured pursuant to covenant, must take into account the amount so insured.

"Pay the Premiums . . . out of the Income."—The section does not alter the law as between tenant for life and remainderman as to the ultimate incidence of the payments, *re Baring*

(1893) 1 Ch 61. The tenant for life of leaseholds, the lease of which contains a covenant to insure, is bound to insure during the continuance of his interest, re *Gjers* (1899) 2 Ch. 54, re *Betty* (1899) 1 Ch. 821; but not if there be no covenant to insure, re *Betty*, at p. 829. If there be no such obligation to insure the trust property, it would seem that a tenant for life, out of whose income the trustee acting under this section has paid insurance premiums, has a right to be recouped out of capital.

"**Without obtaining the Consent.**"—Apart from the Act, such consent would be necessary, unless there were a covenant to insure, which the tenant for life was bound to perform. See the previous note.

Subsection 2. "Which a Trustee is bound forthwith to convey."—The language of this subsection raises a difficult question. Is the subsection intended only to exclude a bare trustee, or is it intended to exclude any trustee whose *cestuis que trust* are all *sui juris*. It seems probable, that the above words are taken from Mr. Dart's definition of a bare trustee, which was discussed in detail by Jessel, M R., in *Morgan v Swansea Urban Sanitary Authority*, 9 C D. 582, but the final clause of that definition, viz. "and has been requested by them so to convey it," which was considered by Jessel, M.R, as essential to its meaning, is not reproduced in the present subsection. The subsection, literally construed, would appear to lead to the result that where all the *cestuis que trust* are *sui juris*, a trustee, even if he has active duties to perform, and holds for persons in succession, is given no power to insure by this section, but it is difficult to believe that such was the intention.

Subsection 3.—The reference to "instrument creating the trust" appears to show that the section only applies to trusts created by an instrument It is open to question whether an administrator is a trustee within the section.

For definitions of "trustee," "convey," "instrument," and "transfer," see section 50, *infra.*

Section 19.—(1.) A trustee of any leaseholds for lives or years which are renewable from time to time, either under any covenant or contract, or by custom or usual practice, may, if he thinks fit, and shall, if thereto required by any person having any beneficial interest, present or future, or contingent, in the leaseholds, use his best endeavours to obtain from time to time a renewed lease of the same hereditaments on the accustomed and reasonable terms, and for that purpose may from time to time make or concur in making a surrender of the lease

Sect. 19.

Power of trustees of renewable leaseholds to renew and raise money for the purpose.

Sect. 19. for the time being subsisting, and do all such other acts as are requisite : Provided that, where by the terms of the settlement or will the person in possession for his life or other limited interest is entitled to enjoy the same without any obligation to renew or to contribute to the expense of renewal, this section shall not apply unless the consent in writing of that person is obtained to the renewal on the part of the trustee.

(2.) If money is required to pay for the renewal, the trustee effecting the renewal may pay the same out of any money then in his hands in trust for the persons beneficially interested in the lands to be comprised in the renewed lease, and if he has not in his hands sufficient money for the purpose, he may raise the money required by mortgage of the hereditaments to be comprised in the renewed lease, or of any other hereditaments for the time being subject to the uses or trusts to which those hereditaments are subject, and no person advancing money upon a mortgage purporting to be under this power shall be bound to see that the money is wanted, or that no more is raised than is wanted for the purpose.

(3.) This section applies to trusts created either before or after the commencement of this Act, but nothing in this section shall authorise any trustee to do anything which he is in express terms forbidden to do, or to omit to do anything which he is in express terms directed to do, by the instrument creating the trust.

This section replaces sections 10 and 11 of the Trustee Act, 1888, which are repealed by the present Act. See section 51, and Schedule, *infra*

Provisions similar to the above were originally contained in Lord Cranworth's Act, 23 & 24 Vict c. 145, sections 8, 9 These sections were repealed by the Settled Land Act, 1882, but not re-enacted until 1888.

"A Trustee."—See notes to subsection 3, *infra*.

Subsection 2.—The section does not alter the law as to how the expenses of renewal are to be borne as between tenant for life and remainderman, *re Baring, Jeune* v *Baring* (1893) 1 Ch 61 In the absence of express direction in the settlement as to how fines are to be borne, the principle is as follows :— the portion of the fine to be paid by the remainderman is to be ascertained by reference to the actual enjoyment of the tenant for life, and must be paid with compound interest up to the death of the tenant for life, and simple interest from that time until payment, *Bradford* v. *Brownjohn*, 3 Ch. 711; *Isaac* v. *Wall*, 6 C.D. 706. In *re Baring*, *supra*, it was suggested that the amounts should be ascertained before the tenant for life's death by actuarial valuation, but it seems this cannot be done without either the consent of all parties or order of the Court. See *re Baring*, *supra*, at p. 70.

The cases where the settlement provides for payment of fines may be divided under three heads (see *Bradford* v. *Brownjohn*, *supra*, *per* Selwyn, L.J.), viz —

1. The expense to be raised by sale or mortgage of the estate, in this case the tenant for life loses the rents of the part sold and keeps down the interest in case of mortgage.

2. The same provision is made by means of a sale or mortgage of another estate, in which case the tenant for life of that estate is in a similar position. *Ainslie* v. *Harcourt*, 28 Beav. 313, is an instance of both these classes.

3. The expenses of renewal are directed to be paid out of the rents and profits, in which case the whole burthen is thrown upon the tenant for life, as in *Solley* v *Wood*, 29 Beav 482.

There is a further class of cases in which the settlement provides for payment " out of rents and profits or by mortgage." In these cases the Court throws the onus on the successive tenants in proportion to their interests, see *Jones* v. *Jones*, 5 Hare 440   See further as to this subject, Lewin on Trusts, 10th edit., Ch. 15.

Subsection 3.—The reference to "instrument creating the trust" appears to show that the section only applies to trusts created by an instrument.   It is open to question whether an administrator is a trustee within the section.

For definitions of "trust," "trustee," "instrument," and "mortgage," see section 50, *infra*.

Power of trustee to give receipts

Section 20.—(1.) The receipt in writing of any trustee for any money, securities, or other personal property or effects payable, transferable, or deliverable to him under any trust or power shall be a sufficient discharge for the same, and shall effectually exonerate the person paying, transferring, or delivering the same from seeing to the application or being answerable for any loss or misapplication thereof.

(2.) This section applies to trusts created either before or after the commencement of this Act.

G

Sect. 20.

This section replaces, with merely verbal alterations, section 36 of the Conveyancing and Law of Property Act, 1881, which section is repealed by the present Act. See section 51, and Schedule, *infra*.

Previous efforts had been made to modify by statute the strict rules of the Court of Chancery on the subject of the responsibility of person paying money to trustees.

By 7 & 8 Vict. c. 76, section 10, it was enacted that the *bonâ fide* payment to and receipt of any person to whom any money should be payable on any express or implied trust, or for any limited purpose, should effectually discharge the person paying the same from seeing to the application thereof, unless the contrary be expressly declared by the instrument creating the trust or security. The enactment took effect on the 1st January, 1845, and did not apply to instruments executed before that date. It was repealed in the same year by 8 & 9 Vict. c. 106, section 1, as from the 1st October, 1845.

By Lord St. Leonards's Act (22 & 23 Vict. c 35), section 23, it was enacted that the *bonâ fide* payment to, and receipt of, any person to whom any purchase or mortgage money should be payable upon any express or implied trust, should effectually discharge the person paying the same from seeing to the application thereof, unless the contrary be expressly declared in the instrument creating the trust or security. This section has not been repealed. It seems the better opinion is, that this clause applies only to trusts created since the Act, Lewin, 10th edit., p. 518.

By Lord Cranworth's Act (23 & 24 Vict. c. 145), section 29, a more extensive power was given to trustees of instruments executed since the Act. The enactment extended to any money, not merely purchase or mortgage money, and there was no provision as to contrary intention. This enactment was repealed by the Conveyancing and Law of Property Act, 1881.

"**The Receipt in Writing.**"—As to payment to a solicitor or banker, see section 17, *ante*, p. 75.

"**Under a Trust or Power.**"—The section only applies if the property is receivable by the trustee under a trust or power. A person not validly appointed trustee cannot give a good discharge for trust money paid to him. A person having money to pay to a trust is not bound to accept the trustee's receipt under this section. If there be circumstances which make it reasonable for him to decline to be satisfied with the statutory receipt, he will not be responsible for the costs of any consequent legal proceedings. Cf. *Hockey* v. *Western* (1898) 1 Ch. 350.

Payment by a debtor, for the express purpose of discharging his debt to an estate, to his own agent who happens to be (but not to the debtor's knowledge) one of the trustees, is not sufficient to discharge the debtor. *Miller* v. *Douglas*, 56 L J. Ch. 91.

For the law apart from statute, see Lewin, 10th edit., 519, *et seq.*

For definitions of "trust," "trustee," "property," and "securities," see section 50, *infra.*

Section 21.—(1.) An executor or administrator may pay or allow any debt or claim on any evidence that he thinks sufficient.

(2.) An executor or administrator, or two or more trustees, acting together, or a sole acting trustee where by the instrument, if any, creating the trust a sole trustee is authorised to execute the trusts and powers thereof, may, if and as he or they may think fit, accept any composition or any security, real or personal, for any debt or for any property, real or personal, claimed, and may allow any time for payment for any debt, and may compromise, compound, abandon, submit to arbitration, or otherwise settle any debt, account, claim, or thing whatever relating to the testator's or intestate's estate or to the trust, and for any of those purposes may enter into, give, execute, and do such agreements, instruments of composition or arrangement, releases, and other things as to him or them seem expedient, without being responsible for any loss occasioned by any act or thing so done by him or them in good faith.

(3.) This section applies only if and as far as a contrary intention is not expressed in the instrument, if any, creating the trust, and shall have effect subject to the terms of that instrument, and to the provisions therein contained.

(4.) This section applies to executorships, administratorships and trusts constituted or created either before or after the commencement of this Act.

This section replaces section 37 of the Conveyancing and Law of Property Act, 1881 (repealed by the present Act, see section 51, and Schedule, *infra*), which itself took the place of section 30 of Lord Cranworth's Act (23 & 24 Vict. c. 145). The last-mentioned section only applied to executors, and only to wills signed or confirmed by codicil after the 28th August, 1860.

Sect. 21.   "**An Executor . . . may pay or allow any Debt or Claim.**"—Co-executors, however numerous, are regarded in law as an individual person, and by consequence the acts of any one of them, in respect of the administration of the effects, are deemed to be the acts of all; for they have all a joint and entire authority over the whole property. Williams on Executors, 9th edit., 816; *re Macdonald* (1897) 2 Ch. 181; *Astbury* v. *Astbury* (1898) 2 Ch. 111.

It is conceived that the effect of subsection 1 is that where a payment by an executor or administrator is attacked by the legatees, the question to be decided is, not was the evidence on which he acted sufficient to justify him, but did he, in making the payment, in good faith think that a debt or claim binding on the estate was proved. *Jones* v. *Owens*, 47 L T 61, at p. 64 The executor or administrator must in good faith think a debt or claim is established. The subsection does not authorise him to make payments of claims which he knows are neither debts nor enforceable claims An executor or administrator may pay a debt, if satisfied with the evidence of its existence, although the creditor's remedy be barred by the Statutes of Limitation, *Midgley* v *Midgley* (1893) 3 Ch. 282, unless it has been judicially declared to be barred *ib*, or unless an administration action be pending *ib*, and, it would seem, notwithstanding the dissent of a co-executor. *Smith* v. *Everett*, 27 Beav. 446; but see as to this, *Midgley* v. *Midgley, supra; Astbury* v *Astbury* (1898) 2 Ch. 111. This is, however, the solitary exception to the rule that he is not entitled to pay claims which are not binding on the estate, Williams on Executors, 9th edit., 1698, he cannot pay claims which cannot be enforced by reason of the Statute of Frauds, *re Rownson*, 29 C D. 358, at p. 368.

"**Or Administrator.**"—These words are new. It was thought that on the authority of *re Clay and Tetley*, 16 C.D. 3, the section in the Conveyancing and Law of Property Act, 1881, did not apply to an administrator, even with the will annexed.

"**An Executor or Administrator may . . . accept any Composition, etc.**"—As to one of several executors acting alone, see *supra*. Apart from statute an executor or administrator who accepted composition or security, allowed time, compounded, abandoned, submitted to arbitration, or otherwise compromised, did so at his own peril. For if attacked in respect of such act the *onus* was on him to prove benefit to the estate. See Williams on Executors, 1696, 1697, *Blue* v. *Marshall*, 3 P. Wms 381; *Forshaw* v. *Higginson*, 8 D.M. & G. 827.

"**Two or more Trustees acting together.**"—This does not mean that less than the whole body of trustees can exercise the powers given.

"**Sole Trustee authorised, etc.**"—Under section 22, *infra,* p. 85, a sole surviving trustee may, unless forbidden by the instrument creating the power or trust, exercise or perform a power or trust originally given to or vested in two or more trustees jointly.

"Compromise, compound, abandon."—The section of Lord Cranworth's Act was held to extend to claims of every kind, including the claim of a person to be one of a class of residuary legatees, *re Warren*, 1884 W.N. 181. The section does not empower executors to compromise questions relating to the validity of the will or the testamentary capacity of the testator *Abdallah* v. *Rickards*, 4 Times L R. 622, but they can compromise a debt due from one of themselves, *re Houghton*, *Hawley* v. *Blake* (1904) 1 Ch. 622, not following *dictum* to the contrary in *de Cordova* v *de Cordova*, 4 A.C. 692, at p. 703. For instances of compromise, see *West of England Bank* v. *Murch*, 23 C D. 138, where, under special circumstances, the power to compromise was held to justify a sale of a business in consideration of shares and debentures (this case must not, however, be taken as an authority of general application, see the cases cited in notes to section 13, "Trust for sale or power of sale," *ante*, p 67); and *re Trenchard* (1902) 1 Ch 378.

"In Good Faith"—See *Jones* v. *Owens*, 47 L.T. 61, at p 64, *ante*, p. 84; *re Houghton*, *supra*.

Subsection 3—In the Conveyancing and Law of Property Act, 1881, th s subsection was in terms limited to trustees. The words "as regards trustees" are now omitted, and having regard to the definition of "trust" in section 50, it seems that this subsection applies to executors or administrators.

Subsection 4.—The language of the repealed section is retained, although by section 50 of this Act the expression "trust" appears to be sufficient to include executorships and administratorships.

For definitions of "trust," "trustee," "instrument," and "property," see section 50, *infra*.

Section 22.—(1). Where a power or trust is given to or vested in two or more trustees jointly, then, unless the contrary is expressed in the instrument, if any, creating the power or trust, the same may be exercised or performed by the survivor or survivors of them for the time being.

(2.) This section applies only to trusts constituted after or created by instruments coming into operation after the thirty-first day of December one thousand eight hundred and eighty-one.

This section is a re-enactment, with verbal alterations, of section 38 of the Conveyancing and Law of Property Act, 1881, which section is repealed by this Act. See section 51, and

Sect. 22

Schedule, *infra*. The omission of express reference to executors and executorships in the present section is, of course, due to the extended meaning given to the term "trustee" by section 50 of the present Act.

It is to be observed that the section relates only to "surviving" trustees, and not generally to "remaining" or "continuing" trustees. It would thus appear not to apply to the following cases, viz. :—

(*a*) Renunciation by an executor. This is dealt with by section 77 of the Probate Act, 1857 (20 & 21 Vict. c. 77), which is as follows: "Where any person after the commencement of this Act renounces Probate of Will of which he is appointed executor, or one of the executors, the rights of such person in respect of the executorship shall wholly cease, and the representation to the testator, and the administration of his effects, shall and may, without any further renunciation, go, devolve, and be committed in like manner as if such person had not been appointed executor." As to the case of an executor dying without having taken probate, or not appearing to a citation, see section 16 of the Probate Act, 1858 (21 & 22 Vict. c. 95).

(*b*) Renunciation of a power by one who has accepted or acted under it. This is dealt with by section 52 of the Conveyancing and Law of Property Act, 1881, which is as follows. (1) "A person to whom any power, whether coupled with an interest or not, is given, may by deed release, or contract not to exercise, the power. (2) This section applies to powers created by instruments coming into operation either before or after the commencement of this Act."

(*c*) Disclaimer of a power before accepting or acting under it. This case is dealt with by section 6 of the Conveyancing Act, 1882, which is as follows: "(1) A person to whom any power, whether coupled with an interest or not, is given, may by deed disclaim the power, and, after disclaimer, shall not be capable of exercising or joining in the exercise of the power. (2) On such a disclaimer, the power may be exercised by the other or others, or the survivors or survivor of the others, of the persons to whom the power is given, unless the contrary is expressed in the instrument creating the power. (3) This section applies to powers created by instruments coming into operation either before or after the commencement of this Act"

(*d*) Disclaimer, not merely of a power, but of the whole of the trusts and trust estate; retirement of a trustee under section 11 of the present Act, or otherwise; replacement of a trustee under section 10 or 25 of the present Act; removal of a trustee by the Court, or under section 10 of the present Act, or otherwise; in all of which cases the question whether powers can be exercised by the other or others of the trustees must, it is submitted, be decided in accordance with the general principles referred to below.

The general principles, independently of statutory enactment, applicable to the survivorship of trusts and powers, will be found in Chance on Powers, section 653; Sugden on Powers,

8th edit., p. 128, Vaisey on Settlements, p. 347; Lewin on
Trusts, 10th edit., p. 278, Farwell on Powers, 2nd edit., p. 452.
They may be summarised as follows :—

(1) As co-trustees have an authority coupled with an estate
or interest, their office is impressed with the quality of survivorship. Thus, if land be vested in two trustees upon trust to
sell, and one of them die, the other may sell, and this is so
even if the land is not vested in them, for "the trust or power
imperative is the estate." Cf. Lewin, pp. 278, 726. In like
manner the offices of executors and of administrators survive.

(2) The rule of survivorship applies not only to trusts, or
powers imperative, but also to such discretionary powers as
are annexed to the office of trustee, and are meant to form an
integral part of it, cf. Lewin, p. 728; re Smith, Eastick v. Smith
(1904) 1 Ch. 139, although such discretionary powers might
not be exerciseable by the representatives of a last trustee
under section 30 of the Conveyancing and Law of Property
Act, 1881, or otherwise. Cf. Robson v. Flight, 4 De G.J. & S.
608; Vaisey, p. 352.

(3) If the power arises by implication, it attaches to the
office, and may be exercised by the holder of the office for the
time being. Cf. Farwell, p. 461; Sugden, pp. 115-128

(4) A bare power given to two or more by name cannot be
executed by the survivors or survivor. Cf. Sugden, pp. 126-
128; Farwell, p. 454.

(5) Where a power is given nominatim, although in the
character of executors, e.g. "to my executors A and B," it is in
each case a question of intention whether the power is given to
the person or annexed to the office. Cf. Sugden, p. 128;
Farwell, p. 457; and see re Smith, Eastick v. Smith (1904) 1
Ch. 139, infra, p. 88.

As to the effect of the present section in modifying the law
as it applies to powers given to trustees of trusts constituted
after or created by instruments coming into operation after the
31st of December, 1881, the chief question arises on the 4th
rule above stated.

It has been suggested (Vaisey, p. 347) that the effect of
section 38 of the Conveyancing and Law of Property Act, 1881,
was to abolish the doctrine which raised a presumption against
the survivorship of powers, and that even in the case of a bare
power given to two or more by name, the power survives by
virtue of that section. It is submitted, however, that as
section 38 and the present section apply only to "trustees,"
and not to "persons" generally, the above statement is too
wide, and that survivorship only occurs where the donees of
the power are in some sense trustees; and see note to subsection 2, infra.

It is further submitted that the fact that the power is of a
fiduciary character does not of itself make the donee a trustee
within the meaning of the section, although a power to appoint
new trustees, as being in its nature fiduciary, has been held by
the Court of Appeal to be vested in a lunatic " in the character

of trustee" within the meaning of section 128 of the Lunacy Act, 1890. *In re Shortridge* (1895) 1 Ch. 278. It can scarcely be contended that the effect of the section is that a power to appoint amongst children (a fiduciary power), given to husband and wife, can be exercised by the survivor without express words to that effect in the instrument creating the power.

It is further submitted that it is not sufficient that the donees be in fact trustees if the power is not given to them as such; *e.g.* in the above case, though the husband and wife were the trustees or amongst the trustees of the instrument, if the power were given to them *nominatim*, it is submitted that the power would not survive (see, however, Farwell, p. 455). The true test appears to be whether or not the power is given to the donees in their capacity of trustees or executors. Cf. *Crawford* v. *Forshaw* (1891) 2 Ch. 261; *In re Smith, Eastick* v. *Smith* (1904) 1 Ch. 139.

The judgment of Farwell, J., in the case last mentioned, summarises the law as follows :—"The result of the authorities and of sections 22 and 37 of the Trustee Act is, in my opinion, this : Every power given to trustees which enables them to deal with or affect the trust property is *prima facie* given them *ex officio* as an incident of their office, and passes with the office to the holders or holder thereof for the time being; whether a power is so given *ex officio* or not depends in each case on the construction of the document giving it, but the mere fact that the power is one requiring the exercise of a very wide personal discretion is not enough to exclude the *prima facie* presumption, and little regard is now paid to such minute differences as those between ' my trustees,' ' my trustees A. and B.,' and ' A. and B , my trustees.' The testator's reliance on the individuals to the exclusion of the holders of the office for the time being must be expressed in clear and apt language."

Subsection 2.—It should be noticed that the date upon which it depends whether in a particular case the section applies or not, is not that at which the powers or trusts in question are given or vested, but that at which the trusts of which the donee is trustee were constituted. Thus, if by an instrument executed after 1881 a power were given to the executors of the will of a testator, who had died before that year, the section would not apply. This is made clear by reference to the language of the repealed section 38 of the Conveyancing and Law of Property Act, 1881: "This section applies only to executorships and trusts constituted after, etc." The fact that the scope of the section is restricted by reference to the date of the constitution of the original trusteeship or executorship, though not likely to be of frequent practical importance, is of interest as supporting the view stated above that the section does not apply to powers vested in persons who are not trustees of some constituted trust.

For definitions of "trust," "trustee," and "instrument," see section 50, *infra*.

Section 23.—A trustee acting or paying money in good faith under or in pursuance of any power of attorney shall not be liable for any such act or payment by reason of the fact that at the time of the payment or act the person who gave the power of attorney was dead or had done some act to avoid the power, if this fact was not known to the trustee at the time of his so acting or paying.

Sect. 23.

Exoneration of trustees in respect of certain powers of attorney.

Provided that nothing in this section shall affect the right of any person entitled to the money against the person to whom the payment is made, and that the person so entitled shall have the same remedy against the person to whom the payment is made as he would have had against the trustee.

This section is in substitution for section 26 of Lord St. Leonards's Act (22 & 23 Vict. c. 35), which section is repealed by this Act. See section 51, and Schedule, *infra*. The repealed section was as follows: "No trustee, executor, or administrator making any payment or doing any act *bonâ fide* under or in pursuance of any power of attorney shall be liable for the moneys so paid or the act so done, by reason that the person who gave the power of attorney was dead at the time of such payment or act, or had done some act to avoid the power, provided that the fact of the death or of the doing of such act as last aforesaid, at the time of such payment or act *bonâ fide* done as aforesaid by such trustee, executor, or administrator, was not known to him: Provided always, that nothing herein contained shall in any manner affect or prejudice the right of any person entitled to the money against the person to whom such payment shall have been made, but that such person so entitled shall have the same remedy against such person to whom such payment shall be made as he would have had against the trustee, executor, or administrator if the money had not been paid away under such power of attorney."

Section 47 of the Conveyancing and Law of Property Act, 1881, which is not repealed, enacts as follows · "(1) Any person making or doing any payment or act, in good faith, in pursuance of a power of attorney, shall not be liable in respect of the payment or act by reason that before the payment or act the donor of the power had died or become lunatic, of unsound mind, or bankrupt, or had revoked the power, if the fact of death, lunacy, unsoundness of mind, bankruptcy, or revocation was not at the time of the payment or act known to the person making or doing the same. (2) But this section shall not affect any right against the payee of any person interested in any money so paid; and that person shall have the like remedy against the payee as he would have had against the payer if

Sect. 23. the payment had not been made by him. (3) This section
applies only to payments and acts made and done after the
commencement of this Act "

Section 47 of the Conveyancing and Law of Property Act
appears to be intended to extend to all persons, whether trustees
or not, the protection given by the earlier Act to trustees and
executors, and in some respects, noted below, to make that protection more effective. It is not altogether clear what is the
reason for the enactment of the present section, nor, if it is
merely intended to assert that trustees are entitled to the same
privilege as other persons, why the somewhat narrower language
of the earlier section has been adopted in preference to that of
the later Act.

"Acting or paying Money . . . under or in Pursuance of
any Power of Attorney."—This phrase, although strictly applicable only to cases in which the trustee is the donee of the
power, cannot here be so restricted without depriving the section
of its principal value, but must be taken to apply to cases in
which the trustee acts on the faith of powers given to other
persons, e g. pays purchase-money to a vendor who acts as
donee of a power of attorney. That this is intended is apparent
from the terms of the proviso to the section. The words
"pay   by attorney" in the marginal note to section 47 of
the   ncing and Law of Property Act, 1881, should
pr   "payment by or to attorney."

"   ttorney"—A power of attorney is a formal
instrum   ecuted by one empowering another to act in his
stead. It ust for some purposes, but not for all, be by deed
See Jarman's Conveyancing, 3rd edit., vol. 8.

"Act to avoid the Power."—The modes in which a power of
attorney may be determined apart from statutory provisions
are dealt with by Mr. Jarman (Conveyancing, 3rd edit., vol. 8).
They are (1) mutual agreement, (2) revocation, either (a)
express or (b) implied, e g. cesser of power of principal over
subject-matter, lunacy of principal, bankruptcy of principal,
death of principal; (3) renunciation of attorney, either (a)
express or (b) implied, e g bankruptcy of attorney; (4)
exhaustion of power, e.g. where given for a particular purpose
only, (5) expiration of time limited, either expressly or impliedly,
for the exercise of the power.

"Notice of Revocation."—" On the whole, the rule laid down
by Mr. Justice Story (Agency, 470) seems trustworthy, viz.,
that as to the attorney the revocation generally takes effect
from the time when revocation by act of the principal is made
known to him; and as to third persons when it is made known
to them and not before," Jarman's Conveyancing, 3rd edit.,
vol. 8, p 35, and this rule appears to apply to revocation by
death of the principal, his bankruptcy, and insanity.

Effect of the Section.—The language of the section is not
so wide as that of section 47 of the Conveyancing and Law of

Property Act, 1881, as it omits express reference to the bankruptcy, lunacy, and unsoundness of mind of the principal. Probably bankruptcy comes within the phrase, "some act to avoid the power," but it is difficult to suppose that lunacy and unsoundness of mind can do so. The question does not, however, appear to be one of substance if (as is submitted is the case) section 47 of the Conveyancing and Law of Property Act, 1881, applies to trustees, or if the law apart from statute is as stated above.

It would seem clear that neither this section nor section 47 of the Conveyancing and Law of Property Act, 1881, gives any protection in the case of determination of the power in any of the above modes (3), (4), or (5), and that the trustee is therefore bound to satisfy himself that the power has not been so determined.

Irrevocable Powers —Apart from statute, powers given for valuable consideration cannot be expressly revoked, but if not for valuable consideration, though expressed to be irrevocable, may yet be revoked at any time. Cf. Jarman's Conveyancing, 3rd edit., vol. 8, p. 35; and Story on Agency, 9th edit., pp. 579, *et seq.*

Section 8 of the Conveyancing Act, 1882, contains express provision making irrevocable powers of attorney given for valuable consideration and expressed to be irrevocable; and section 9 of the same Act contains similar provisions as to powers of attorney, whether given for valuable consideration or not, expressed to be irrevocable for a fixed time. These sections apply only in favour of a purchaser. They do not depend on the absence of notice.

For definition of "trustee," see section 50, *infra.*

Section 24.—A trustee shall, without prejudice to the provisions of the instrument, if any, creating the trust, be chargeable only for money and securities actually received by him notwithstanding his signing any receipt for the sake of conformity, and shall be answerable and accountable only for his own acts, receipts, neglects, or defaults, and not for those of any other trustee, nor for any banker, broker, or other person with whom any trust moneys, or securities may be deposited, nor for the insufficiency or deficiency of any securities, nor for any other loss, unless the same happens through his own wilful default; and may reimburse himself, or pay or discharge out of the trust premises, all expenses incurred in or about the execution of his trusts or powers.

This section replaces section 31 of Lord St. Leonards's Act (22 & 23 Vict c. 35), which section is repealed by this Act. See section 51, and Schedule, *infra*. The two sections are virtually identical in expression, except that the repealed section commences, "Every deed, will, or other instrument creating a trust, either expressly or by implication, shall, without prejudice to the clauses actually contained therein, be deemed to contain a clause in the words, or to the effect following." The repealed section therefore only applied to trustees under an instrument, whilst the present section applies to all trustees as defined by section 50, including executors and administrators.

"**Without Prejudice to the Provisions of the Instrument.**"— The instrument creating the trust may extend or restrict the protection given by this section as between the trustees and beneficiaries. *Pass* v. *Dundas*, 43 L.T. N.S. 665; 29 W.R. 332. As against creditors, however, a testator, it is submitted, cannot extend the protection, for creditors are not, like legatees, bound by the terms of the will. *Doyle* v. *Blake*, 2 Sch. & Lef. 239, 245.

"**Shall . . . be chargeable only for.**"—Before the passing of Lord St. Leonards's Act, it was usual to insert in every will or settlement provisions similar to those of the present section, but such a clause was not strictly necessary, for equity infuses such a proviso into every trust deed. *Dawson* v. *Clarke*, 18 Ves. 247, 254; and cf. remarks of Lord Selborne, *In re Brier*, 26 C.D. at p 243.

"**Notwithstanding his signing any Receipt for the Sake of Conformity.**"—As it is necessary for all co-trustees to join in giving a receipt, it was very early decided that in equity, though not in law, it was competent to a trustee to show that the money acknowledged to have been received by all was in fact received by one *Brice* v *Stokes*, 11 Ves. 319, 324. But as to executors, the rule was not identical, for since one executor could give a valid receipt, the joining of his co-executor in giving the receipt was considered to be a voluntary act or interference, for the consequences of which he must be held responsible. Thus it would appear that if two executors joined in giving a receipt to a debtor, both would have been liable, though only one received the money, for the debtor requiring the discharge of the executor who has not received the money amounts to saying, "I make this payment to you both, and not to him only who actually receives the money." *Doyle* v. *Blake*, 2 Sch. & Lef. 231, 242. The question may arise whether the effect of the present section (which, by virtue of the definition of "trustee" in section 50, applies to executors and administrators, as well as to trustees in the strict sense) is to alter the rule as to the liability of executors in such a case. It is submitted that the section has no such effect, and that an executor who has joined in giving a receipt must now, as formerly, in order to escape liability, prove special circumstances to show that his joining in giving the receipt was a mere formality, and raised no presumption that the money was, though not received by him, yet under his control. For a full discussion of the earlier law on the subject, see Lewin on Trusts, p. 287.

"Accountable only for his own Acts . . . Wilful Default."— These words, although very wide and general, in fact do little if anything, to protect trustees. The comments of Mr. David- son (Precedents, 2nd edit., vol. iii. pp. 183, 184) [on the clause formerly usually inserted in settlements, and the form of which is virtually identical with the present clause, may be usefully referred to here . " It is considered, and probably with justice, that trustees attach a certain degree of importance to this clause, and it has been suggested that this arises from its being satisfactory for them to see what they are told is the rule of equity made an express part of the contract, instead of being left to an implication of which they can know nothing. It may be thought doubtful, however, whether the real inducement to the insertion of the clause in question was not in general a belief very naturally inspired by its language, that it carried with it a degree of protective force, and tempered the rigorous doctrines applicable to the administration of trusts with a certain latitude and indulgence. If in acting on this natural though unfounded impression, trustees were induced to deviate from the strict line of duty to which they would otherwise have considered it incumbent to adhere, it must be acknowledged that the real operation of the clause was anything but protective."

"Not for those of any other Trustee."—These words, of course, give no protection to a trustee who, by any neglect or default of his own, places it in the power of his co-trustee to cause a loss to the trust estate. Thus in *Brice* v. *Stokes*, 11 Ves. 319, 327, a trustee who had joined in giving a receipt was made liable, not for so joining, but because he subsequently permitted his co-trustee to keep, and deal with, the money. See also *Walker* v. *Symonds*, 3 Sw. 1, and other cases referred to in Lewin on Trusts, 10th edit, p. 286. To authorise leaving moneys under the control of a co-trustee, a special clause is necessary *Wilkins* v. *Hogg*, 10 W.R. 47, *Pass* v. *Dundas*, 29 W.R. 332.

"Nor for any Banker, etc."—Whilst trustees cannot delegate the execution of the trust, they may avail themselves of the services of others, wherever such employment is according to the usual course of business Lord Watson, in *Learoyd* v. *Whiteley*, 12 App. Cas at p. 734, Lord Selborne, in *Speight* v. *Gaunt*, 9 App. Cas at p. 5. But trustees will not be protected in respect of defaults of agents employed otherwise than in the usual course of business. Thus if trust funds are left in the hands of solicitors awaiting investment, the trustees will be responsible for any consequent loss, for they are not entitled to treat solicitors as bankers ; see *Wyman* v. *Paterson* (1900)

A C. 271, *ante*, p 77., and in such a case, relief under section 3 of the Judicial Trustees Act, 1896, will not be given, *Wynne* v. *Tempest* (1897) W.N. 43. The judgments in *Wyman* v *Paterson* demonstrate the liability of trustees in such circumstances even·when the instrument creating the trust contains special indemnity provisions going beyond the provisions of the present section. Again, a trustee is bound to exercise proper care in the selection of the agent. See *Robinson* v. *Harkin* (1896) 2 Ch. 415, a case in which trustees were held liable for not having exercised proper care in the selection of a broker, and having improperly left the trust fund in his hands.

As to appointing a solicitor or banker to receive payment of moneys receivable by the trustee, see section 17, *supra*.

As to the duties of trustees in investing trust funds, and the employment of valuers therein, see sections 1 and 8, *supra*.

" Insufficiency or Deficiency of any Securities."—The section will not protect the trustee if the investment, when made, was not both authorised and proper. See note, " Real securities," *ante*, p. 20; and section 9, *ante*, p 46.

As to retention of unauthorised securities, see notes to section 4 of the Amendment Act of 1894, *post*, p. 176. See Judicial Trustees Act, 1896, section 3 (p. 184, *infra*), for power for the Court to relieve a trustee from liability for breaches of trust in cases in which the trustee has acted " honestly and reasonably."

As to the liability of retiring trustees, see *Head* v. *Gould* (1898) 2 Ch 250.

" And may reimburse himself."—This, like the earlier part of this section, is merely an expression of what has long been recognised as the rule of equity. " It is in the nature of the office of a trustee, whether expressed in the instrument or not, that the trust property shall reimburse him all the charges and expenses incurred in the execution of the trust." Lord Eldon, in *Worrall* v. *Harford*, 8 Ves. at p. 8; and see *In re Raybould, Raybould* v. *Turner* (1900) 1 Ch. 199; *Ecclesiastical Commissioners* v. *Pinney* (1900) 2 Ch. 736; *In re Frith, Newton* v *Rolfe* (1902) 1 Ch. 342; *Hardoon* v. *Belilios* (1901) A.C. 118, *Wise* v. *Perpetual Trustee Co.* (1903) A.C. 139. The expenses must of course be properly incurred. *Re Beddoe, Downes* v. *Cottam* (1893) 1 Ch. 547, a case in which a trustee had unreasonably defended an action; *In re Hodgkinson, Hodgkinson* v. *Hodgkinson* (1895) 2 Ch. 190, a case in which the judge, on the hearing of a summons, declined to make an order as to costs. (But costs incurred through the mistaken but not unreasonable conduct of a trustee will be allowed him. *In re Jones, Christmas* v. *Jones* (1897) 2 Ch. 190.) *How* v. *Winterton* (1902) W.N. 230, a case in which the payment of a voluntary school rate was allowed as part of a trustee's costs, charges, and expenses. Generally as to what charges and expenses may be properly charged against the trust fund, see Lewin, 10th edit., p. 750.

Expenses incurred in the execution of the trust will be borne by capital or income in proportion to the benefit conferred on each. *Carter* v. *Sebright*, 26 B. 374   Thus the costs of the appointment of new trustees under a power, including, apparently, the costs of the donee of the power, will fall on the corpus of the trust estate. *Harvey* v. *Olliver* (1887) W.N. 149. As to costs of appointment by the Court, see section 38, *infra*.

The right of the trustee to reimbursement is precluded by his own, but not by his co-trustee's default. *In re Frith, Newton* v. *Rolfe* (1902) 1 Ch. 342

In the absence of express provision to the contrary, a trustee may not make a profit out of the trust by charging for his services, professional or otherwise, *re Fish* (1893) 2 Ch. 413. As to what charges are authorised by the usual express power, see *Clarkson* v. *Robinson* (1900) 2 Ch. 722.

As to the right of trustees to indemnity by the *cestuis que trust* personally where the *cestuis que trust* are *sui juris* and absolutely entitled, see Lewin, 10th edit., p. 761; *Hardoon* v. *Belilios, supra; Wise* v. *Perpetual Trustee Co., supra,* and where the *cestuis que trust* has induced a breach of trust, see section 45, *infra*.

For definitions of "instrument," "trust," "trustee," and "securities," see section 50, *infra*.

PART III.

POWERS OF THE COURT.

Appointment of New Trustees and Vesting Orders.

Section 25.—(1.) The High Court may, whenever it is expedient to appoint a new trustee or new trustees, and it is found inexpedient, difficult, or impracticable so to do without the assistance of the Court, make an order for the appointment of a new trustee or new trustees either in substitution for or in addition to any existing trustee or trustees, or although there is no existing trustee. In particular and without prejudice to the generality of the foregoing provision, the Court may make an order for the appointment of a new trustee in substitution for a trustee who is convicted of felony, or is a bankrupt.

(2.) An order under this section, and any consequential vesting order or conveyance, shall not operate further or otherwise as a discharge to any former or continuing trustee than an appointment of new trustees under any power for that purpose contained in any instrument would have operated.

(3.) Nothing in this section shall give power to appoint an executor or administrator.

This section is a consolidation of sections 32 and 33 of the Trustee Act, 1850 (13 & 14 Vict c 60), sections 8 and 9 of the Trustee Extension Act, 1852 (15 & 16 Vict c. 55), and section 147 of the Bankruptcy Act, 1883 (46 & 47 Vict. c. 52), which sections are repealed by the present Act   See section 51, and Schedule, *infra*.

It must be remembered that the present section does not deal exhaustively or generally with the powers of the Court in the matter of appointment of trustees. This section, and the sections replaced by it, merely provide a simple and expeditious method of appointing new trustees in comparatively simple cases, substituting proceedings by petition or summons in place of a suit or action.

The general jurisdiction of the Court to remove and replace trustees remains unaffected by these statutory provisions. Cf *Letterstedt* v. *Broers*, 9 App. Cas 371 ; Lewin on Trusts, 10th edit., p. 793 ; and see *re Martin's Trusts*, 34 C D. 618.

Further statutory power is given to the Courts by the Judicial Trustees Act, 1896 (see p. 180, below). As to the power to appoint new trustees without the assistance of the Court, see section 10, *supra*, p. 48.

"The High Court may, etc "—In spite of the very wide language of section 32 of the Trustee Act, 1850, it was very early decided that the section gave no power to remove a trustee desirous of continuing *Re Hodson's Settlement*, 9 Hare 118 ; *re Blanchard*, 3 De G.F. & J. 131 ; and in *re Combs*, 51 L.T. 45, the Court of Appeal approved this decision. This restriction on the scope of the enactment was removed in certain specific cases, viz in the case of a felon by section 8 of the Trustee Extension Act, 1852, in the case of a bankrupt by section 147 of the Bankruptcy Act, 1883. It should be noted that section 147 of the Bankruptcy Act, 1883, expressly authorised the removal of a bankrupt "whether voluntarily resigning or not." It would appear that the omission of these words in the present section does not restrict the jurisdiction, *re Betts*, *McLean* v. *Betts*, 41 S.J. 209, and it has also been held that, under the present section, the Court has power to remove a felon trustee against his will. *In re Dawson's Trusts*, (1899) W.N. 134

The present section, in consolidating the above enactments, appears to treat the replacing of a felon or bankrupt trustee not as exceptional but as typical instances of the exercise of tho power of the Court to appoint new trustees in substitution for existing trustees. It is submitted, however, that the interpretation put upon section 32 of the Trustee Act, 1850, in re Combs (cited above), is applicable to the present section, and that, accordingly, the Court will not, upon petition or summons, remove a trustee who is desirous of continuing, except in the specified cases of felony and bankruptcy. It would thus appear that the power of the Court as to removal of trustees under this section is in this respect more restricted than the power given to individuals under section 10.

"**Whenever it is expedient to appoint a New Trustee.**"— The section enables the appointment of new trustees of constructive, as well as of express, trusts (see definition of trustee in section 50, *infra*), but not the appointment of an executor or administrator (see subsection 3). That new trustees of constructive trusts cannot be appointed under section 10, see note, "A trustee," *ante*, p 50. It has been held expedient to appoint new trustees in the following cases :—

1 Where a trustee is an infant. *Re Gartside's Estate*, 1 W.R. 196, *re Arrowsmith*, 6 W R. 642, *re Porter's Trust*, 2 Jur N S. 349. In a case in which the infant was one of three trustees under a will, the order was expressed to be without prejudice to any application by the infant to be restored on coming of age *Re Shelmerdine*, 33 L J Ch. 474.

2. Where there is a sole trustee, *re Dickinson*, 1 Jur. N.S. 724, *re Brackenbury*, 10 Eq. 45; or an insufficient number of trustees, *re Boycott*, 5 W.R 15, *re Gregson*, 34 C.D. 209

3. Where numerous persons are trustees Thus in the case of *Shepherd* v. *Churchill*, 25 B. 21, upon a partition, the shares of the parties being very minute and complicated, the Court, to save expense, declared each of the parties trustee as to the shares allotted to the others of them, and then appointed a new trustee in his place and vested the property in such new trustee, with directions to convey the allotted shares. See also *Lees* v. *Coulton, infra*.

4. Where unborn persons, on coming into existence, will be trustees. Where in a partition action a sale was decreed of land in which unborn issue might take legal estates, such issue were declared to be trustees within the meaning of the Trustee Act, 1850, for the purpose of appointing a new trustee in their place *Lees* v. *Coulton*, 20 Eq. 20

5. Where there is no personal representative of a last or sole trustee. *Davis* v. *Chanter*, 4 Jur. N.S 272; *re Matthews*, 26 B. 463, and see also *re Davis's Trust*, 12 Eq 214; *re Williams' Trusts*, 36 Ch. D. 231; *re Pilling's Trusts*, 26 Ch. D. 432; *re Stocken's Settlement* (1893) W.N. 203

6 Where all trustees have died in the testator's lifetime. *Gunson* v. *Simpson*, 5 Eq 332; *re Smirthwaite's Trusts*, 11 Eq. 251; *re Williams' Trusts*, 36 Ch D. 231.

7. Where no trustee is appointed *Dodkin* v. *Brunt*, 6 Eq. 580; *re Davis's Trusts*, 12 Eq. 214, *re Moore*, 21 Ch. D. 778;

Sect. 25. *re Gillett's Trusts* (1876) W N. 251; 25 W R. 23; and see note, "Although there is no existing trustee," *infra*, p. 102.

8. Where a trustee has gone to reside abroad permanently. *Re Bignold's Settlement*, 7 Ch 223, cf. also *re Earl of Stamford* (1896) 1 Ch. 288; *re Walker* (1901) 1 Ch. 259; *Hutchinson* v. *Stephens*, 5 Sim. 498 (as to what constitutes absence abroad); and see also *re Gardner*, 10 Ch. D. 29, and *post*, p 107

9. Where the trustee has absconded. *Re Renshaw's Trusts*, 4 Ch. 783; and as to vesting property in the other trustees in such a case, without appointing a new trustee, see *Dugmore* v. *Suffield* (1896) W.N. 50; *re Lees' Trusts* (1896) 2 Ch. 508; *re Fitzherbert's Trusts* (1898) W N. 58.

10. Where a trustee is incapable through age or physical infirmity. *Re Lemann's Trust*, 22 Ch. D. 633; *re Phelps' Settlement*, 31 Ch. D. 351; *re Dewhirst's Trusts*, 33 Ch. D 416; *re Martin's Trusts*, 34 Ch D. 618, *re Barber*, 39 Ch. D. 187; *re Weston's Trusts* (1898) W.N. 151.

11. Where the trustee is a lunatic or mentally infirm. *Re Boyce*, 4 D.G J. & S. 205; *re Vickers*, 3 Ch. D 112 (As to the want of jurisdiction in the Chancery Court to make a vesting order in the case of a lunatic trustee, see *infra*, p 104.)

12. Where the trustee is a bankrupt. *Coombes* v. *Brookes*, 12 Eq. 61, *re Barker*, 1 Ch. D. 43; *re Adams' Trusts*, 12 Ch. D. 634; *re Foster*, 55 L.T N.S. 479 (In the last-cited case, although the trustee has obtained his discharge.) *Re Betts*, *McLean* v. *Betts*, 41 S.J. 209.

13 Where the trustee is a felon. *Re Dawson's Trusts* (1899) W.N. 134, S.C. (reported as *re Danson*), 43 S J. 706

14. Where a vesting order is required. *Re Davies*, 3 M. & G. 278, *re Stocken's Settlement* (1893) W.N. 203.

"Inexpedient, difficult, or impracticable so to do without the Assistance of the Court."—In general where there are persons in existence able and willing to exercise the power of appointment of new trustees, contained in the instrument, or given by section 10 of the present Act, the Court has no power under this section to appoint new trustees. *Re Sutton* (1885) W.N 122; *re Gibbon's Trusts* (1882) W N. 12; *re Higginbotham* (1892) 3 Ch 132. But in *re Humphrey*, 1 Jur N.S. 921; *re Somerset* (1887) W.N. 122, in which cases the persons having the power to appoint were resident abroad, and it was not shown whether or not they were willing to appoint, the Court exercised its power under this section. The Court will appoint under this section in the case of a person having power to appoint (under the trust instrument or under section 10 of the present Act) being a lunatic or mentally infirm. *In re Sparrow*, 5 Ch. 662 As to the jurisdiction in lunacy in such a case, see Lunacy Act, 1890 (53 Vict c. 5), sections 128 and 129; *re Shortridge* (1895) 1 Ch. 278; and note, "No such person able and willing to act," p. 54, *supra*. It has been held inexpedient to appoint without the assistance of the Court in a case in which a vesting order is required. *In re Davies*, 3 M. & G. 278; and see *re Stocken's Settlement* (1893) W.N. 203. In cases in which an additional trustee is required, and no vacancy exists, there is no power under section 10, nor under the usual provisions of trust instruments, to make the appointment without the assistance of the Court, and in such cases the Court will appoint. *Re Gregson*, 34 C.D. 209.

"Make an Order."—As stated above, the Court has, independently of statutory provisions, inherent jurisdiction to appoint a trustee in an action, whenever such appointment is necessary. The power to appoint by order as apart from a decree was first conferred in certain cases by section 22 of Lord St. Leonards's Trustee Act, 1830 (11 Geo. 4. and 1 Will. 4. c. 60), and in general terms by the sections of the Trustee Act, 1850, which are replaced by the present section.

What Persons are eligible for Appointment.—For the general principles in accordance with which the Court exercises its discretion in selecting trustees, see *In re Tempest*, 1 Ch. 485; *Tempest v. Camoys*, 58 L.T 221; *Forster v. Abraham*, 17 Eq. 351; *re Earl of Stamford* (1896) 1 Ch. 288 The general rule is that the Court will not appoint a tenant for life one of the trustees, although it may do, and sometimes has done, so in special circumstances. *Forster v Abraham*, 17 Eq. 351; *ex parte Clutton*, 17 Jur 988, *re Currie*, 10 C.D 93; *re Price* (1883) W.N. 202; *Tempest v. Camoys*, 58 L.T. 221 The same rule applies to beneficiaries generally, *re Conybeare*, 1 W.R. 458; *re Clissold*, 10 L.T. 642; *re Burgess* (1877) W N. 87; *re Lightbody*, 52 L T. 40, also to a near relative, *Wilding v. Bolder*, 21 B. 222; and to the husband of a beneficiary, *re Parrott* (1881) W.N 158, *re Hattett*, 18 W.R 416; (unless in the case of a very small fund, *re Knight*, 26 C D. 82); and also to the solicitor of any of the beneficiaries, *re Earl of Stamford* (1896) 1 Ch. 288; and possibly also to the agent of the estate, *re Freeman's Settlement*, 37 C D. 148. In appointing a beneficiary the Court has in some cases required an undertaking by him to at once appoint new trustees if he should become sole trustee, *re Hattet*; *re Burgess*; *re Lightbody*, *supra*.

Formerly, the Court, though it sometimes appointed an unmarried woman trustee, *re Campbell*, 31 B. 176, as a rule refused to do so, except when special circumstances were proved. *Brook v. Brook*, 1 Beav. 531, *Berkley v. Berkley*, 9 Ch. 720. But although the Court still exercises special care in such a case, *re Peake* (1894) 3 Ch. 520, such appointments are now frequently made, *re Dickinson* (1902) W.N. 104. Since a married woman cannot convey trust estates without the concurrence of her husband, *re Harkness and Allsopp* (1896) 2 Ch. 358 (unless she is a bare trustee within section 16 of the present Act, see notes, p. 73, *supra*), and does not become personally liable as debtor in respect of a breach of trust, *re Turnbull* (1900) 1 Ch. 180, it is submitted that, in spite of the

Sect. 25. alteration in her position effected by the Married Women's Property Act, 1882 (see especially sections 18 and 24), she is still not a fit person to be appointed a trustee by the Court, except in special circumstances. The exception of the husband from liability by virtue of section 24 of the last-mentioned Act affords an additional reason against such an appointment.

The Court has probably no power to appoint a corporation to be trustee. *Per* North, J., *In re Brogden, Billing* v. *Brogden* (1888) W.N. 238.

In special circumstances the Court has appointed persons out of the jurisdiction. *Re Freeman's Settlement*, 37 C.D. 148; *re Cunard*, 27 W R. 52; *re Simpson* (1897) 1 Ch. 256

The Number of Trustees to be appointed.—The general rule is that on the appointment of a new trustee or new trustees the original number of trustees will be made up.

Where, however, only one was originally appointed the Court will act on the well-recognized principle that it is not desirable that the administration of a trust shall be in the hands of a sole trustee, *re Dickinson*, 1 Jur. N.S. 724, *re Porter*, 2 Jur N.S 349, and will appoint two or more trustees, *exparte Tunstall*, 4 De G. & S 421; except in special cases, as when the trust is to be immediately wound up, when a sole trustee may be appointed, *re Reynault*, 16 Jur. 233. Where one alone was originally appointed, and no vacancy has occurred, the Court will sometimes, though not as a matter of right, appoint an additional trustee. *Grant* v. *Grant*, 34 L.J. Ch. 641; *re Brackenbury*, 10 Eq. 45

Where more than one trustee was originally appointed, the Court will, when it appears desirable, increase the original number either under its original jurisdiction in a suit, *Birch* v. *Cropper*, 2 De G. & S. 255; *Plenty* v. *West*, 16 Beav. 356, *D'Adhemar* v. *Bertrand*, 35 Beav. 19; or under its statutory powers, *re Welch*, 3 My. & Cr. 292; *re Boycott*, 5 W.R. 15, *re Gregson*, 34 Ch. D. 209. In filling up a vacancy the Court will only in special cases, as when the trust is to be immediately wound up, *re Marriott*, 18 L.T. 749, or it is found impossible to find persons to serve as trustees, *Bulkeley* v. *Earl of Eglinton*, 1 Jur. N.S. 994; *re Fowler* (1886) W.N. 183, reduce the original number of trustees, and will probably never appoint a sole trustee where more than one were originally appointed, *re Ellison*, 2 Jur. N.S. 62; *West of England Bank* v. *Murch*, 23 Ch. D. 138

At one time the power of the Court to appoint less than the original number was utilized to effect the discharge of a trustee, the other trustees being reappointed in place of themselves and the retiring trustee, *re Shipperdson's Trusts*, 49 L.J. (N.S.) Ch. 619, *re Harford's Trusts*, 13 Ch. D. 135. But later decisions laid down the rule that the Court has no power to make such order, *In re Colyer*, 50 L J. (N.S.) Ch. 79, *re Aston*, 23 Ch. D. 217; *re Gardiner*, 33 Ch D. 590; *re Chetwynd* (1902) 1 Ch. 692, except perhaps where the trustees have virtually no duty to perform, *Davies* v. *Hodgson*, 32 Ch. D. 226. Another possible exception is in the case of the absolute impossibility of securing a new trustee, *re Mace's Trusts* (1887) W.N. 232, but it seems questionable whether this decision can be reconciled with the other authorities, and especially with *re Gardiner's Trusts*, cited above. In cases such as that of an absconding trustee, coming within section 26, subsection 2 of the present Act, the necessity of appointing a new trustee may be dispensed with, and the property at once vested in the other trustees, to the exclusion of the absconding trustee, *re Watson*, 19 Ch. D. 384 (overruling *re Nash*, 16 Ch. D. 503); *re Martyn*, 26 Ch. D. 745; *re Leon* (1892) 1 Ch 348; *Dugmore* v. *Suffield* (1896) W.N. 50, *re Lees* (1896) 2 Ch. 508; *re Fitzherbert* (1898) W N. 58

As to the voluntary retirement of one trustee and the vesting of the property in the continuing trustees, see section 11, *supra*.

"A New Trustee"—The Court has no power in ordinary circumstances to reappoint the existing trustees for the purpose of making a consequential vesting order   This device, though formerly resorted to, *re Dalgleish's Settlement*, 4 C.D. 143; *re Crowe's Trust*, 14 C.D. 610, was disproved in *re Vicat*, 33 C.D. 103, and *re Dewhirst's Trusts*, 33 C.D 416, except in cases in which there is a reasonable question whether the existing trustees have been validly appointed. The proper course is to obtain a vesting order under some other subsection than subsection 1 of sections 26 and 35 of the present Act. If none such apply, one of the trustees should retire so as to enable the Court to appoint a new trustee in his place. *In re Stocken's Settlement* (1893) W.N. 203.

New Trustee of Part of Trust Property.—Although section 25 contains no such express provision as that of section 10 (2) (*b*) (see notes to section 10 (2), *supra*, p. 57), the Court can appoint separate sets of trustees thereunder, *re Paine's Trusts*, 28 C D. 725; *re Hetherington's Trusts*, 34 C.D. 211; *re Moss's Trusts*, 37 C.D. 513; *re Cotterill's Trusts* (1869) W.N. 183; *re Cunard's Trusts*, 27 W R 52; *re Aston's Trusts*, 25 L.R Ir. 96; as also in an administration action, *re Grange, Cooper* v. *Todd* (1881) W.N 50. Where there were no existing trustees the Court appointed new trustees of part only of the trust property, *Savile* v. *Couper*, 36 C.D. 520, *re Moss's Trusts*, *supra; re Nesbitt's Trusts*, 19 L.R. Ir. 509.

"In substitution for."—As to the removal of a trustee against his will, see commencement of note to this section, *ante*, p. 96. As to the power of the Court to discharge a trustee under this section from part only of the trusts, see notes to section 10, subsection 2, *supra*, p. 57. As to increasing or reducing the number of trustees, see *ante*, p. 100.

"In addition to"—The Court has power under this section to appoint additional trustees when no vacancy has occurred,

Sect. 25. *re Boycott*, 5 W.R. 15; *re Gregson*, 34 C.D. 209. No such power is given to individuals by section 10. As to increasing or reducing the number of trustees, see *ante*, p. 100.

"**Or although there is no Existing Trustee.**"—The section authorises the appointment of a new trustee or new trustees (1) if there be an existing trustee or existing trustees (and then either in substitution for or in addition to any existing trustee or trustees), or (2) if there be no existing trustee. The Trustee Act, 1850, did not contain this phrase, "although there is no existing trustee," and the suggestion was made that in a case in which all the trustees appointed by a will had disclaimed, the Act gave no power to appoint. See *re Tyler's Trusts*, 5 De G. & S. 56; *re Hazeldine*, 16 Jur. 853. The phrase was accordingly inserted by section 9 of the Trustee Extension Act, 1852, to meet this objection. The question is, however, still left open whether the Act gives a power to appoint trustees of a will where no trustees have been appointed by the testator, or whether in such a case the Court can only appoint by virtue of its inherent jurisdiction, *Dodkin* v. *Brunt*, 6 Eq. 580. As to merely constructive trusts, however, it is probable that this question will seldom arise, as, in almost every case, some person can be found who may be regarded as trustee; *e g* the heir or executor of testator, *re Davis's Trust*, 12 Eq 214; *re Moore*, 21 Ch. D. 778. Cf also cases of *Gunson* v. *Simpson*, 5 Eq 332; *re Williams' Trusts*, 36 Ch. D. 231; *re Smirthwaite's Trusts*, 11 Eq. 251, in which cases all trustees named in the will predeceased the testator, and the testator's heir was held to be a trustee.

"**Who is convicted of Felony, or is a Bankrupt.**"—See note, "The High Court may, etc.," p. 96, *supra;* and "Whenever it is expedient to appoint a new trustee (12), (13)," p. 98, *supra*. As to the effect of felony on the vesting of trust property, see section 48, *post*, p. 159.

"**Shall not operate further or otherwise as a Discharge.**"— As to the liability of a retiring trustee for breaches of trust committed by his successor when the breaches of trust were in contemplation at the time of the retirement and appointment, see *Head* v. *Gould* (1898) 2 Ch. 250.

"**Power to appoint an Executor or Administrator.**"—The express negation of jurisdiction to appoint an executor or administrator is introduced in the present section owing to the construction which (in reliance on the definition of "trustee" as including an executor or administrator) had been attempted to be placed on the corresponding section of the Trustee Act, 1850. *Re Moore*, 21 C.D. 778; *Brown* v. *Burdett*, 40 C.D. at p. 253. Later cases decided that the Act of 1850 did not give power to appoint a new executor, or a new trustee to perform the duties of an executor, but only power to appoint a trustee in place of an executor when all the duties of executor had been performed. *In re Willey* (1890) W.N. 1; *Eaton* v. *Daines* (1894) W.N. 32.

Further as to this question, and the absence of any provision Sect. 25. similar to this subsection in section 10 of this Act, see notes on p. 50, *supra*.

Practice.—See Trustee Act Rules (Order 54 (*b*) of Rules of Supreme Court), and notes thereon, *post*, p. 202.

For definitions of "trustee" and "bankrupt," see section 50, *infra*, p. 161.

Section 26.—In any of the following cases, Sect. 26.
namely :—

Vesting orders as to land.

> (i.) Where the High Court appoints or has appointed a new trustee ; and
>
> (ii.) Where a trustee entitled to or possessed of any land, or entitled to a contingent right therein, either solely or jointly with any other person—
>> (*a*) is an infant, or
>> (*b*) is out of the jurisdiction of the High Court, or
>> (*c*) cannot be found ; and
>
> (iii.) Where it is uncertain who was the survivor of two or more trustees jointly entitled to or possessed of any land ; and
>
> (iv.) Where, as to the last trustee known to have been entitled to or possessed of any land, it is uncertain whether he is living or dead ; and
>
> (v.) Where there is no heir or personal representative to a trustee who was entitled to or possessed of land and has died intestate as to that land, or where it is uncertain who is the heir or personal representative or devisee of a trustee who was entitled to or possessed of land and is dead ; and
>
> (vi.) Where a trustee jointly or solely entitled to or possessed of any land, or entitled to a contingent right therein, has been required, by or on behalf of a person entitled to require a conveyance of the land or a release of the right, to convey the land or to release the right, and has wilfully refused or neglected to convey the land

or release the right for twenty-eight days after the date of the requirement;

the High Court may make an order (in this Act called a vesting order) vesting the land in any such person in any such manner and for any such estate as the Court may direct, or releasing or disposing of the contingent right to such person as the Court may direct.

Provided that—

(a) Where the order is consequential on the appointment of a new trustee the land shall be vested for such estate as the Court may direct in the persons who on the appointment are the trustees; and

(b) Where the order relates to a trustee entitled jointly with another person, and such trustee is out of the jurisdiction of the High Court or cannot be found, the land or right shall be vested in such other person, either alone or with some other person.

Subsection (i.).—This subsection replaces section 34 of the Trustee Act, 1850 (13 & 14 Vict. c. 60), which section is repealed by the present Act. See section 51, and Schedule, *infra*

In spite of the general language of the subsection, no jurisdiction is thereby given on an appointment of a new trustee to make a vesting order affecting property vested in a lunatic, unless, indeed, such lunatic is an infant, or out of the jurisdiction within the meaning of subsection (ii.).

The Trustee Act, 1850, by sections 32, 34, and 35, made provision for the appointment of new trustees by the Court of Chancery, and for the vesting of the trust property in the new trustees. The wide language of these sections would doubtless have been held to include the particular case of the appointment in place of a lunatic trustee, and the necessary vesting order thereon, but for the fact that, by sections 3, 4, and 5 of the same Act, there is special provision for the making of vesting orders in the case of lunatic trustees, not by the Court of Chancery, but by the Lord Chancellor, in Lunacy. It was accordingly held that, although a trustee could be appointed by the Court of Chancery in place of a lunatic trustee, no order divesting the property from him could be made except in lunacy. By section 10 of the Trustee Extension Act, 1852 (15 & 16 Vict. c. 55), power was given to the Lord Chancellor in Lunacy to make an order for the appointment of new trustees in every case in which, under the Trustee Act, 1850, he had jurisdiction to make a vesting order. Consequently, in the case of a lunatic trustee there was jurisdiction in Lunacy to appoint a new trustee, and to make a vesting order as to the property vested in the lunatic, and there was jurisdiction in Chancery to appoint a new trustee, but not as a rule to make a vesting order. *Re Ormerod*, 3 De G. & J. 249; *re Boyce*, 4 D.J. & S. 205; *re Sparrow's Trusts*, 5 Ch. 662; *re Vickers*, 3 C.D. 112. The repeal and substantial re-enactment by the Lunacy Act, 1890, of the sections of the Trustee Act, 1850, dealing with lunatics, and the passing of the Trustee Act, 1893, have left the law on this point unchanged. See the judgment of Stirling, J., in *re M* (1899) 1 Ch. 79, in which the whole question and the earlier authorities are fully discussed.

It has been decided that there is jurisdiction in Chancery to make a vesting order in the case of a lunatic trustee, if the lunatic trustee is an infant, *re Arrowsmith*, 6 W.R. 642 (and see *re Edwards*, 10 C.D. 605, and Lunacy Act, 1890, section 143), or out of the jurisdiction, *re Gardner's Trusts*, 10 C.D. 29; *Caswell* v. *Sheen*, 69 L.T. N.S. 854; and cf. *Herring* v. *Clark*, 4 Ch. 167; for in the cases of infant trustees and trustees out of the jurisdiction, express provision was made by sections 7 to 12 of the Trustee Act, 1850, for vesting the property by order of the Court of Chancery, apart from any appointment of new trustees. Where, however, the sole jurisdiction to make a vesting order depends on the fact of the appointment of new trustees, no such order can be made in Chancery of property vested in a lunatic. *In re Mason*, 10 Ch. 273. It is submitted that the law has in this respect been unaffected by the Lunacy Act, 1890, and the Trustee Act, 1893. Cf. *re M.*, above referred to.

In certain cases vesting orders must be made and entituled both in Chancery and Lunacy, viz. when property has to be divested from both a lunatic and a sane trustee. This necessity occurs whenever a new trustee is appointed in place of a lunatic one of two or more trustees, for it is not sufficient to divest the property from the lunatic and vest his share in the continuing and new trustees, but the whole property must be divested from the old trustees and vested in the continuing and new trustees as joint tenants. *In re Pearson*, 5 C D. 982; *re Ohell*, 49 L.T. N.S. 196. In such cases the order is made by the Lords Justices in Lunacy under the Lunacy Act, and in Chancery under their Chancery jurisdiction and by virtue of the present section. As to the Chancery jurisdiction of the Lords Justices, see *re Platt*, 86 C D. 410; *re Farnham* (1896) 1 Ch. 836.

An exceptional case of similar nature is that of property in Ireland being vested in an English lunatic trustee. Since the Lunacy Act, 1890 (53 Vict. c 5), does not extend to Ireland, the Judge in Lunacy has no jurisdiction thereunder to vest land or stock in Ireland, and accordingly the Chancery jurisdiction has to be resorted to for the appointment of a new

Sect. 26. trustee and the consequent vesting order (Lewin, 819). *Re Davies*, 3 Mac. & G 278 ; *re Hodgson*, 11 C.D. 888 ; *re Lamotte*, 4 C.D. 325 ; *re Smyth*, 55 L T. N.S 37.

As to the distinction between that physical weakness and decay which may make an appointment of new trustees and consequent vesting order by the Chancery Court expedient, and that mental weakness and decay which gives rise to the jurisdiction in lunacy, see *re Lemann's Trusts*, 22 C.D. 633 ; *re Phelps' Settlement Trusts*, 31 C.D 351 , *re Dewhirst's Trusts*, 33 C D. 416 ; *re Martin's Trusts*, 34 C.D. 618 , *re Barber*, 39 C D. 187 ; *re Weston's Trusts* (1898) W.N. 151 ; and cf. section 116 of the Lunacy Act, 1890 (53 Vict. c 5).

The Court will not, for the purpose of making this subsection available, reappoint the existing trustees. See *re Dewhirst's Trusts*, 33 C D. 416, overruling *In re Dalgleish's Settlement*, 4 C.D. 143 , and see note, " A new trustee," to section 25, *supra*, p. 101. The Court will, however, appoint a new trustee for the purpose of making a vesting order under this subsection. *Re Davies*, 3 M. & G 278 ; *re Stocken's Settlement* (1893) W.N. 203.

The subsection only applies where the appointment is made by the Court. Thus, where an appointment of new trustees is desired and a vesting order is necessary, application should be made for appointment of new trustees by the Court. The subsection applies to appointments by the Court under its ordinary as well as under its statutory jurisdiction. *Re Hughes's Settlement*, 2 H. & M. 695, a case in which trustees of a settlement who had obtained an order in a suit for the transfer of a mortgage debt to themselves, were held to be " new trustees " of the mortgage within the meaning of section 34 of the Trustee Act, 1850.

For definition of " trustee," see section 50, *infra*.

Subsection (ii).—This subsection replaces sections 7 to 12 of the Trustee Act, 1850, so far as those sections applied to trustees. As to mortgagees, see section 28 of the present Act. The subsection deals with three only of the various ways in which a trustee becomes incapable of acting. It appears to be a matter for regret that " bankruptcy," " felony," " unfitness," and " unwillingness to act," were not included in the subsection, so as to enable the Court in such cases to vest the property in the other trustees without the necessity of appointing a new trustee. See note, " A new trustee," to section 25, *supra*, p 101 ; and see concluding paragraph of note, " The number of trustees to be appointed," *ante*, p. 100.

It may even be suggested that in place of any detached list of cases, in which the Court is authorised to make a vesting order, general language such as that used in section 25 might well have been employed.

The case of a lunatic trustee is dealt with by the Lunacy Act, 1890, but in cases where the lunatic trustee is an infant, or out of the jurisdiction, vesting orders may be made by the High Court under the present subsection. See *re Arrowsmith*,

6 W R. 642; 4 Jur. N.S. 1123; *In re Gardner's Trust*, 10 C.D. 29; section 143 of the Lunacy Act, 1890; and note to subsection (1.), *supra*, p. 105.

The Court is authorised to make a vesting order as to land upon a judgment for sale or mortgage by section 30, and upon a judgment for specific performance by section 31, and in cases covered by those sections a vesting order will not be made under the present section. *Re Carpenter*, Kay 418; and note, "General effect of sections 30 and 31," *infra*, p. 118.

"**Entitled to or possessed of.**"—This phrase replaces the expression "seised or possessed of" in section 7 of the Trustee Act, 1850. As to this change of phraseology, see note to the definition of "possessed" in section 50, *infra*, p. 166. It seems clear that both expressions include vested interests of a freehold or leasehold nature either in possession or reversion.

"**Either solely or jointly with any other Person.**"—Where the legal estate in land is vested in two persons, either as tenants in common or as joint tenants, one of whom is alone beneficially entitled, the other is "solely" entitled upon trust. *McMurray* v. *Spicer*, 5 Eq. 527. Where the legal estate in copyholds is vested in coparceners as trustees, each coparcener is "jointly" entitled. *Re Greenwood's Trusts*, 27 C.D. 359.

(a) "**Is an Infant.**"—The case of an infant trustee is now only likely to occur in the cases of constructive trusts, when a last surviving trustee of copyholds has died intestate leaving an infant customary heir, for neither section 4 nor section 30 of the Conveyancing and Law of Property Act, 1881, which vest trust estates in the personal representative instead of in the heir of a deceased trustee, apply to copyholds. See Copyhold Act, 1894 (section 88), replacing Copyhold Act, 1887 (section 45); *re Mills*, 37 C.D. 312; 40 C.D. 14; *re Beaufort* (1898) W.N. 148; nor does section 1 of the Land Transfer Act, 1897, apply to copyholds.

(b) "**Is out of the Jurisdiction of the High Court.**"—This phrase refers not to merely temporary absence, as on a voyage. *Hutchinson* v. *Stephens*, 5 Sim. 498 (a case under Lord St Leonards's Trustee Act, 1830, 11 Geo. 4., 1 Wm. 4. c. 60) See also *re Mais*, L J. Ch. 875; *re Earl of Stamford* (1896) 1 Ch. 288; and *re Walker* (1901) 1 Ch. 259, as to what constitutes absence abroad; and cf. the language of section 10 of the present Act, which gives power to appoint if a trustee "remains out of the United Kingdom for more than twelve months." It seems that a trustee may be treated as out of the jurisdiction although he appears by counsel. *Stillwell* v. *Ashley*, cited in Seton on Decrees, 6th edit, p. 1247.

Cases in which the Court has made vesting orders under this subsection or section 9 (the corresponding section) of the Trustee Act, 1850, which it in part replaces, are *re Skitter*, 4 W.R. 791, in which case, on the death of a mortgagee intestate after going into possession, the heir was considered a

Sect. 26.

trustee for the executors (cf. section 29, *infra*); *Hooper* v. *Strutton*, 12 W.R. 367, in which case the heir of an owner of land was held a trustee for his executors, to whom he had given a power of sale; *re Stanley's Trust* (1893) W.N. 30, in which case service on the heir of a sole trustee was dispensed with on the grounds that in the circumstances it was extremely unlikely he could have any claim for costs.

(c) "**Cannot be found.**"—Cases in which the Court has made vesting orders under this subsection or section 9 (the corresponding section) of the Trustee Act, 1850, which it in part replaces, are *Wilks* v. *Groom*, 6 De G.M. & G. 205, in which case, on the disclaimer by all the trustees of a will, land was held to have vested in the heir of the deceased owner, and after a failure to discover on inquiry who was the heir, a vesting order was made by the Court; *re General Accident Assurance Corporation, Limited* (1904) 1 Ch 147, where a limited company trustee after voluntary liquidation, was dissolved, and it was held that the case came within this subsection; Buckley, J., however, dissents from this decision, *re Niger Patent Enamel Co.* (1904) W.N. 99, 120, *re Barber*, 58 L.T. 303, in which case an estate vested by way of mortgage in an absconded trustee was by the order of the Court vested in the persons beneficially interested in the mortgage, *re Walker's Mortgage Trusts*, 3 C.D. 209, in which case a mortgage was vested in three trustees, one of whom went abroad and could not be found, and on the receipt of the mortgage money by the other trustees from an intending transferee, a vesting order was made of the estate of the absconding trustee (see notes on "trustee," in section 50, *infra*, p. 168, as to when that term includes a mortgagee) *Dugmore* v *Suffield* (1896) W.N. 50, in which case mortgage estates were vested in four trustees, one of of whom absconded, and the estate of the absconding trustee was vested in the other trustees; *re Lees' Settlement Trusts* (1896) 2 Ch. 508, a similar case; (in the last cited-case it appears to be suggested that the present subsection is wider than the section replaced, but it is submitted that there is nothing to support this suggestion,) *re Fitzherbert's Settlement Trusts* (1898) W.N. 58, a similar case.

For definitions of "trustee," "possessed," "land," and "contingent right," see section 50, *infra*.

Subsection (iii)—This subsection replaces section 13 of the Trustee Act, 1850, which is repealed by the present Act. See section 51, and Schedule, *infra*.

"**Entitled to or possessed of.**"—See note on these words under subsection (ii.).

For definitions of "trustee," "possessed," and "land," see section 50, *infra*.

Subsection (iv.)—This subsection replaces section 14 of the Trustee Act, 1850, which is repealed by the present Act. See section 51, and Schedule, *infra*.

As to the presumption of death arising from the fact that a person has not been heard of for seven years, see *re Phene's Trust*, 5 Ch. 139; *re Lewes Trusts*, 6 Ch 356; *Hickman* v. *Upsall*, 20 Eq. 136, *re Corbishley's Trusts*, 14 C.D. 846; *re Rhodes*, 36 C.D 586; *re Benjamin* (1902) 1 Ch 723.

"**Entitled to or possessed of.**"—See note on these words under subsection (ii.)

For definitions of "trustee," "possessed," and "land," see section 50, *infra*.

Subsection (v.).—This subsection replaces section 15 of the Trustee Act, 1850, which section is repealed by the present Act. See section 51, and Schedule, *infra* The repealed section applied to the cases "when any person seised of any lands upon any trust shall have died intestate as to such lands without an heir, or shall have died and it shall not be known who is his heir or devisee," and was held not to apply to leaseholds, *re Mundel's Trusts*, 8 W R. 683.

"**Heir or Personal Representative.**"—Since neither section 4 nor section 30 of the Conveyancing and Law of Property Act, 1881, applies to copyholds or customary freeholds, the word "heir" is still required in the present section. The words "personal representative" are necessary for the case of freeholds as well as of leaseholds.

"**Entitled to or possessed of.**"—These words, replacing the words "seised of," have the effect of extending the operation of this subsection to leaseholds as well as freeholds and copyholds. See also notes on these words under subsection (ii).

"**Uncertain who is, etc.**"—Where the validity of the will was disputed, it was held that it was uncertain who was the personal representative within the meaning of section 29, *re Cook's Mortgage* (1895) 1 Ch. 700.

"**Devisee.**"—This word is necessary for the like reasons stated above for the retention of the word "heir."

For definitions of "trustee," "possessed," "land," and "devisee," see section 50, *infra*

Subsection (vi.).—This subsection replaces section 2 of the Trustee Extension Act, 1852 (15 & 16 Vict c 55) The repealed section replaced sections 17 and 18 of the Trustee Act, 1850, under which the power of the Court arose only upon a written refusal to convey, or neglect, or refusal so to do, after tender of a proper deed. As to the inconvenience of such restriction, see *Rowley* v. *Adams*, 14 B. 130.

"**Entitled to or possessed of**"—See note on these words under subsection (ii.), *supra*, p. 107.

"**Has been required.**"—No special form of requisition is essential, but some demand must be proved to have been made.

Sect. 26.

"**Persons entitled to require.**"—A person who has purchased the beneficial interest in the land from the beneficiaries is (in the absence of dispute as to title) a person entitled to require a conveyance or surrender from the trustee. *Re Mills*, 40 C.D. 14; *re O'Donnell*, 19 W.R. 522.

An assignee of a mortgage is entitled to require a surrender by the mortgagor of copyholds in accordance with a covenant in the mortgage deed, *re Crowe's Mortgage*, 13 Eq. 26 A purchaser of land sold under a decree of the Court is entitled to require a conveyance from the person in whom the land is vested, *Rowley* v *Adams*, 14 B. 130. Where a trustee has been appointed out of Court in place of a trustee who had absconded, and the absconding trustee refuses to convey, an order will be made under this subsection on the application of the persons entitled to appoint and the continuing and new trustees, *re Keeley*, 53 L.T. 487. A beneficiary absolutely entitled to land is entitled to require a conveyance by trustees in whom it is vested, *re Grayson*, 27 W.R. 534, *Brader* v. *Kerby* (1872) W.N. 174. A person who had obtained a decree for specific performance declaring the defendant a trustee for the purpose of granting a lease, is a person entitled to require a conveyance, and although in such a case a vesting order will not be made, the Court will appoint a person to execute the lease on behalf of the defendant if he refuse to grant the lease. *Derham* v. *Kiernan*, I R. 5 Eq. 217.

"**Wilfully refused or neglected**"—A refusal of a trustee to convey has been held not to be wilful within this provision, if the title of the person asking for the conveyance is disputed, and the trustee entertain a *bonâ fide* doubt as to it, *re Mills*, 40 C D. 14, though, in earlier cases, this rule was not always observed, *re Grayson*, 27 W.R. 534

"**For Twenty-eight Days.**"—The Court has no jurisdiction to make an order upon a petition presented before the expiration of the twenty-eight days, *re Knox* (1895) 1 Ch. 538; (1895) 2 Ch. 483 (a decision on the similar language of section 35). In *Knight* v *Knight* (1866) W.N. 114, a motion for a vesting order in a suit was ordered to stand over until the expiration of the twenty-eight days.

"**The High Court may make an Order.**"—As to the Chancery jurisdiction of the Lords Justices in Lunacy, see *ante*, p. 105.

"**A Vesting Order.**"—Before the passing of the Trustee Act, 1850 (13 & 14 Vict. c. 60), the Court had no power to vest land or other property by decree or order. It had, however, power by virtue of several statutes, and especially of Lord St. Leonards's Trustee Act (11 Geo. 4., 1 Wm. 4, c. 60), either to direct trustees under disability to convey or to appoint persons to convey for them. The right to appoint persons to convey is reserved as an alternative in the present Act (see section 33, *infra*). Both Lord St. Leonards's Trustee Act and the Trustee Act, 1850, contained sections authorising the making of such

orders on petition. The present Act does not contain similar
sections, but leaves the form of proceedings to be dealt with by
the Rules of Court. For these, see *post*, p 191.

With regard to property, the title to which is registered
under the Land Transfer Acts, 1875 and 1897, Rule 151 of
the Land Transfer Rules, 1903, provides that, when the power
of disposing of registered land has by order of Court become
vested in some person other than the registered proprietor,
and the registered proprietor refuses to execute a transfer,
or his execution of a transfer cannot be obtained, or can only
be obtained after undue delay or expense, the registrar may,
after due notice under the rules to such proprietor, and on
production of the land certificate, and such evidence as he
may deem sufficient, make such entry in or correction of the
register as under the circumstances he shall think fit. The
power conferred on the registrar by rule 151 is extended by
Rule 174 to registered charges. The Land Transfer Acts and
Rules do not, it is conceived, in any way affect the power of
the Court to make an order vesting *the land* under the Trustee
Act, 1893 (cf. *Capital and Counties Bank* v. *Rhodes* (1903)
1 Ch. 657), but the vesting order requires to be followed by
the rectification of the register either under Rule 151 of the
Land Transfer Rules, 1903, or section 95 of the Land Transfer
Act, 1875, which gives any Court of competent jurisdiction
general power to order rectification of the register. The procedure prescribed by Rule 151 is troublesome and expensive,
and the right practice would seem to be, where an order vesting
registered land is sought, to ask, in addition, for an order for
rectification of the register under section 95. An office copy
of the order would then be served on the registrar pursuant
to Rule 310, and he is bound by section 96 of the Act of 1875
to obey the order.

With regard to land out of the jurisdiction, see section 41,
infra, and notes thereon; and section 2 of the Act of 1894,
infra.

Section 27.—Where any land is subject to a
contingent right in an unborn person or class of
unborn persons who, on coming into existence would,
in respect thereof, become entitled to or possessed
of the land on any trust, the High Court may make
an order releasing the land from the contingent
right, or may make an order vesting in any person
the estate to or of which the unborn person or class
of unborn persons would, on coming into existence,
be entitled or possessed in the land.

This section re-enacts, with verbal amendments, section 16
of the Trustee Act, 1850 (13 & 14 Vict. c. 60), which section

Sect. 27. is repealed by the present Act. See section 50, and Schedule, *infra.*

The circumstances contemplated by this section are only likely to occur in the case of constructive trusts. As to the necessity for a judgment declaring the rights of the parties in the case of certain constructive trust, see note to section 30, "General effect of sections 30 and 31," *infra*, p. 118.

"**Contingent Right.**"—All rights of unborn persons are necessarily contingent.

"**Unborn Persons.**"—This phrase, it is submitted, must here, as in section 30 of the Trustee Act, 1850, be given a meaning wider than its popular sense, and will include, *e g.*, the heirs of a living person, and generally "any person so far not in existence as that he could not be properly made a party to an action." Cf. judgment of Jessel, M.R., in *Basnett* v. *Moxon*, 20 Eq. 182.

For cases in which the power given to the Court by section 16 of the Trustee Act, 1850, has been exercised, see *Wake* v. *Wake*, 1 W.R. 283, and cases noted under section 31, *infra*.

"**Entitled to or possessed of.**"—See note on these words under subsection (ii) of section 26, *supra*, p. 107.

For definitions of "land," "contingent right," "possessed," and "trust," see section 50, *infra*

Practice.—See *post*, p. 193.

Sect. 28.

Vesting order in place of conveyance by infant mortgagee.

Section 28.—Where any person entitled to or possessed of land, or entitled to a contingent right in land, by way of security for money, is an infant, the High Court may make an order vesting or releasing or disposing of the land or right in like manner as in the case of an infant trustee.

This section replaces sections 7 and 8 of the Trustee Act, 1850 (13 & 14 Vict. c. 60), so far as they relate to infant mortgagees. Those sections are repealed by the present Act. See section 51, and Schedule, *infra*. As to the earlier history of this enactment see note to section 29, p. 114, *infra*.

The effect of the section, stated shortly, is that where a mortgagee is an infant the Court may make a vesting order in like manner as in the case of an infant trustee. That a mortgagee is not, during the continuance of the mortgage, a trustee for the mortgagor, see definition of trustee in section 50, *infra*, and notes thereon, p. 168, *infra*

Since the Conveyancing and Law of Property Act, 1881, came into force, the case of an infant mortgagee of other than copyhold land is not likely to be of very frequent occurrence, for by virtue of section 30 of that Act (replacing section 4 of the Vendor and Purchaser Act, 1874) mortgage estates now devolve upon the personal representatives, and do not pass to

the heir or devisee, see note, "Is an infant," *ante*, p. 107. The
case of an infant personal representative does not often occur, for
in the event of the sole executor being an infant, administration
durante minoritate may be granted by the Probate Division of
the High Court. The case of contingent rights in land other
than copyholds being vested in an infant by way of security can
hardly now occur.

For an example of an order vesting in executors of a deceased
mortgagee the legal estate in copyholds outstanding in an infant
heir, see *re Franklyn* (1888) W.N. 217.

"**As in the Case of an Infant Trustee.**"—Section 26, subsection 2, provides that where a trustee entitled to or
possessed of any land, or entitled to a contingent right therein,
either solely or jointly with any other person, is an infant, the
High Court may make an order (in this Act called a vesting
order) vesting the land in any such persons in any such manner
and for any such estate as the Court may direct, or releasing
or disposing of the contingent right to such person as the
Court may direct.

The effect of a vesting order under this section is as if the
infant mortgagee had been a person of full capacity and had
executed a conveyance or release to the effect intended by the
order. See section 32, *infra*

For forms of order, see Seton on Decrees, 6th edit., pp. 1230
and 1235.

Practice.—See *post*, p. 193

For definitions of "land," "possessed," "contingent right,'
and "trustee," see section 50, *infra*.

Section 29.—Where a mortgagee of land has
died without having entered into the possession
or into the receipt of the rents and profits thereof, Vesting order
in place of
and the money due in respect of the mortgage has conveyance
been paid to a person entitled to receive the same, by heir, or
devisee of
or that last-mentioned person consents to any order heir, etc , or
for the reconveyance of the land, then the High personal representative
Court may make an order vesting the land in such of mortgagee.
person or persons in such manner and for such
estate as the Court may direct in any of the following
cases, namely—

(*a*) Where an heir or personal representative or
devisee of the mortgagee is out of the
jurisdiction of the High Court or cannot
be found; and

(*b*) Where an heir or personal representative or
devisee of the mortgagee on demand made

I

by or on behalf of a person entitled to require a conveyance of the land has stated in writing that he will not convey the same or does not convey the same for the space of twenty-eight days next after a proper deed for conveying the land has been tendered to him by or on behalf of the person so entitled; and

(c) Where it is uncertain which of several devisees of the mortgagee was the survivor; and

(d) Where it is uncertain as to the survivor of several devisees of the mortgagee or as to the heir or personal representative of the mortgagee whether he is living or dead; and

(e) Where there is no heir or personal representative to a mortgagee who has died intestate as to the land, or where the mortgagee has died and it is uncertain who is his heir or personal representative or devisee.

This section re-enacts, with some verbal amendments, section 19 of the Trustee Act, 1850 (13 & 14 Vict c 60), which section is repealed by the present Act. See section 51, and Schedule, *infra*.

See the definition of trustee in section 50. A mortgagee, so long as the mortgage money has not been repaid to him, is not a trustee within the meaning of the present Act.

This section, with section 28, is intended to deal with cases of difficulty in obtaining the reconveyance or transfer of the mortgage security, owing to the incapacity of the mortgagee to convey It must be noted that while incapacity arising from infancy is dealt with by section 28 in general terms, incapacity arising from other causes is only dealt with by section 29 in cases in which the mortgagee is the heir, personal representative, or devisee of a deceased mortgagee.

The explanation of the existence and of the form of the present section is to be found in the history of the successive statutory enactments dealing with mortgagees under disability. Cf. Lewin, 3rd (1857) edit., pp. 836, 888.

Under the provisions of 7 Anne, c. 19, an infant trustee or mortgagee of land was empowered by the direction of the Court of Chancery by an order made on petition to convey the lands as if he were of age.

Similar provisions were contained in Lord St. Leonards's
Trustee Act (11 Geo. 4. and 1 Will. 4. c. 60), section 6.

Section 8 of the last-mentioned Act contained provisions similar to those of the present section, but dealing only with trustees, and not with the heirs of a deceased mortgagee. Owing, however, to the language of a reference to section 8 of Lord St. Leonards's Trustee Act, contained in section 2 of the Escheat and Forfeiture Act (4 & 5 Will. 4. c. 23), the judges held themselves bound to construe section 8 as applying to mortgagees as well as trustees, *exparte Whitton*, 1 Keen 278.

An Amending Act (1 & 2 Vict. c. 69) was then passed to restrict the application of section 8 of Lord St. Leonards's Trustee Act to the case of trustees, excluding mortgagees, and this Act made provision for the case of a deceased mortgagee in language virtually identical with that of the present section. See *Spunner* v. *Walsh*, 10 Ir. Eq Rep 214

The Trustee Act, 1850, in section 7 re-enacted section 6 of Lord St. Leonards's Trustee Act, in sections 9 to 18 re-enacted section 8 of Lord St. Leonards's Trustee Act, and in section 19 re-enacted the enabling provisions of 1 & 2 Vict. c 69.

Since a person in whom mortgage estates are vested becomes a constructive trustee, either when all moneys secured by the mortgage have been paid off, or when the right to receive the mortgage money is vested in another person, *re Skitter's Mortgage Trust*, cited below, and since both the Trustee Act, 1850, and the present Act contain provisions for making vesting orders in the case of constructive trustees under disability, it appears at least doubtful whether the provisions contained in the present section were necessary, either in the Trustee Act, 1850, or in the present Act.

The case of the infancy of an heir devisee or personal representative of a deceased mortgagee is covered by section 28.

The case of the lunacy of either of these is dealt with by the Lunacy Act, 1890 (53 Vict. c 5), section 135.

"**Without having entered into Possession.**"—The section does not apply where the mortgagee has gone into possession. The importance of this restriction, however, is greatly diminished, if not entirely abolished, if the decision in the case of *re Skitter's Mortgage Trusts*, 4 W R 791, is good law. In that case it was held that a vesting order could be made under section 9 of the Trustee Act, 1850, vesting in the executors mortgage estates which had devolved on the heir of an intestate mortgagee, although the mortgagee had shortly before her death gone into possession. If this case was rightly decided, it would appear that the present section is altogether unnecessary (and see note, *supra*), for in every case provided for by the present section the Court could hold, as in the case cited, that the heir, devisee, or personal representative, was a trustee within the meaning of section 9 of the Trustee Act, 1850, and section 26 of the present Act. *Re Skitter's Mortgage Trust* has never been overruled, though some doubt as to its authority seems to have been suggested, see *re Lea's Trust*, 6 W.R. 482.

"**Reconveyance of the Land.**"—This phrase appears to suggest that only a reconveyance to a mortgagor, and not a transfer to another mortgagee, is contemplated by the section. It is conceived, however, that the extended meaning given by the Court to this word in the repealed section will also be given to it in the present Act. The narrower meaning, excluding "transfer," was given to the word by Turner, V.C., in *re Meyrick's Estate*, 9 Hare 116, but this decision was overruled by the Lords Justices in *re Boden's Trust*, 1 De G.M. & G. 57. The later decision has been followed in *re Lea's Trust*, 6 W.R. 482. In these cases the transfer was from the heir to the executors or administrator.

"**Where an Heir or Personal Representative**"—The words "or personal representative" did not occur in the repealed section 19 of the Trustee Act, 1850. When that Act was passed, mortgage estates in freehold land, on the death of the mortgagee, devolved, as other real estate, upon his heir or devisee. Now, however, in accordance with section 30 of the Conveyancing and Law of Property Act, 1881 (44 & 45 Vict c. 41), as modified by section 45 of the Copyhold Act, 1887 (50 & 51 Vict. c. 78), and section 88 of the Copyhold Act, 1894 (57 & 58 Vict. c. 46), while copyhold and customary land still devolves upon the devisee or heir, mortgage freeholds pass, on the death of the mortgagee to his personal representative. It is probably due to this alteration of the law that the reference to the personal representative has been introduced in the present section. No provision for the case of mortgagees of leaseholds was made by section 19 of the Trustee Act, 1850, probably because it was thought that in the case of a security which would vest in personal representatives no difficulty could arise. By parity of reasoning it would seem that the case of freeholds since 1881 need not have been provided for. The provision which has, however, been made, would probably apply to a mortgagee of leaseholds. The provision would seem to be of little practical value, for if, *e g.*, the personal representative is abroad or cannot be found, there would be no one entitled to receive the money. In *re Cook's Mortgage* (1895) 1 Ch. 700, where an order was made under this section, the money had been paid to the mortgagee before his death, so that the case was one of a deceased trustee, and it is submitted a vesting order could have been made under section 26, subsection (v.).

"**If a Proper Deed for conveying the Land has been tendered.**"—It is not clear why the somewhat burdensome requirements of the corresponding portion of the repealed section should have been retained in the present section. It would have been a simple matter to have adopted the language of subsection 6 of section 26, which deals with the analogous case of a trustee who refuses or neglects to convey. For an

example of the difficulty caused in the case of copyholds by the
language of the present section, see *Rowley* v. *Adams*, 14 Beav
130, a decision on section 17 of the Trustee Act, 1850, the
language of which was similar to that of the present section.
Section 17 was repealed and re-enacted in simpler language by
section 2 of the Trustee Extension Act, 1852, the language of
which is similar to that of section 26, subsection (vi.) of the
present Act.

"Where there is no Heir"—In this case the petition or
summons must be served on the Crown.   *Re Minchin*, 2
W R. 179.

"Where it is uncertain who is his Personal Representative."
—Such a case has arisen where the validity of a will appointing
executors was being disputed in the Probate Division.   *Re
Cook's Mortgage* (1895) 1 Ch. 700, in which case a vesting order
was made under this section   See *supra*, p 116.

Practice.—See *post*, p. 193.

Section 30.—Where any court gives a judgment or makes an order directing the sale or
mortgage of any land, every person who is entitled Vesting order
consequential
to or possessed of the land, or entitled to a con- on judgment
tingent right therein [as heir, or under the will of for sale or
mortgage of
a deceased person, for payment of whose debts the land.
judgment was given or order made], and is a party
to the action or proceeding in which the judgment or
order is given or made or is otherwise bound by the
judgment or order, shall be deemed to be so entitled
or possessed, as the case may be, as a trustee within
the meaning of this Act; and the High Court may,
if it thinks expedient, make an order vesting the
land or any part thereof for such estate as that
Court thinks fit in the purchaser or mortgagee or in
any other person.

This section replaces section 29 of the Trustee Act, 1850
(13 & 14 Vict c. 60), and section 1 of the Trustee Extension
Act, 1852 (15 & 16 Vict. c. 65), which sections are repealed by
the present Act. See section 51, and Schedule, *infra.*
The words within [   ] were repealed by section 1 of the
Trustee Act, 1893, Amendment Act, 1894 (57 & 58 Vict. c. 10).
See p. 175, *infra.*
The provisions of section 14 of the Judicature Act, 1884
(47 & 48 Vict. c. 61), should be compared with the present
section. They are set out in the note to section 31, p. 123,
infra.

Sect. 30.

The General Effect of Sections 30 and 31 of the present Act must be discussed as a whole, and involves the consideration of the sections which they replace.

The early sections of the Trustee Act, 1850, gave power to the Court by order, on petition, to vest in other persons estates and interests in land previously vested in mortgagees or in persons who were trustees within the meaning of the Act, and section 16 of the same Act extended the power to the case of unborn persons who, upon coming into existence, would become trustees of land.

The object of sections 29 and 30 of the Act appears to have been to enlarge the class of persons to be considered as trustees within the meaning of the Act for the purpose of such vesting orders.

Section 29 of the Trustee Act, 1850, was as follows: "And be it enacted that when a decree shall have been made by any Court of Equity directing the sale of any lands for the payment of the debts of a deceased person, every person seised or possessed of such lands or entitled to a contingent right therein as heir or under the will of such deceased debtor, shall be deemed to be so seised or possessed or entitled, as the case may be, upon a trust within the meaning of this Act; and the Court of Chancery is hereby empowered to make an order wholly discharging the contingent right under the will of such deceased debtor of any unborn person." It will be observed that this section only deals with the single case of a decree having been made directing the sale of land for the payment of debts.

Section 30 of the Trustee Act, 1850, contained provisions virtually identical with those of section 31 of the present Act, and had therefore a much wider operation than section 29, as it embraced all cases in which a decree had been made for the conveyance of lands. Both sections, however, were limited to cases in which a *decree* has been made, in this respect following the lines of sections 16 to 18 of Lord St. Leonards's Trustee Act, 1830 (11 Geo 4. and 1 Will. 4. c. 60), which sections dealt with conveyance of property vested in constructive trustees.

It appears to have been very early discovered that the restriction of section 29 to sales for the payment of debts (thus excluding, *e.g.*, a sale for payment of costs, *Weston* v. *Filer*, 5 De G. & Sm. 608), was inconvenient, and section 1 of the Trustee Extension Act, 1852 (15 & 16 Vict. c. 55), enacted as follows: "When any decree or order shall have been made by any Court of Equity directing the sale of any lands for any purpose whatever, every person seised or possessed of such land or entitled to a contingent right therein being a party to the suit or proceeding in which such decree or order shall have been made and bound thereby or being otherwise bound by such decree or order, shall be deemed to be so seised or possessed or entitled (as the case may be) upon a trust within the meaning of the Trustee Act, 1850; and in every such case it shall be lawful for the Court of Chancery, if the said Court shall think it expedient for the purpose of carrying such sale into effect, to make an order vesting such lands or any part thereof for such estate as the Court shall think fit either in any purchaser or in such other person as the Court shall direct; and every such order shall have the same effect as if such person so seised or possessed or entitled had been free from all disability and had duly executed all proper conveyances and assignments of such lands for such estate." It will be observed that this section applies not only to sales for any purpose, but also to sales directed by orders as distinct from decrees.

The result of these three sections therefore appears to have been that the class of persons to be considered as trustees within the meaning of the Acts for the purpose of vesting orders was declared to contain, (1) the heirs and devisees of a debtor in cases in which a decree has been made for sale of the lands for the purpose of payment of debts, (2) parties to a suit (and persons claiming under them) in which a decree has been made for the conveyance of lands, and (3) persons entitled to land being parties to a suit or proceeding (and other persons bound thereby) in which a decree or order shall have been made directing the sale of lands for any purpose whatever.

Section 30 of the Trustee Act, 1893, as originally enacted, re-enacted the provisions of section 29 of the Trustee Act, 1850, only enlarging its scope by the inclusion of mortgages as well as sales, and sales directed by orders as well as by decrees. Section 1 of the Trustee Act, 1893, Amendment Act, 1894, by repealing the words "as heir, or under the will of a deceased person, for payment of whose debts the judgment was given or order made," in effect enlarged the scope of section 30 so as to include all the cases provided for by section 1 of the Trustee Extension Act, 1852.

Section 31 of the Trustee Act, 1893, re-enacts, with merely verbal amendments, section 30 of the Trustee Act, 1850, replacing the word "decree" by the word "judgment."

It seems, at least, open to doubt whether the effect of sections 30 and 31 of the present Act, and of the three sections which they replace, is to enlarge (as appears to have been intended) the power of the Court to make vesting orders, by increasing the class of persons to be considered trustees within the meaning of the Act. It would appear to be at least arguable that, had none of these sections been passed, the Courts of Equity would, in accordance with the general principles of Equity, have regarded as constructive trustees, and thus trustees within the meaning of the Acts, all those persons who under those sections the Court may declare to be trustees. The corresponding sections of the Act of 1830 were of service because that Act contained no such definition of trustee, but it is suggested that the operation of the Trustee Act, 1850, and the Trustee Act, 1893 (which have such definition), would have been wider had the sections in question been omitted.

Thus, in *re Angelo*, 5 De G. & Sm. 278, a case in which the above-mentioned sections (which deal only with land) do not

Sect. 30.   apply, a mortgagor who had authorised a sale of stocks and shares was regarded as a trustee for the purchaser, and the Court, upon petition, vested the shares in the purchaser. The question arose as to land in *re Carpenter*, Kay 418, in which case, upon the death of a vendor intestate after the approval of a draft surrender, but before execution, it was argued that his infant heir was a trustee within the meaning of the Trustee Act, 1850, and that the Court would make a vesting order as to the land, the case of *re Angelo* being relied upon. Page Wood, V.C. (afterwards Lord Hatherley), however, referred to section 29 of the Trustee Act, 1850, and section 1 of the Trustee Extension Act, 1852, "as showing that in cases of real estate the constructive trust must first have been declared by a decree of the Court; and said that the reason of that was that there might always be a question whether the contract could be enforced by a suit for specific performance, and it would be extremely inconvenient to declare the vendor to be a trustee upon a petition on which that point could not be decided." In the case of *re Colling*, 32 Ch. D. 333, it was decided that Ann Colling, a person of unsound mind, whose freeholds had been sold by the guardians of the poor under the Lunacy Regulation Act, 1862, and who had died after the title was proved, but before the conveyance was executed, could not be held a trustee within the meaning of the Trustee Act, 1850. Fry, L J., referring to the case of *re Carpenter*, in his judgment said: "I think that Lord Hatherley laid down the correct principle. In section 29 the obtaining a decree for sale for the payment of the debts of a deceased person is treated as a condition precedent. So in section 30 a decree for specific performance or conveyance is made a condition precedent. The first section of the Act of 1852 provides for the case where an order has been made for the sale of any lands for any purpose whatever The Legislature appear to me to have meant that in cases of contract the Act in general should only apply in favour of a purchaser where there has been a decree or order on which his right is founded; and without saying that in no case where there is no decree or order can a vendor be held a trustee, I think that we cannot in the present case treat Ann Colling as having become a trustee of the property."

The exceptional case in which it appears that a vendor can, without a decree or order, be held a trustee, is that in which the contract for sale has been executed by the payment of purchase-money. In *re Cuming*, 5 Ch. 72, Giffard, L.J., in his judgment said: "I think that the distinction drawn between an executed and an unexecuted contract is sound. Where there is only a contract for sale a suit is necessary to declare the vendor a trustee; but where the contract has been executed by payment of the purchase-money and a formal covenant to surrender, I think that no suit is necessary." So also in the case of a mortgage of copyholds, by covenant to surrender, the mortgagor was held, on receipt of the mortgage moneys, to be a trustee for the mortgagee, *re Crowe's*

Mortgage, 13 Eq. 26. The case of *re Collingwood's Trust*, 6 W.R. 536, is not an exception to the rule, as it was decided on the ground that the trust was express and not constructive. Other cases illustrating the rule are *re Weeding's Estate*, 4 Jur. N.S. 707, in which an option to purchase contained in a lease was exercised after the death of the lessor, and it was held that an infant devisee could not be held to be a trustee until there should have been a decree; *re Propert*, 22 L.J. Chancery 948, in which it was held that a covenant to assign the last day of the term does not make the mortgagor a trustee; *Oust* v. *Middleton*, 9 W.R. 242, a case of a contract to grant a building lease; *re Burt*, 9 Hare 289, a case of partnership; *re Martin* 34 C.D. 618, a case of a purchase in the name of a third person. The case of *re Pagani* (1892) 1 Ch. 236, may be usefully referred to. In that a case a vendor sold a lease and business, part of the purchase-money being payable only at the end of five years. Before the expiration of that time the vendor became a lunatic. It was decided that he was a trustee within section 135 of the Lunacy Act, 1890, which Act contains a definition of trustee similar to that in the Trustee Act, 1850, and the Trustee Act, 1893. This decision may be explained on the grounds that, as the Lunacy Act, 1890, contains no provisions similar to sections 29 and 30 of the Trustee Act, 1850, the rule that in cases of real estate a decree is necessary before a vesting order can be made of land of a constructive trustee does not apply to cases under the Lunacy Act. The case of *re Beaufort's Will* (1898) W.N. 148 (in which a vesting order was made, without a judgment, of the interest of an infant heir in copyholds, agreed to be sold by a vendor who died before the title was approved) appears to have been decided without reference to the authorities.

For the general principle that a vendor who has contracted to sell, and whose title has been accepted, is a constructive trustee for the purchaser, see *Lysaght* v *Edwards*, 2 Ch. D. 499, in which the question is elaborately discussed by Jessel, M.R.

Section 4 of the Conveyancing and Law of Property Act, 1881, enacts that where at the death of any person there is subsisting a contract enforceable against his heir or devisee for the sale of the fee simple or other freehold interest descendible to his heirs general, his personal representatives shall have power to convey.

It must be noted that for "decree or order" in section 1 of the Trustee Extension Act, 1852, is substituted "judgment or order" in section 30 of the present Act, and for "decree" in section 30 of the Trustee Act, 1850, is substituted "judgment" in section 31 of the present Act There is no definition of the word "judgment" in the present Act, nor in the Interpretation Act, 1889 (52 & 53 Vict. c 63). As to the use of the word in the Judicature Acts and Rules of the Supreme Court, see Judicature Act, 1873 (36 & 37 Vict. c. 66), section 100, and section 19 and notes thereon in the Annual Practice, and cases there referred to. But no general definition applicable to other

Sect. 30. Acts is there contained, *exparte Chinery*, 12 Q.B.D. at p. 345. It is submitted, therefore, that the word "judgment" in sections 30 and 31 applies only to judgments of the nature of "decrees" before the Judicature Acts, and that the substitution of "judgment" for "decree" does not extend the operations of these sections.

"**Gives a Judgment or makes an Order.**"—That a judgment or order is a condition precedent, and as to meaning of judgment, see note above, "General effect of sections 30 and 31."

"**Sale or Mortgage.**"—Section 29 of Trustee Act, 1850, and section 1 of Trustee Extension Act, 1852, applied only to sales. The inclusion of mortgage is new. As to a sale directed in a partition action, see note to section 31, *infra*, p 124, "Sale in lieu of partition." Where the Court has decreed a sale in a foreclosure action, a vesting order as to the equity of redemption of the infant mortgagor was refused as being unnecessary, as all equitable estates were bound by the order for sale, *re Williams*, 5 De G. & Sm. 515, a case decided, before the Act of 1852 came into force, under section 7 of the Trustee Act, 1850, but which applies in principle to cases under the present section.

"**Every Person.**"—It was decided in *Beckett* v. *Sutton*, 19 Ch. D. 646, that section 1 of the Trustee Extension Act, 1852, was not limited (as suggested by the last words of that section) to persons under disability, and it would seem clear that the present section is not so limited. At first sight it would appear that in this respect the section, instead of being restrictive in effect (as suggested in the note, "General effect of sections 30 and 31," above), gives important powers to the Court, viz. to vest in other persons interests of trustees who are under no disability. But this can in a proper case be done apart from this section by first appointing a new trustee and then vesting. *Shepherd* v. *Churchill*, 25 B. 21; *Lees* v. *Coulton*, 20 Eq. 20. That these words include a person of unsound mind not so found, see *Herring* v *Clark*, 4 Ch. 167; and a lunatic so found, see *re Stamper*, 46 L.T. 372.

"**Otherwise bound by the Judgment or Order.**"—That unborn persons are, apart from this Act, bound by a judgment, see *Basnett* v. *Moxon*, 20 Eq. 182, and they would therefore appear to be within the section as being "entitled to a contingent right" in the land, and "bound by the judgment or order." Section 29 of the Trustee Act, 1850, contained a specific reference to unborn persons which is omitted from the present section. Cf. *Wake* v. *Wake*, 17 Jur. 545. As to the general provisions for vesting the contingent rights of unborn persons, see section 27, *supra*.

"**Make an Order Vesting, etc.**"—This may be an order in the action without a separate petition, *Wood* v. *Beetlestone*, 1 K. & J. 213; and this is presumably still the law, though section 43 of the Trustee Act, 1850, has been repealed without

re-enactment. Whether made in an action or not, the application may be by summons, O. 55, 13a (c) of Rules of Supreme
Court. For form of summons, see Daniell's Chancery Forms,
2109 ; and for forms of orders, see Seton, p. 1268. Generally as
to practice, see *post*, p. 191.

As to the persons who may make the application, see
section 36, *infra*.

For definitions of " mortgage," " land," " possessed," " contingent right," and " trustee," see section 50, *infra*.

Section 31.—Where a judgment is given for
the specific performance of a contract concerning
any land, or for the partition, or sale in lieu of *Vesting order consequential*
partition, or exchange, of any land, or generally *on judgment*
where any judgment is given for the conveyance *for specific performance,*
of any land either in cases arising out of the *etc.*
doctrine of election or otherwise, the High Court
may declare that any of the parties to the action are
trustees of the land or any part thereof within the
meaning of this Act, or may declare that the interests
of unborn persons who might claim under any party
to the action, or under the will or voluntary settlement of any person deceased who was during his
lifetime a party to the contract or transactions concerning which the judgment is given, are the interests
of persons who, on coming into existence, would be
trustees within the meaning of this Act, and thereupon the High Court may make a vesting order
relating to the rights of those persons, born and
unborn, as if they had been trustees.

This section is a re-enactment of section 30 of the Trustee
Act, 1850 (13 & 14 Vict. c. 60), as extended by section 7 of the
Partition Act, 1868 (31 & 32 Vict. c. 40), to "cases where in
suits for partition the Court directs a sale instead of a division
of the property." Section 30 of the Trustee Act, 1850, and
section 7 of the Partition Act, 1868, are repealed by the present
Act. See section 51, and Schedule, *infra*.

For the general operation of section, 30 and 31, see note to
section 30, *supra*, p 118.

The provisions of section 14 of the Judicature Act, 1884
(47 & 48 Vict. c. 61), should be compared with the present section,
and are as follows : " Where any person neglects or refuses
to comply with a judgment or order directing him to execute
any conveyance, contract, or other document, or to indorse
any negotiable instrument, the Court may, on such terms and

Sect. 31.
conditions (if any) as may be just, order that such conveyance, contract, or other document shall be executed, or that such negotiable instrument shall be indorsed by such person as the Court may nominate for that purpose; and in such case the conveyance, contract, document, or instrument so executed or indorsed shall operate and be for all purposes available as if it had been executed or indorsed by the person originally directed to execute or indorse it."

"Where a Judgment is given."—That a judgment should have been given is a condition precedent to the operation of this section. See the note to section 30 last referred to.

"Specific Performance of a Contract concerning any Land." —A contract to take a lease is not within the section, *Grace* v. *Baynton* (1877) W.N. 79, but a contract to grant a lease is within the section, *Hall* v. *Hale*, 51 L.T. N.S. 226 ; *Cowper* v. *Harmer*, 57 L.J. Ch. 460. In *ex parte Mornington*, 4 De G.M. & G. 537, in a specific performance suit, section 30 of the Trustee Act, 1850, was held to apply to the exercise of a power of jointuring. For examples of the application of section 30 of the Trustee Act, 1850, to contracts for the sale of land, see note to section 30 (*supra*, p. 118), "General effect of sections 30 and 31."

"For the Partition."—For cases in which vesting orders have been made in partition actions, see *Bowra* v. *Wright*, 4 De G. & S 265 ; *Stanley* v. *Wrigley*, 3 Sm. & G 18 ; *Shepherd* v. *Churchill*, 25 Beav. 21.

"Sale in Lieu of Partition."—Section 7 of the Partition Act, 1868, provided that "section 30 of the Trustee Act, 1850, shall extend and apply to cases where in suits for partition the Court directs a sale instead of a division of the property." For cases in which vesting orders have been made upon a decree for sale in a partition action, see *Basnett* v. *Moxon*, 20 Eq 182 ; *Lees* v. *Coulton*, 20 Eq. 20 ; *Beckett* v. *Sutton*, 19 Ch D. 646 ; *Caswell* v. *Sheen* (1893) W N. 187 ; 69 L T. N.S. 854 In the case of *Beckett* v. *Sutton*, Chitty, J , held that in spite of the fact that section 7 of the Partition Act, 1868, refers expressly to section 30 of the Trustee Act, 1850, and omits any reference to section 29 of that Act, the last-mentioned section applies to cases in which a sale is directed in a partition action. It will appear, therefore, that sections 30 and 31 of the present Act both apply to such a case.

"Conveyance of any Land either in Cases arising out of the Doctrine of Election or otherwise."—For a case of election, see *re Montagu, Faber* v. *Montagu* (1896) 1 Ch. 549, where a vesting order was made of the interest of an infant tenant in tail; and cf. section 18 of Lord St. Leonards's Trustee Act, 1830 (11 Geo. 4. and 1 Will. 4, c. 60).

For instances in foreclosure actions, see *Lechmere* v *Clamp*, 31 Beav. 578 ; *Foster* v *Parker*, 8 Ch. D. 147 , *Mellor* v. *Porter*, 25 Ch. D. 158.

"**Interests of Unborn Persons.**"—For the meaning and effect of this phrase, see the judgment of Jessel, M.R., in *Basnett* v. *Moxon*, 20 Eq 182; and see also *Lees* v. *Coulton*, 20 Eq. 20; *Hargreaves* v. *Wright*, 1 W R. 108.

"**As if they had been Trustees.**"—It must be borne in mind that the section does not give power to the Court to make a vesting order in every case in which a decree for sale or conveyance has been made, but only in those cases in which, were the person whose interest is being dealt with a trustee, an order could be made, *i.e.* those cases enumerated in section 26 of the present Act. Thus in *Shepherd* v. *Churchill*, 25 Beav. 21, where a vesting order was desired of the various interests of numerous persons, the object was obtained by declaring the persons trustees and appointing a new trustee in their place, and then making a vesting order as upon the appointment of new trustees. See the similar case of *Lees* v. *Coulton*, 20 Eq. 20, in which it was held that the appointment of a new trustee and consequent vesting order ought to be the subject of subsequent application, and not be made by the decree. Cf. also *Caswell* v. *Sheen*, 69 L.T. N.S. 854.

Practice—See *post*, p 191.

As to the person who may make the application, see section 36, *infra;* and as to effect of vesting order, see section 32

For definitions of "land," "conveyance," "trustee," and "rights," see section 50, *infra*.

Section 32.—A vesting order under any of the foregoing provisions shall in the case of a vesting order consequential on the appointment of a new trustee, have the same effect as if the persons who before the appointment were the trustees (if any) had duly executed all proper conveyances of the land for such estate as the High Court directs, or if there is no such person, or no such person of full capacity, then as if such person had existed and been of full capacity and had duly executed all proper conveyances of the land for such estate as the Court directs, and shall in every other case have the same effect as if the trustee or other person or description or class of persons to whose rights or supposed rights the said provisions respectively relate had been an ascertained and existing person of full capacity, and had executed a conveyance or release to the effect intended by the order.

Sect. 32.   This section consolidates provisions to the same effect contained in sections 7 to 15, 19, and 34 of the Trustee Act, 1850 (13 & 14 Vict. c. 60), and sections 1, 2, and 8 of the Trustee Extension Act, 1852 (15 & 16 Vict. c. 55).

It deals first with the case of vesting orders made on the appointment of new trustees (section 26 (i.)), and as to these provides separately for the cases of the former trustees being (1) existing and of full capacity, and (2) non-existent, or not of full capacity. In the first case the operation of the order is as though those persons had duly executed all proper conveyances, and in the second case as if such persons had existed and been of full capacity, and had duly executed all proper conveyances.

As to vesting orders made otherwise than on the appointment of new trustees, viz. under section 26, (ii.) to (vi.), and sections 27 to 31, the section does not deal separately with the case of persons of full capacity and those not of full capacity, but provides generally that the operation of the order is to be as if the person to whose rights the said sections respectively relate had been an ascertained and existing person of full capacity, and had executed a conveyance to the effect intended by the order. That this does not have the effect of restricting the operation of such vesting orders to the case of persons under disability, see *Beckett* v. *Sutton*, 19 Ch. D. 646, a decision on similar language in section 1 of the Trustee Extension Act, 1852 (15 & 16 Vict. c. 55).

That the effect of a vesting order dealing with the rights of an infant tenant in tail is to bar the estate tail and remainders over, see re *Montagu, Faber* v. *Montagu* (1896) 1 Ch 549.

It is submitted that a vesting order dealing with the rights of a tenant for life could not vest the fee simple although under the Settled Land Acts and other statutes a tenant for life can deal with the fee simple. Cf. *Wood* v. *Beetlestone*, 1 K. & J. 213.

As to Copyholds.—The section applies to vesting orders as to copyhold and customary land by virtue of the definitions of the word "land" in the Interpretation Act, 1889 (52 & 53 Vict. c. 63), and section 50 of the present Act. The effect, therefore, of a vesting order as to copyholds is as though the former trustee, or person whose rights are thereby dealt with, had made a surrender. Admittance is still necessary, except in the case provided for by subsection 1 of section 34 of the Act. A mandamus can be obtained to enforce admittance, re *Lane and Irving*, 12 W.R. 710.

Since a vesting declaration under section 12 cannot be made as to copyholds, and since section 30 of the Conveyancing and Law of Property Act, 1881, does not apply to the devolution of copyholds (see note, "Is an infant," *supra*, p. 107), vesting orders as to copyholds must frequently be required.

As to the general effect of vesting orders as to copyhold, see *Bristow* v. *Booth*, L.R. 5 C.P. 80. As to the fines payable, see

Bristow v. *Booth; Paterson* v. *Paterson,* 2 Eq. 31; and cf. *Hall* v. *Bromley,* 35 C.D. 642.

The consent of the lord of the manor is not necessary (1 Jur. N.S, 418), and he is not a necessary party to the application, *Paterson* v *Paterson,* 2 Eq. 31.

For forms of orders vesting copyholds, see Seton, pp. 1236, 1237, and 1251.

Further as to vesting orders as to copyholds, see section 34, *infra.*

For definitions of "trustee," "conveyance," land," and "rights," see section 50, *infra.*

Section 33.—In all cases where a vesting order can be made under any of the foregoing provisions, the High Court may, if it is more convenient, appoint a person to convey the land or release the contingent right, and a conveyance or release by that person in conformity with the order shall have the same effect as an order under the appropriate provision.

This section re-enacts, with merely verbal alterations, section 20 of the Trustee Act, 1850 (13 & 14 Vict. c. 60), which section is repealed by the present Act. See section 51, and Schedule, *infra.* Before the Act of 1850 there was no provision for the making of vesting orders, but under the provisions of Lord St. Leonards's Trustee Act, 1830 (11 Geo. 4 & 1 Will. 4. c. 60), the Court could appoint a person to convey.

For a similar provision see section 14 of the Judicature Act, 1884 (47 & 48 Vict. c. 61), set out in the note to section 31, *supra,* p. 123.

The procedure authorised by this section will probably be found convenient in the case of a sale in lots, as it avoids the necessity of a large number of vesting orders, while at the same time it enables each purchaser to have his own deed of conveyance. Cf. *Hancox* v *Spittle,* 3 Sm & G. 478.

For forms of orders, see Seton, 6th edit., pp. 1261 and following.

As to form of conveyance. "The conveyance should contain a recital showing that it is made in obedience to the order of the Court, and should be executed by the person appointed to convey in his own name" (Lewin, 10th edit., p 810). It has been held that an express covenant for quiet enjoyment cannot be given by a person appointed to grant a lease, *Cowper* v. *Harmer,* 57 L.J Ch. 460, but it is suggested that the correctness of this decision is not beyond doubt, seeing that the implied covenant is more onerous than the usual express covenant; and cf. *re Ray* (1896) 1 Ch. 468.

As to the effect of a conveyance on behalf of a tenant in

Sect. 33. tail, see *Caswell* v. *Sheen*, '9 L.T. N.S. 854; *re Montagu, Faber* v.'
Montagu (1896) 1 Ch. 549; and on behalf of a tenant for life,
Wood v. *Beetlestone, supra,* p. 126.

For definitions of "convey," "conveyance," "land," and
"contingent right," see section 50, *infra.*

Sect. 34.

Effect of
vesting order
as to copy-
hold.

Section 34.—(1.) Where an order vesting copyhold land in any person is made under this Act with
the consent of the lord or lady of the manor, the
land shall vest accordingly without surrender or
admittance.

(2.) Where an order is made under this Act
appointing any person to convey any copyhold land,
that person shall execute and do all assurances and
things for completing the assurance of the land;
and the lord and lady of the manor and every other
person shall, subject to the customs of the manor
and the usual payments, be bound to make admittance to the land and to do all other acts for
completing the assurance thereof, as if the persons
in whose place an appointment is made were free
from disability and had executed and done those
assurances and things.

This section re-enacts, with verbal amendments, section 28
of the Trustee Act, 1850 (13 & 14 Vict. c. 60), which section
is repealed by the present Act. See section 51, and Schedule,
infra.

The marginal note to the section is somewhat misleading,
the general effect of a vesting order as to copyholds (as other
land) being dealt with by section 32. By virtue of the definition
of "land" in section 50, the sections of the Act which enable
the Court to make vesting orders of land apply to copyhold
and customary land. Accordingly by virtue of section 32,
where a vesting order is made as to copyholds, no surrender
is necessary, for "conveyance" in that section includes surrender
of copyholds (cf. section 50). The present section is therefore
only ancillary to the sections above referred to. Cf. *Bristow* v.
Booth, L R 5 C.P 80; and see note "As to copyholds," p. 126,
supra.

"**With the Consent.**"—The consent may be given either in
Court or by writing properly verified. The latter is the proper
course to be adopted, *Ayles* v *Cox,* 17 B. 584. For form of
consent and of affidavit verifying the signature thereto, see
Daniell's Chancery Forms, pp. 1080, 1081; and see Daniell's
Chancery Practice, p. 1782.

For form of order vesting copyholds with the consent of the lord of the manor, see Seton, p. 1236.

"Without Surrender or Admittance."—The first subsection dispenses with the necessity for admittance in cases in which the consent of the lord of the manor has been obtained to the making of the vesting order. Without such consent the Court has no power to dispense with the necessity for admittance.

The second subsection provides for admittance in the case of the appointment, under the provisions of section 33, of a person to surrender copyholds. The necessity for this subsection is not evident, as it would appear that the combined operations of sections 32 and 33 would effect all that is desired.

"Subject to the Customs of the Manor and the Usual Payments."—See *Bristow* v. *Booth*, L.R. 5 C.P. 80; and note, "As to copyholds," to section 32, *supra*, p. 126

For an order appointing a person to assure copyholds, see *re Heys's Will*, 9 Hare 221.

For definitions of "land" and "convey," see section 50, *infra*.

Section 35.—(1.) In any of the following cases, namely :—

   (i.) Where the High Court appoints or has appointed a new trustee ; and

   (ii.) Where a trustee entitled alone or jointly with another person to stock or to a chose in action—

      (*a*) is an infant, or

      (*b*) is out of the jurisdiction of the High Court, or

      (*c*) cannot be found ; or

      (*d*) neglects or refuses to transfer stock or receive the dividends or income thereof, or to sue for or recover a chose in action, according to the direction of the person absolutely entitled thereto for twenty-eight days next after a request in writing has been made to him by the person so entitled, or

      (*e*) neglects or refuses to transfer stock or receive the dividends or income thereof, or to sue for or

K

recover a chose in action for twenty-eight days next after an order of the High Court for that purpose has been served on him; or

(iii.) Where it is uncertain whether a trustee entitled alone or jointly with another person to stock or to a chose in action is alive or dead,

the High Court may make an order vesting the right to transfer or call for a transfer of stock, or to receive the dividends or income thereof, or to sue for or recover a chose in action, in any such person as the Court may appoint :

Provided that—

(a) Where the order is consequential on the appointment by the Court of a new trustee, the right shall be vested in the persons who, on the appointment, are the trustees; and

(b) Where the person whose right is dealt with by the order was entitled jointly with another person, the right shall be vested in that last-mentioned person either alone or jointly with any other person whom the Court may appoint.

(2.) In all cases where a vesting order can be made under this section, the Court may, if it is more convenient, appoint some proper person to make or join in making the transfer.

(3.) The person in whom the right to transfer or call for the transfer of any stock is vested by an order of the Court under this Act, may transfer the stock to himself or any other person, according to the order, and the Banks of England and Ireland and all other companies shall obey every order under this section according to its tenor.

(4.) After notice in writing of an order under this section it shall not be lawful for the Bank of England or of Ireland or any other company to transfer any stock to which the order relates or to

Sect. 35.

pay any dividends thereon except in accordance with the order.

(5.) The High Court may make declarations and give directions concerning the manner in which the right to any stock or chose in action vested under the provisions of this Act is to be exercised.

(6.) The provisions of this Act as to vesting orders shall apply to shares in ships registered under the Acts relating to merchant shipping as if they were stock.

Subsection (i.)—This subsection replaces section 35 of the Trustee Act, 1850 (13 & 14 Vict. c. 60), which section is repealed by the present Act. See section 51, and Schedule, *infra*.

In spite of the general language of the subsection, no jurisdiction is thereby given, on an appointment of a new trustee, to make a vesting order affecting property vested in a lunatic, unless such lunatic is an infant or out of the jurisdiction within the meaning of subsection (ii.), *re M.* (1899) 1 Ch. 79. See note to subsection (i.) of section 26, *supra*, p. 104.

Generally as to this subsection, see notes to subsection (i.) of section 26, *supra*, p. 104 (the corresponding provision dealing with vesting orders as to land).

The Court will not, for the purpose of making this subsection available, reappoint the existing trustees, *re Dewhirst's Trusts*, 33 C.D. 416, overruling *re Dalgleish's Settlement*, 4 C.D. 143, and *re Crowe's Trusts*, 14 C.D. 610. The Court will, however, appoint a new trustee for the purpose of making a vesting order under this section, *re Stocken's Settlement* (1893) W.N. 203.

In a case in which trust funds had been invested on unauthorised investments, Romilly, M.R., appointed a new trustee in place of a trustee who had gone abroad, but refused to make any order respecting the transfer of the investments, lest by doing so he should sanction a breach of trust, *re Harrison*, 22 L.J. Ch. 69; but in *re Peacock*, 14 C.D. 212, another case in which trust funds had been invested in unauthorised investments, the Court of Appeal made an order for appointment of new trustees, with the right to call for the transfer of the funds to themselves *or to any purchaser or purchasers*, the trustees undertaking to hold the proceeds on the trusts of the settlement.

Subsection (ii.).—This subsection deals with the cases formerly provided for by sections 22, 23, 24, and 25 of the Trustee Act, 1850 (13 & 14 Vict. c. 60), and sections 2, 3, 4 and 5 of the Trustee Extension Act, 1852 (15 & 16 Vict. c. 55), which sections are repealed by the present Act. See section 51, and Schedule, *infra*.

In the case of this subsection, as in the case of subsections (ii.) to (vi.) of section 26 (containing the corresponding provisions as to land), it seems a matter of regret that the cases of bankruptcy, felony, unfitness, and unwillingness to act were not dealt with, so as to enable the Court to vest the right to call for transfer of the stock in the other trustees without the necessity of appointing a new trustee See note to subsection (ii.) of section 26, *supra*, p. 106. In one respect the present section is more defective than section 26, as the case of there being no personal representative of a last surviving trustee, or of its being uncertain who is such personal representative, provided for in the case of land by section 26, subsection (v.), is not dealt with by the present section. See *re Ellis*, 24 B. 426 , *re Herbert*, 8 W.R. 272; *re Stocken's Settlement Trusts* (1893) W.N 202; *re Cane's Trusts* (1895) 1 I R. 172; and in this case the expedient of appointing the person beneficially entitled or some other person a new trustee has to be resorted to, so that the vesting order may be made under subsection (1). See also next note.

"**Trustee entitled.**"—This will presumably include the personal representatives of a deceased trustee in whose sole name stock is standing. This case was specifically provided for by section 25 of the Trustee Act, 1850 (13 & 14 Vict c. 60), which section is repealed by but not re-enacted in the present Act. It has been held that where the trustee of an English will died domiciled in Scotland, his executor who had proved the will in Scotland and not in England, as being entitled to prove the will in England, was his personal representative within the meaning of that section, *re Trubee's Trusts* (1892) 3 Ch. 55. In that case North, J., expressed himself to be following *re Price's Settlement* (1883) W.N. 202, but since in that case the expedient of appointing a new trustee was resorted to, it can hardly be claimed as a precedent. *Re Ellis's Settlement*, 24 B. 426, and *re Dickson* (1872) W.N. 223 , 27 L T. N.S. 671, however, appear to shew that persons entitled to prove the will were "personal representatives" within section 25 of the Trustee Act, 1850. Such persons will not be held to be "entitled to" stock within the present subsection, for until probate they cannot compel transfer in the books of the company, *re Cane's Trusts* (1895) 1 I.R. 172. In the case therefore of the executor of a last trustee not proving, as in other cases in which there is no personal representative of a sole trustee of stock, a new trustee must be appointed in order to obtain a vesting order, as suggested in the last note, *supra.*

"**Is an Infant.**"—The question whether an infant, in whose name (either solely or jointly with other persons) stock, to which he is beneficially entitled, has been transferred, can be declared a trustee of such stock, for the purposes of this subsection, has been raised in several cases. In *re Findlay*, 32 Ch. D. 221, 641, an order was made declaring the infant a trustee, and vesting the right to call for a transfer of the stock in other persons. The Bank of England, however, refused to act on the order, on the ground that the Court had no jurisdiction to declare the infant a trustee, and the validity of the order was not insisted upon by the parties to the application. The only reported decision supporting the position so taken up by the Bank of England appears to be *re Westwood*, 6 N.R. 61, 316, but an order similar to that made in *re Findlay* had been made in *Sanders v. Homer*, 25 Beav. 467, *Rives v. Rives* (1866) W.N. 144; *Gardner v. Cowles*, 3 C D. 304; *re Harwood*, 20 C.D. 536; and, since the date of *re Findlay* has been made, in *re Barnett* (1889) W.N. 216.

The chief inconvenience of allowing stock to remain in the name of an infant is the difficulty that arises in dealing with the dividends. This inconvenience is partly removed by the provisions of section 32 of 11 Geo 4 and 1 Will. 4. c 65, which is as follows: "And be it further enacted that it shall be lawful for the Court of Chancery, by an order to be made on the petition of the guardian of any infant in whose name any stock shall be standing or any sum of money, by virtue of an Act for paying off any stock and who shall be beneficially entitled thereto, or if there shall be no guardian, by an order to be made in any cause depending in the said Court to direct all or any part of the dividends due or to become due in respect of such stocks, or any such sum of money to be paid to any guardian of such infant or to any other person according to the discretion of such Court for the maintenance and education or otherwise for the benefit of such infant, such guardian or other person to whom such payment shall be directed to be made being named in the order directing such payment, and the receipt of such guardian or other person for such dividends or sum of money or any part thereof, shall be as effectual as if such infant had attained the age of twenty-one years and had signed and given the same." As to stock transferable in the books of the Bank of England or the Bank of Ireland, section 3 of the National Debt (Stockholders Relief) Act, 1892 (55 & 56 Vict. c. 39), provides as follows: "In the following cases, namely, (a) where an infant is the sole survivor in an account, and (b) where an infant holds stock jointly with a person under legal disability, and (c) where stock has by mistake been brought in or transferred into the sole name of an infant, the bank may, at the request in writing of the parent, guardian, or next friend of the infant, receive the dividends and apply them to the purchase of like stock, and the stock so purchased shall be added to the original investment."

In the case of *Devoy v. Devoy*, 3 Sm. & Giff. 403; 3 Jur. N S. 79, where a father had transferred stock into the joint names of himself, his wife, and an infant child, not intending to part with the ownership or control thereof, the infant was declared a trustee for the father, and the right to call for a transfer of the stock was vested in the father. That case was followed in *Stone v Stone*, 3 Jur. N S. 708, in which case the facts were very similar

"**Out of the Jurisdiction of the High Court.**"—As to the absence which brings a trustee within this phrase, see note to the same words in section 26, subsection (ii.), *supra*, p. 107.

Cases in which the Court has made vesting orders under the subsection or sections 22 and 25 (the corresponding sections) of the Trustee Act, 1850, are *re Angelo*, 5 D.G. & Sm. 278, where a mortgagor of stocks was held a trustee for a purchaser from the mortgagee (see *ante*, p. 119) ; *re Price* (1894) W.N. 169, and *re Lees* (1896) 2 Ch. 508, in which cases a vesting order was made in favour of the trustees, other than the one abroad, without a new trustee being appointed, *re Peyton*, 25 B 317; 2 D.G. & J. 290, in which case an order vesting the right to receive dividends in the trustees, other than the one abroad, was varied by limiting the right to the joint lives of such trustees; *re Blaine* (1886) W.N. 203, and *re Keeley*, 53 L T. 487, in which cases a new trustee, in place of the absent trustee, had been appointed out of Court ; and *re Mainwaring*, 26 B 172, in which case the order was varied by the insertion of an express recital that the trustee was out of the jurisdiction.

"**Neglects or refuses to transfer Stock . . . according to the Direction of the Person absolutely entitled thereto.**"—See and compare the language of subsection (vi) of section 26, *supra*, p. 103, which subsection contains the corresponding provision as to the refusal to convey land. Provision for the case of refusal to transfer stock was formerly contained in sections 23, 24, and 25 of the Trustee Act, 1850.

The expression "person absolutely entitled" has been held to include trustees appointed out of Court, *exparte Russell*, 1 Sim. N.S. 404; *re Ellis*, 24 B. 426; *re Baxter*, 2 Sm. & Giff. App 5; and since subsection (i.) of the present section deals only with the case of new trustees appointed by the Court, the present provision is of very great importance in enabling trustees appointed out of Court to obtain transfer of stocks which cannot be obtained by means of a vesting declaration under section 12, *supra*, p. 63. The expression has also been held to include beneficiaries absolutely entitled, *re White*, 5 Ch. 698, but not a tenant for life, *exparte Russell*, 1 Sim. N.S. 404; *Mackenzie* v. *Mackenzie*, 5 D G. & Sm. 338, except as to dividends already accrued due, *re Hartnall*, 5 D.G. & Sm. 111. It may be noted that section 36, which provided that orders concerning "any land, stock, or chose in action subject to a trust" may be made on the application of "any person beneficially interested in the land, stock, or chose in action," or "any person duly appointed trustee thereof," does not extend the scope of the present subsection so as to include persons beneficially interested otherwise than absolutely. *Exparte Russell*, 1 Sim. N.S. 404; *Mackenzie* v. *Mackenzie*, 5 D.G. & Sm. 338.

Orders under the repealed sections of the Trustee Act, 1850, have been made against an executor of a last surviving trustee, who has not proved, *re Ellis*, 24 B. 426; *re Thornton's Trusts*,

9 W.R. 475, and against one of the next of kin of a testator who, though not appointed executor, was entitled to take out administration, re *Stroud* (1874) W.N. 180. Cf. note on "Trustee entitled," *supra*, p. 132.

"**For Twenty-eight Days.**"—The Court has no jurisdiction under this subsection to make an order upon a petition presented before the expiration of the twenty-eight days, re *Knox* (1895) 1 Ch. 538; (1895) 2 Ch. 483. In *Knight* v. *Knight* (1866) W.N. 114, a motion for a vesting order (of land) in a suit was ordered to stand over until the expiration of the twenty-eight days

"**Neglects** or refuses to transfer Stock . . . after an Order of the High Court has been served on him."—The contingency here contemplated was not provided for by the Trustee Act, 1850, see *Mackenzie* v. *Mackenzie*, 5 D.G. & Sm. 338, and was accordingly dealt with by sections 4 and 5 of the Trustee Extension Act, 1852 (15 & 16 Vict c. 55), which sections are repealed by the present Act. See section 51, and Schedule, *infra*.

The provisions of section 14 of the Judicature Act, 1884 (47 & 48 Vict. c. 61), should be compared with the present section, and are set out in the note to section 31, *supra*, p. 123.

"**Where it is uncertain whether a Trustee . . . is alive or dead.**"—Provision for this event was formerly contained in sections 22 and 25 of the Trustee Act, 1850 (13 & 14 Vict. c 60) ; section 26, subsection (iv.) of the present Act provides for the same event in the case of land.

As to the presumption of death arising from the fact that a person has not been heard of for seven years, see re *Phene's Trust*, 5 Ch. 159; re *Lewes' Trusts*, 6 Ch. 356; *Hickman* v. *Upsall*, 20 Eq. 136; re *Corbishley's Trusts*, 14 C.D 846; *In re Rhodes*, 36 C.D. 586; *In re Benjamin* (1902) 1 Ch. 723. An order was made under the provisions in section 22 of the Trustee Act, 1850, in a case in which one of two trustees in whose names stock was standing appears not to have been heard of for seventeen years, re *Bourke*, 2 D.G.J. & Sm. 426.

"**May make an Order . . . in any such Person as the Court may appoint.**"—The proper form of order for vesting stock, on which there is *no liability*, in trustees, directs that the right to transfer the stock, and to receive the dividends thereon, shall vest in the trustees, *and orders them to transfer the same into their own names to be held by them on the trusts of the instrument.* Seton, 6th edit., 213; re *Gregson* (1893) 3 Ch. 233; re *Joliffe* (1893) W.N. 84; re *Price* (1894) W.N. 169. Cf. re *C.M.G.* (1898) 2 Ch. 324; re *Tweedy*, 28 Ch. D. 529. Where before the transfer took place one of the new trustees died, the words "or the survivor of them" and a direction to transfer into "their or his names or name" were, by consent of all parties, added to the order, re *Glanville* (1877) W.N. 248; (1878) W.N. 21. The usual form of order, when shares not

Sect. 35.

fully paid are to be vested, directs that the right to transfer the shares *to any purchaser or purchasers*, and to receive dividends, shall vest in the trustees, the trustees undertaking to hold the proceeds of sale thereof (if any) upon the trusts of the instrument. Seton, 6th edit., p. 1213; *New Zealand Trust and Loan Co.* (1893) 1 Ch. 403. As to form of order vesting *unauthorised* investments in new trustees, see *re Peacock*, 14 Ch. D. 212 (*ante*, p. 131); Seton, 6th edit., p. 1212.

Where part of the property was inadvertently omitted, a further order was made vesting the omitted property, *re Hopper* (1886) W.N. 41; 54 L.T. 267.

Where the order vests the right to transfer in a person beneficially entitled, it would seem that the order ought to direct him to transfer into his own name. See arguments in *re Gregson* (1893) 3 Ch. 233, a case of appointment of new trustees, but it is conceived the arguments apply to all vesting orders of stock.

Recitals are not usually inserted in vesting orders except in orders to be acted upon by the bank; or in orders made in Chambers; in the latter case, as there is no formal statement of the facts, as in a petition, it is convenient, and in the former case the bank require that the following facts be stated, viz. (1) that the persons in whose name the stock stands are trustees; (2) that one of the cases provided for by the Act has occurred; and (3) that the applicants are beneficially interested or otherwise come within section 37. See *re Ellis*, 24 Beav. 426, *re Mainwaring*, 26 Beav. 172; Seton, 6th edit., p 1248.

"Where the Order is consequential on the Appointment by the Court of a New Trustee, etc."—Similar provision to that contained in this proviso was formerly made by section 35 of the Trustee Act, 1850 (13 & 14 Vict. c 60). As to vesting orders on the appointment of a new trustee by the Court, see notes to subsection 1 (1) of the present section.

"Where the Person whose Right is dealt with by the Order was entitled jointly, etc."—Similar provisions to that contained in this proviso were formerly made by sections 22 and 24 of the Trustee Act, 1850 (13 & 14 Vict. c. 60).

Subsection 2. "Appoint some Proper Person to make or join in making the Transfer."—Similar provision was formerly made by section 20 of the Trustee Act, 1850 (13 & 14 Vict. c 60). Section 33 of the present Act makes provision for the appointment of a person to convey land.

Subsection 3.—Similar provisions were formerly contained in section 26 of the Trustee Act, 1850 (13 & 14 Vict. c. 60), and section 6 of the Trustee Extension Act, 1852 (15 & 16 Vict. c. 55). Having regard to the importance of keeping the bank books clear, the Court will place a very strict interpretation on any section where there is room for argument. *Re Smyth's Settlement*, 4 D.G. & Sm. 499. The Bank of England has been diligent in raising questions on the construction of the repealed

sections of the Trustee Act, 1850, and on the forms of vesting
orders thereby authorised. Cf. *re Glanville* (1877) W N. 248 ;
(1878) W N. 21 ; *re Ellis*, 24 Beav. 426 ; *re Mainwaring*,
26 Beav. 172 ; *re Gregson* (1893) 3 Ch. 233.

As to the indemnity to the bank in acting on any vesting
order under the Act, see section 49, *infra*.

Subsection 4.—Similar provision was contained in section 26
of the Trustee Act, 1850 (13 & 14 Vict. c. 60). In many cases
it may be expedient to immediately give notice under this
subsection to the bank or company of the making of the order,
so as to protect the stock in the interval between the making
and the drawing up of the order.

Subsection 5.—Similar provision was contained in section 31
of the Trustee Act, 1850 (13 & 14 Vict. c. 60). It is under
this subsection that when the right to transfer stock is vested,
the order proceeds to say to whom the same is to be transferred.
See *supra*, p. 135.

Subsection 6.—This subsection replaces section 10 of the
Merchant Shipping Act, 1855 (18 & 19 Vict. c. 91), which
enacted that shares in ships registered under the Merchant
Shipping Act, 1854 (17 & 18 Vict c. 104), should be deemed to
be included in the word "stock" as defined by the Trustee Act,
1850, and that the provisions of such last-mentioned Act should
be applicable to such shares accordingly. It is not evident
why the definition of stock in section 50, "so far as relates to
vesting orders made by the Court under this Act," is not made
to include shares in ships.

Section 36.—(1.) An order under this Act for
the appointment of a new trustee or concerning any
land, stock, or chose in action subject to a trust, Persons entitled to
may be made on the application of any person apply for orders
beneficially interested in the land, stock, or chose in
action, whether under disability or not, or on the
application of any person duly appointed trustee
thereof.

(2.) An order under this Act concerning any
land, stock, or chose in action subject to a mortgage
may be made on the application of any person beneficially interested in the equity of redemption,
whether under disability or not, or of any person
interested in the money secured by the mortgage.

This section is a re-enactment of section 37 of the Trustee
Act, 1850 (13 & 14 Vict. c. 60), which section is repealed by the
present Act. See section 51, and Schedule, *infra*.

Sect. 36.

"**Beneficially interested in.**"—A person having a contingent interest in a trust fund comes within the section, *re Sheppard's Trust*, 4 D.G.F. & J. 423; but a person having a mere possibility would presumably not be included. Cf. *Davis* v. *Angel*, 31 Beav. 223. Where a sale has been decreed, and the purchase-money paid, the purchaser comes within the section, *Ayles* v. *Cox*, 17 Beav. 584, and in such a case the purchaser should make the application, as it has been suggested that the vendors are not persons "beneficially interested in the land" within the meaning of the section, *Rowley* v. *Adams*, 14 Beav. 130, though plaintiffs in a creditor's administration action in which a sale has been made have been held to be within the section, *re Wragg*, 1 De G.J. & S. 356. Where the sale is in lots, the purchasers of several lots may, to save expense, join in one application, *Rowley* v *Adams*, *supra*. Committees of a lunatic *cestui que trust* are not beneficially interested within the meaning of the section, *re Bourke*, 2 D.G.J. & Sm. 426.

"**Person duly appointed Trustee.**"—A constructive trustee appears, therefore, not to be authorised to apply under the Act for an order

It should be noted that this section deals only with procedure, and does not extend the jurisdiction of the Court to make orders in cases not provided for in earlier sections. See *exparte Russell*, 1 Sim. N.S. 404, 408; *Mackenzie* v. *Mackenzie*, 5 D.G. & Sm. 338, 341.

Practice.—As to practice generally, see *post*, p. 191.

For definitions of "trust," "trustee," "land," "stock," and "mortgage," see section 50, *infra*; and as to the inclusion of shares in ships in vesting orders as to "stocks," see section 35, subsection 6, *supra*, p. 131.

Sect. 37.

Powers of new trustee appointed by Court.

Section 37.—Every trustee appointed by a court of competent jurisdiction shall, as well before as after the trust property becomes by law, or by assurance, or otherwise, vested in him, have the same powers, authorities, and discretions, and may in all respects act as if he had been originally appointed a trustee by the instrument, if any, creating the trust.

This section re-enacts, with verbal amendments, section 33 of the Conveyancing and Law of Property Act, 1881 (44 & 45 Vict. c. 41), which section is repealed by the present Act. See section 51, and Schedule, *infra*. The repealed section replaced the provision contained in section 27 of Lord Cranworth's Act (23 & 24 Vict. c. 145), that every trustee appointed by the Court, whether before or after the passing of the Act, should have the same powers, authorities, and discretions, and might in all respects act, as if he had been originally nominated a trustee by the instrument creating the trust.

Section 33 of the Trustee Act, 1850 (13 & 14 Vict. c 60), which section is repealed by the present Act (see section 50, and Schedule, *infra*), enacted that the person or persons appointed trustees by order under that Act should have all the same rights and powers as he or they would have had if appointed by decree in a suit duly instituted.

That in many cases trustees appointed by the Court, whether by decree or by order, could not, apart from express statutory provision, exercise the powers and discretions given to the trustees by the instrument, see Lewin, 10th edit, pp. 722, 723, and the cases there cited.

Although the present section is not, as were sections 27 of Lord Cranworth's Act and 33 of the Conveyancing and Law of Property Act, expressed to apply to appointments made before as well as those made after the passing of the Act, it would seem clearly not to be intended to be restricted to the latter.

Although the language of the present section and the repealed sections is very general, it is to be assumed that it will not operate to vest in a new trustee powers and discretions which are expressly, or by necessary implication, restricted to the trustees originally appointed by the instrument creating the trust. It is suggested that the same tests which would decide whether the power and discretion would survive to the other or others in the event of the death of one trustee, will also serve to decide whether the power or discretion is one which, on the appointment by the Court of a new trustee, becomes vested in him. See notes to section 22, *supra*, p. 85.

There appears to be a singular lack of authority as to the operation of the sections in question. In the case of *Cooper* v. *Macdonald*, 35 Beav. 504 (decided five years after Lord Cranworth's Act came into force), it was held that a trustee appointed by the Court could not exercise a power to appoint new trustees given by the settlement to the surviving trustees or trustee. It does not appear from either report of this case that Lord Cranworth's Act was referred to. The true *ratio decidendi* of this case obviously was that the power to appoint only arose in accordance with the language of the will in the event of the death of an original trustee, or one appointed under the power in the will, and had not arisen by the death of a trustee appointed by the Court. (The statutory power for surviving trustees to appoint on the death of any trustee, whether appointed by the Court or not, did not apply in the case under discussion, for the early part of section 27 of Lord Cranworth's Act only applies to instruments created after that Act.)

For the similar provision in the case of the appointment by individual donees, see section 10 (3), *supra*, p. 49.

" **The Same Powers and Discretions.**"—This does not include

Sect. 37.

the duties incident to the office of personal representative of a deceased person. See *ante,* p 102.

For definitions of "trust," "property," and "instrument," see section 50, *infra.*

Sect. 38.

Power to charge costs on trust estate

Section 38.—The High Court may order the costs and expenses of and incident to any application for an order appointing a new trustee, or for a vesting order, or of and incident to any such order, or any conveyance or transfer in pursuance thereof, to be paid or raised out of the land or personal estate in respect whereof the same is made, or out of the income thereof, or to be borne and paid in such manner and by such persons as to the Court may seem just.

This section replaces section 51 of the Trustee Act, 1850, which section is repealed by the present Act. See section 51, and Schedule, *infra.* Several verbal alterations occur, and one substantial amendment, viz. the insertion of the words "and by such persons," as to which, see the note below.

The section is required because the Court, acting under the jurisdiction by way of petition and summons given to it by the Act, "is not exercising its ordinary jurisdiction in which it has a jurisdiction to dispose of costs." See judgment of Romilly, M.R., in *re Primrose,* 23 Beav. at p. 599; and *re Sparks,* 6 Ch. D. 361.

"**Order appointing a New Trustee.**"—The general rule, applicable to appointments by the Court or by individuals, is that the costs, charges, and expenses of all parties, incurred in and about the appointment of new trustees, and the transfer to them of the trust estate, are properly chargeable against the *corpus* of the trust fund. *Harvey* v. *Olliver,* 57 L T. 239; *ex parte Davies,* 16 Jur 882; *re Parby,* 29 L.T. (O.S.) 72. But where remaindermen made application for the appointment of additional trustees unnecessarily, they were ordered to pay the costs of the appointment, *re Brackenbury,* 10 Eq. 45; and trustees retiring without adequate reasons, or whose conduct has been unreasonable, or vexatious, have been disallowed their costs, or even ordered to pay the costs of the appointment. *Porter* v. *Watts,* 21 L.J. Ch. 211, *Richardson* v. *Grubb,* 16 W.R. 176; *re Wiseman,* 18 W.R. 574; *re Adams,* 12 Ch. D. 634, *re Knox's Trusts* (1895) 1 Ch. 538, (1895) 2 Ch. 483.

If the trustees are appointed for distinct trust funds the costs must be apportioned. *Re Grant,* 2 J. & H. 764; *re Allen* (1887) W.N. 132.

"**Vesting Order.**"—The costs of a vesting order under section 35, subsection 1 (e), were thrown upon the trustees, whose unreasonable refusal to transfer had rendered the application necessary, *re Knox's Trusts* (1895) 1 Ch. 538, (1895) 2 Ch. 483. A vesting order rendered necessary by the infancy, lunacy, or other disability of a mortgagee, or his representative, will usually be at the expense of the mortgagor. *King* v. *Smith*, 6 Hare 473; Fisher on Mortgage, 5th edit., p. 902. A vesting order necessary to complete a conveyance on sale by private contract, *Bradley* v. *Munton*, 16 B. 294, and *Purser* v. *Darby*, 4 K. & J 41, or under the decree of the Court, *Ayles* v. *Cox*, 17 Beav 584, will, as a rule, be borne by the vendor.

"**Of and incident to.**"—In *re Fellowes*, 2 Jur. N.S. 62, the words "incidental and consequent on the inquiry" were struck out of the petition.

"**In such Manner.**"—Costs of appointment of new trustees and vesting order as to realty have been ordered to be raised by a charge on the inheritance. *Exparte Davies*, 16 Jur 882; *re Crabtree*, 14 W R. 497.

"**By such Persons.**"—These words do not occur in the repealed section of the Trustee Act, 1850. It was at least extremely doubtful whether the earlier Act gave jurisdiction to the Court to make a respondent personally responsible for the costs of the petition, *re Primrose*, 23 Beav 590; *re Sparks*, 6 Ch. D. 361; *re Woodburn's Will*, 1 D.G. & J. 333; *re Wiseman*, 18 W.R. 574; and the Judicature Act, 1873, did not remove the difficulty, *re Sarah Knight's Will*, 26 Ch D. 82; *re Mills*, 34 Ch. D. at p. 33. No such question arises under the present section, *re Knox's Trusts* (1895) 1 Ch. 538, (1895) 2 Ch. 483.

For definitions of "trustee," "conveyance," "transfer," and "land," see section 50, *infra*.

Section 39.—The powers conferred by this Act as to vesting orders may be exercised for vesting any land, stock, or chose in action in any trustee of a charity or society over which the High Court would have jurisdiction upon action duly instituted, whether the appointment of the trustee was made by instrument under a power or by the High Court under its general or statutory jurisdiction.

This section re-enacts, with verbal amendments, section 45 of the Trustee Act, 1850 (13 & 14 Vict. c. 60), which section is repealed by the present Act. See section 51, and Schedule, *infra*.

"**The Powers . . . may be exercised.**"—The sanction of the Charity Commissioners to the application to the Court is requisite under section 17 of the Charitable Trusts Act, 1853, in the case of all endowed charities subject to the jurisdiction of the commissioners.

"Over which the High Court would have Jurisdiction upon Action duly instituted."—See *re Davenport's Charity*, 4 De G.M. & G. 839 ; and section 28 of the Charitable Trusts Act, 1853 (16 & 17 Vict. c. 137).

"By Instrument under a Power."—These words replace the phrase "by any power contained in any deed or instrument" in the repealed section, and will include an appointment made by surviving trustees under section 10 of the present Act, *re Coates and Parsons*, 34 C.D. 70 ; see also, *ante*, p. 51. Trustees can also be appointed under the Trustees Appointment Acts, 1850 to 1890 ; by the Court under the Charitable Trusts Act, the consent of the Charity Commissioners to the application being first obtained ; or by the Commissioners themselves.

For definitions of "trustee," "land," and "stock," see section 50, *infra*.

Section 40.—Where a vesting order is made as to any land under this Act or under the Lunacy Act, 1890, or under any Act relating to lunacy in Ireland, founded on an allegation of the personal incapacity of a trustee or mortgagee, or on an allegation that a trustee or the heir or personal representative or devisee of a mortgagee is out of the jurisdiction of the High Court or cannot be found, or that it is uncertain which of several trustees or which of several devisees of a mortgagee was the survivor, or whether the last trustee or the heir or personal representative or last surviving devisee of a mortgagee is living or dead, or on an allegation that any trustee or mortgagee has died intestate without an heir or has died and it is not known who is his heir or personal representative or devisee, the fact that the order has been so made shall be conclusive evidence of the matter so alleged in any court upon any question as to the validity of the order ; but this section shall not prevent the High Court from directing a reconveyance or the payment of costs occasioned by any such order if improperly obtained.

This section is a re-enactment, with merely verbal amendments, of section 44 of the Trustee Act, 1850 (13 & 14 Vict. c. 60), and section 104 of the Lunacy Act, 1890 (53 & 54 Vict. c. 5), which sections are repealed by the present Act. See section 51, and Schedule, *infra*.

As to the evidence required of the allegations before an Sect. 40.
order is made, see *Collinson* v. *Collinson*, 3 De G.M. & G. 409.

"**Where a Vesting Order is made as to any Lands.**"—It must be noted that this section has no application to appointments of new trustees, nor to vesting orders as to stock, in this respect being more restricted than section 49, *infra*, p. 161.

As to amending an order made on mistake as to facts, see *re Clinton, Jackson* v. *Claney* (1882) W.N. 176.

The protection given by this section affords a strong inducement to obtain a vesting order of the Court, rather than to rely on a vesting declaration under section 10, in those cases in which the adoption of either of these two courses is possible.

It should be noted that the present section deals only with the facts on which an order is based, and not the jurisdiction of the Court or the parties to the proceedings, as to which see section 49, *infra*, p. 161; and cf. section 70 of the Conveyancing and Law of Property Act, 1881 (44 & 45 Vict c. 41).

"**Personal Incapacity.**"—This seems to refer to the infancy of a trustee, or mortgagee, provided for by sections 26 (ii.)a and 28, but not to bankruptcy, felony, or other unfitness or incapacity upon which no vesting order can be directly founded, although such unfitness or incapacity may give the Court power to appoint a new trustee under section 25, and make a consequential vesting order under section 26 (i.).

"**That any Trustee or Mortgagee has died Intestate without an Heir.**"—The language of the present section has not been altered to cover the case of there being no personal representative provided for in sections 26 (v.) and 29 (e).

For definitions of "land," "trustee," "mortgagee," and "devisee," see section 50, *infra*.

Section 41.—The powers of the High Court in Sect. 41.
England to make vesting orders under this Act shall extend to all land and personal estate in Her Majesty's dominions, except Scotland.

Application of vesting order to land out of England

This section replaces section 54 of the Trustee Act, 1850, which was as follows: "And be it enacted that the powers and authorities given by this Act to the Court of Chancery in England shall extend to all lands and personal estate within the dominions, plantations, and colonies belonging to Her Majesty (except Scotland)." That section is repealed by the present Act. See section 51, and Schedule, *infra*.

"**High Court.**"—The expression is defined by section 13 (3) of the Interpretation Act, 1889 (52 & 53 Vict. c. 63). "The expression 'High Court,' when used with reference to England or Ireland shall mean Her Majesty's High Court of Justice in England or Ireland, as the case may be" The powers therefore given to the High Court by other sections of the present

Sect. 41.   Act are given equally to the High Court in England and the High Court in Ireland. The present section, however, is expressly restricted to the High Court in England, and there is no section in the present Act defining the jurisdiction of the High Court in Ireland. It is submitted that in the absence of such definition the jurisdiction must extend over real and personal property situate in England and Ireland, for the Act extends to both England and Ireland. It may be remarked that the Trustee Act, 1850, only gave to the Court of Chancery in Ireland jurisdiction over land and personal property in Ireland (see Trustee Act, 1850, section 55). Now, by virtue of section 2 of the Trustee Act, 1893, Amendment Act, 1894 (57 Vict. c. 10), the High Court in Ireland is, as from the 18th June, 1894, given concurrent jurisdiction with the High Court in England over land and personal estate in "Her Majesty's dominions, except Scotland." See p. 175, below.

Under section 54 of the Trustee Act, 1850, the Court in England made orders vesting real and personal property in Ireland, re Hewitt's Estate, 6 W.R. 537 ; re Taitt's Trusts (1870) W N. 257 ; re Lamotte, 4 Ch. D. 325 ; re Hodgson, 11 Ch D. 888 ; re Steele (1885) W.N. 218 ; and land in Canada, re Schofield, 24 L.T. O.S 322 ; re Groom, 11 L.T. N.S. 336.

"Vesting Order."—As to the advantage of a vesting order from the Court over a vesting declaration under section 10 in respect of the scope of operation, see p. 143, above.

"Personal Estate."—As to the locality of bonds and shares, re Clark, McKecknie v. Clark (1904) 1 Ch. 294.

"Her Majesty's Dominions."—The expression is not defined either in the present Act or in the Interpretation Act, 1889. It is presumably used as including all places over which the authority of the Legislature extends. Cf. section 18 of the Interpretation Act, 1889 (52 & 53 Vict. c 63).

"Scotland."—That the Act as a whole "does not extend to Scotland," see section 52, infra.

For definition of "land," see section 50, infra.

Payment into Court by Trustees.

Sect. 42.

Payment into Court by trustees.

Section 42.—(1.) Trustees, or the majority of trustees, having in their hands or under their control money or securities belonging to a trust, may pay the same into the High Court; and the same shall, subject to rules of Court, be dealt with according to the orders of the High Court.

(2.) The receipt or certificate of the proper officer shall be a sufficient discharge to trustees for the money or securities so paid into Court.

(3.) Where any moneys or securities are vested in any persons as trustees, and the majority are desirous of paying the same into court, but the concurrence of the other or others cannot be obtained, the High Court may order the payment into court to be made by the majority without the concurrence of the other or others; and where any such moneys or securities are deposited with any banker, broker, or other depositary, the Court may order payment or delivery of the moneys or securities to the majority of the trustees for the purpose of payment into court, and every transfer, payment, and delivery made in pursuance of any such order shall be valid and take effect as if the same had been made on the authority or by the act of all the persons entitled to the moneys and securities so transferred, paid, or delivered.

This section replaces (1) the Legacy Duty Act, 1796 (36 Geo. 3. c. 52), section 32, which enabled executors and administrators to pay shares of legatees who were infants or beyond the seas into Court. The provisions of that Act (including section 32, see Lewin, 10th edit. 409) were by 45 Geo. 3. c. 28, section 7, declared to apply to trustees and owners of real estate charged with legacies "as fully and amply as if . . . repeated and re-enacted in this Act"; (2) the Trustee Relief Act, 1847 (10 & 11 Vict. c. 96), sections 1 and 2, which authorised "trustees, executors, administrators, or other persons having in their hands any moneys belonging to any trust whatsoever or the major part of them," and "trustees and other persons" having certain specified stocks standing in their name upon any trust, or the major part of them, on filing an affidavit describing the instrument creating the trust, to pay and transfer the moneys and stock into Court; and (3) the Trustee Relief Act Amendment Act, 1849 (12 & 13 Vict. c. 74), section 1, which extended the provisions of the former Act, by providing for an order being made for payment into Court in case of difficulty in obtaining the consent of all the trustees.

The above-mentioned sections of the Acts of 1796, 1847, and 1849, are repealed by this Act (see section 51, and Schedule), and are re-enacted in a greatly condensed form by the present section; but section 7 of 45 Geo. 3. c. 28 has not been repealed, and it seems open to argument that the owners of real estate charged with a legacy payable to an infant or a person beyond the seas might pay the legacy into Court. The rules of Court, however, do not appear to contemplate, or make provision for, any such payment.

L

Sect. 42.

Section 5 of the Conveyancing and Law of Property Act, 1881, provides, in the case of sale of land, for payment into Court, by the direction of the Court, of a sum of money in discharge of annual or capital sums charged upon the land. That section also contains provisions for the payment in of an additional amount to meet the contingency of further costs, expenses, and interest, thus avoiding the possibility of injustice referred to in the judgment of Romilly, M.R., in *re Buckley's Trusts*, cited below.

"**Trustees having in their Hands or under their Control Money or Securities belonging to a Trust.**"—Having regard to the extended meaning given to "trustee" by section 50 of the present Act, it is apprehended that the omission in the present section of the words "executors, administrators, or other person," which occur in the repealed section of the Act of 1847, will not restrict the operation of the Act. It will still be necessary, however, as under the repealed section of the Act of 1847, to show that the moneys or securities belong to a trust. Under the Act of 1847 it was held that a mortgagee having surplus proceeds of sale in his hands was within the scope of the enactment, *Roberts v. Ball*, 4 W.R 466; and also trustees of a charity, *re Poplar and Blackwell Free School*, 8 Ch. D. 543; but the owner of real estate subject to a charge was not included, *re Buckley's Trusts*, 17 Beav. 110; nor a banking company which had received notice as to conflicting claims to moneys on deposit at the bank, *re Sutton's Trusts*, 12 Ch. D. 175.

Other statutory provisions for payment into Court are, the Life Assurance Companies (Payment into Court) Act, 1896 (59 & 60 Vict. c. 8), providing for the payment into Court by a Life Assurance Company of "any moneys payable by them under a life policy in respect of which, in the opinion of their board of directors, no sufficient discharge can otherwise be obtained;" the Judicature Act, 1873 (36 & 37 Vict. c. 66), section 25 (*b*), authorising any debtor, trustee, or other person liable in respect of a debt or chose in action which has been assigned as therein mentioned, and who has notice of conflicting claims thereto, to pay the same into Court under [this Act].

"**Securities belonging to a Trust.**"—The Trustee Relief Act, 1847, dealing with payment in without an order, applied only to "annuities or stocks standing in the names of the trustees in the books of the Governor & Co., of the Bank of England, or of the East Indian Co., or South Sea Co., or any Government securities." The Trustee Relief Amendment Act, 1849, dealing with payment in on an order, applied to "any moneys, annuities, stocks, or securities." *Re Gledstane* (1878) W.N. 26.

Having regard to the extremely wide meaning given to the word "securities" as used in this section by section 50 of the present Act, it would appear that the old restriction on the range of securities which may be transferred into Court without an order no longer exists. The Court has power to deal with

securities as it may think fit (see subsection 1 of this section),
and would doubtless not allow the retention of securities of a
speculative nature. Cf. Trustee Act, 1893, Rules and note to
rule 4, *infra*, p. 199.

"**May pay the same into the High Court.**"—The Trustee
Relief Acts formerly provided a valuable means of avoiding
the expense of a suit, and were constantly made use of in cases
in which questions arose in the course of administration as to
some particular portion of the trust funds, and a trustee who
commenced a suit instead of making use of these Acts was
bound to justify his action in so doing.

Now that an expeditious and inexpensive method has been
provided for obtaining the opinion of the Court on such
questions without the necessity of a general administration,
the importance of the provisions contained in the present
section is much decreased. A trustee should not avail himself
of the section without sufficient reason, and should consider
whether proceedings by originating summons would not be less
costly and troublesome to the persons interested, *per* Jessel, M.R.,
re Birkett, 9 Ch. D. 576; and trustees who pay money into
Court when the question arising might be decided upon an
originating summons under Order 55, r. 3 of the Rules of
Court, will not be allowed the costs occasioned by such payment
into Court, *per* Kay, J., *re Giles*, 55 L.J. Ch. 695; 34 W.R. 712;
55 L.T. 51.

In some cases, however, payment in may be less expensive
than raising a question on originating summons. Cf. remarks
of Cotton, L.J., in *re Parker's Will*, 39 Ch. D 303.

An executor is not entitled, by paying a legacy, or a lapsed
share of residuary personalty, into Court, to exempt the general
residue from the costs of ascertaining the legatees or next of
kin, *re Gibbon's Will*, 36 Ch. D. 486; *re Giles, supra*; and it is
submitted that the principle is still applicable, for Order 65,
r. 14 (*b*) of the Rules of the Supreme Court, does not, when
there is a general direction to pay testamentary expenses out
of the residuary estate, throw the costs of inquiries as to the
persons entitled to a legacy or share on that particular legacy
or share, *re Baumgarten*, 82 L.T. 711; *re Groom* (1897) 2 Ch.
407. The Court has, however, power to so exempt the residue
under Order 65, r. 14 (*c*).

Trustees of a charity should not pay money into Court
without first applying to the Charity Commissioners, *re Poplar
and Blackwell Free School*, 8 C D. 543, cited *supra*.

By payment into Court, trustees retire from the trust. See
Lewin, p. 412; *re Poplar and Blackwell Free School, supra; re
Murphy's Trust* (1900) 1 I.R. 145.

"**High Court.**"—As to County Court, see section 46, *post*,
p. 156.

Subsection 3.—This subsection, as did the Amending
Act of 1849, which it replaces, makes provision for cases in

Sect. 42. which the majority of trustees are unable to act under the provisions of subsection 1, owing to the fact that the payment authorised by that subsection is only possible with the concurrence of all the trustees in whom the legal control is vested. In such a case this subsection provides for the effectual transfer or payment by virtue of an order of the Court, without the concurrence of the other trustees.

"**Costs of Payment in.**"—The Act makes no provision as to costs of payment in. Since there is no means of obtaining payment of costs out of the fund after payment in, except upon the petition for payment out, the usual practice is to deduct the costs before payment in, *unless the amount of the costs or the necessity for the payment in is disputed, Beaty* v. *Curson*, 7 Eq. 194. Where costs have been improperly deducted the Court cannot order the trustee to refund on the petition for payment out, but an action must be commenced, *re Parker's Will*, 39 Ch. D. 303. Where payment in is made without affidavit, costs cannot be deducted. Cf. Supreme Court Fund Rules, 1894, Form 16, note. Generally as to costs of payment in, see Daniell's Chancery Practice, 1805.

Practice.—See *post*, p. 198.

For definitions of "trustee," "trust," "pay," "payment," "securities," and "transfer," see section 50, *infra*.

Miscellaneous.

Sect. 43.

Power to give judgment in absence of a trustee.

Section 43.—Where in any action the High Court is satisfied that diligent search has been made for any person who, in the character of trustee, is made a defendant in any action, to serve him with a process of the Court, and that he cannot be found, the Court may hear and determine the action and give judgment therein against that person in his character of a trustee, as if he had been duly served, or had entered an appearance in the action, and had also appeared by his counsel and solicitor at the hearing, but without prejudice to any interest he may have in the matters in question in the action in any other character.

This section is a re-enactment, with verbal alterations, of section 49 of the Trustee Act, 1850 (13 & 14 Vict. c. 60), which section is repealed by this Act. See section 51, and Schedule, *infra*. The repealed section was itself a re-enactment of section 24 of Lord St. Leonards's Trustee Act, 1830 (11 Geo. 4. & 1 Will. 4. c 60).

"In any Action."—Section 49 of the Trustee Act, 1850, was restricted to suits in the Court of Chancery. There is no definition of the word "action" in the present Act, nor in the Interpretation Act, 1889 (52 & 53 Vict. c. 63). The word is defined in the Judicature Act, 1873 (36 & 37 Vict. c. 66), section 100, as meaning in that Act "a civil proceeding commenced by writ or in such other manner as may be prescribed by rules of Court; and shall not include a criminal proceeding by the Crown." And this definition includes proceedings commenced by originating summons. *In re Fawsitt, Galland* v. *Burton*, 30 C.D. 231. But the Judicature Act contains no definition applicable to other Acts, *exparte Chinery*, 12 Q.B.D. 345. It would appear that proceedings commenced by originating summons are not necessarily actions within the ordinary meaning of that word as used apart from the Judicature Act, *re Wilson*, 45 C.D. 266; *Lock* v. *Pearce* (1893) 2 Ch. 271; and cf. *re Holloway* (1894) 2 Q.B. 163. In the present section the meaning of the word would appear to be confined to proceedings commenced by writ, though it might be argued that an action commenced by any originating summons to which appearance has to be entered is also within the section. It clearly does not apply to proceedings in which no appearance is entered.

Cases in which the repealed sections were made use of are *De Crespigny* v. *Kitson*, referred to in 12 Sim. p. 163, under the Act of 1850, and *Westhead* v. *Sale*, 6 W.R. 52, and *Burrell* v *Maxwell*, 25 L T. N.S. 655, under the Trustee Act, 1850.

For definition of "trustee," see section 50, *infra*.

Section 44.—(1.) Where a trustee [or other person] is for the time being authorised to dispose of land by way of sale, exchange, partition, or enfranchisement, the High Court may sanction his so disposing of the land with an exception or reservation of any minerals, and with or without rights and powers of or incidental to the working, getting, or carrying away of the minerals, or so disposing of the minerals, with or without the said rights or powers, separately from the residue of the land.

(2.) Any such trustee [or other person], with the said sanction previously obtained, may, unless forbidden by the instrument creating the trust or direction, from time to time, without any further application to the Court, so dispose of any such land or minerals.

(3.) Nothing in this section shall derogate from any power which a trustee may have under the Settled Land Acts, 1882 to 1890, or otherwise.

The words in [ ] are inserted by section 3 of the Trustee Act, 1893, Amendment Act, 1894 (see p. 175, below).

The present section replaces section 2 of the Confirmation of Sales Act, 1862 (25 & 26 Vict. c. 108), which Act is repealed by the present Act. See section 51, and Schedule, *infra*.

The passing of the repealed Act was rendered necessary by the decision in *Buckley* v. *Howell*, 29 B. 546, that a power of sale and exchange does not authorise trustees to sell the lands with a reservation of the minerals. See remarks of Lindley, M.R., and Rigby, L.J., in *re Gladstone* (1900) 2 Ch. 101.

Section 2 of the repealed Act was as follows : "Every trustee and other person now or hereafter to become authorised to dispose of land by way of sale, exchange, partition, or enfranchisement, may, unless forbidden by the instrument creating the trust or power, so dispose of such land with an exception or reservation of any minerals, and with or without rights and powers of or incidental to the working, getting, or carrying away of such minerals, or may (unless forbidden as aforesaid) dispose of by way of sale, exchange, or partition, the minerals, with or without such rights or powers, separately from the residue of the land, and in either case without prejudice to any future exercise of the authority with respect to the excepted minerals, or (as the case may be) the undisposed-of land ; but this enactment shall not enable any such disposition as aforesaid, without the previous sanction of the Court of Chancery, to be obtained on petition in a summary way of the trustee or other person authorised as aforesaid, which sanction once obtained shall extend to the enabling from time to time of any disposition within this enactment of any part or parts of the lands comprised in any order to be made on such petition, without the necessity of any further or other application to the Court."

The present section, as amended, includes a mortgagee with a power of sale, as did also the repealed Act, *re Beaumont's Mortgage Trusts*, 12 Eq. 86; *re Wilkinson's Mortgaged Estates*, 13 Eq. 634. Before the amendment by the Act of 1894 the present section would not, owing to the definition of "trustee" in section 50, have included a mortgagee who was not also a trustee, *re Merchants' Trust and New British Iron Co.*, 38 Solicitors' Journal 253.

For the power of sale given to mortgagees by the Conveyancing and Law of Property Act, 1881, see section 19 of that Act   The language of that section is probably not wide enough to authorise a sale of the surface apart from minerals, or of minerals apart from the surface, without the sanction of the Court under the present section; cf. *re Yates, Batcheldor* v. *Yates*, 38 C.D. 112, in which case it was held by the Court of Appeal that section 19 of the Conveyancing Act did not

authorise the separate sale of trade machinery; and *Born*   **Sect. 44.**
v. *Turner* (1900) 2 Ch. 211, in which case it was held by
Byrne, J., that the section authorised the grant by implication
of an easement over unsold portions of the mortgaged land.

"**Unless forbidden by the Instrument creating the Trust.**"—
It is remarkable that these words are only introduced in the
second subsection, the purpose of which subsection appears
merely to be to dispense with any further application to the
Court when the sanction of the Court has been once obtained.
But though the effect of this is, apparently, to give power to
the Court to sanction a separate sale even in cases in which the
instrument expressly forbids it, the Court would, presumably,
refuse in such a case to give the necessary sanction. The
repealed section clearly gave no power of separate sale in cases
in which the instrument expressly forbade such sale.

"**Nothing in this Act shall derogate.**"—For the powers of
sale and exchange given by the Settled Land Act, 1882, to
tenants for life, see Settled Land Act, 1882, section 3, section
4 (6), and section 17 (and for the exercise of these powers by
the trustees when the tenant for life is an infant, section 60).
Section 5 of the Settled Land Act, 1890, authorises the creation
of easements on a sale or exchange. As to the power of the
tenant for life under the Settled Land Acts to lease the surface
apart from the minerals, see *re Gladstone* (1900) 1 Ch. 101.

The words "without prejudice to any future exercise of
the authority, etc." in the repealed section are omitted in the
present section as unnecessary, *re Thomas's Trusts*, 40 Sol. J. 98.

Practice.—See *post*, p. 196.

For definitions of "trust," "trustee," "land," and "instrument," see section 50, *infra*.

Section 45.—(1.) Where a trustee commits a   **Sect. 45.**
breach of trust at the instigation or request or with
the consent in writing of a beneficiary, the High   **Power to
make bene-**
Court may, if it thinks fit, and notwithstanding that   **ficiary in-**
the beneficiary may be a married woman, entitled for   **demnify for
breach of**
her separate use and restrained from anticipation,   **trust.**
make such order as to the Court seems just, for impounding all or any part of the interest of the
beneficiary in the trust estate by way of indemnity
to the trustee or person claiming through him.

(2.) This section shall apply to breaches of trust
committed as well before as after the passing of this
Act, but shall not apply so as to prejudice any
question in an action or other proceeding which was
pending on the twenty-fourth day of December one

thousand eight hundred and eighty-eight, and is pending at the commencement of this Act.

This section is a re-enactment of section 6 of the Trustee Act, 1888, which section is repealed by this Act. See section 51, and Schedule, *infra*.

Section 6 of the Trustee Act, 1888, was in the main merely a statement of the then existing law. In two points, however, it altered the law, (*a*) in extending the right of impounding to the interest of a married woman restrained from anticipation, and (*b*) in providing that consent, if in writing, may form the basis of a claim to impound.

Neither section 6 of the Act of 1888, nor the present section, displace the previously existing equitable rights and remedies of trustees as against beneficiaries. See the judgment of Romer, J., in *Bolton* v. *Curre* (1895) 1 Ch. at p. 549, which contains the following passage: " But it is now said that section 6 of the Trustee Act, 1888, which was substantially repeated by section 45 of the Trustee Act, 1893, has altered the law. It is contended that the whole of the law as to the impounding of interests to indemnifying trustees is now contained in those sections, and that the formerly existing law on the subject was put an end to by the Act of 1888, unless it was re-enacted by section 6. It is further said that by that section, and the corresponding section of the Act of 1893, the impounding is now put absolutely in the discretion of the Court, and that the interest of a beneficiary is not affected by any equity in favour of the trustees until the Court orders the impounding. . . . I think this contention cannot be sustained. In my opinion section 6 of the Act of 1888 was intended to enlarge the power of the Court as to indemnifying trustees, and to give greater relief to trustees, and was not intended and did not operate to curtail the previously existing rights and remedies of trustees, or to alter the law except by giving greater power to the Court. The discretion given to the Court by section 6, as to whether it will impound or not, is a judicial discretion, and if, prior to the passing of that Act, the Court would, in a proper case, enforce the equity of the trustee, and impound the interest of a beneficiary in the hands of an assignee, then the Court would be bound to do the same in a similar case after the Act. The equity of the trustees exists as much since the Act as before; and if the Court before the Act thought fit, in a proper case, to enforce that equity by impounding, it will equally since the Act think fit to enforce the equity in a similar case, and impound."

As to the general intention of the section, see also the judgments of the Court of Appeal in *Chillingworth* v. *Chambers* (1896) 1 Ch. 685, and especially the passage on p. 707 in the judgment of Kay, L.J.: " The statute does not define the extent of the liability of a concurring beneficiary. The sixth section is rather addressed to describe the case in which the Court may, if it shall think fit, impound all or any part of the interest of the beneficiary by way of indemnity to the trustees, and also to provide that consent of a beneficiary for this purpose must be given in writing." Also the dictum of Davey, L.J., in *re Somerset* (1894) 1 Ch. at p. 275: "Although the power of impounding the interest of the beneficiary is extended by the section to new cases, it is not a new power, and I cannot find any words in the section which have the effect of directing the Court to exercise the statutory jurisdiction on principles different from those on which it acted before the statute."

It would appear, therefore, that the discretion of the Court will be exercised in conformity with the decisions before the 24th December, 1888, except only on the two points above mentioned (consent in writing, and restraint on anticipation), and that the principles on which those decisions were based will still control the action of the Court.

"**At the Instigation or Request or with the Consent in Writing.**"—Before the Act of 1888 mere consent was not enough to create liability, see the judgment of Chitty, J., in *Sawyer* v. *Sawyer*, 28 C.D. at p. 598. The Act in this respect alters the law. The instigation, request, or consent to create liability must be with sufficient knowledge of the facts which make the act or omission a breach of trust, *re Somerset* (1894) 1 Ch. 231. Thus, in the case of an improper investment, knowledge that the proposed investment is a breach of trust must be shown, and the section is not to be construed as if the word "investment" had been inserted instead of "breach of trust" (*per* Lindley, L.J., S.C., p. 265). Full knowledge of the facts is especially essential in the case of married women restrained from anticipation (see cases cited below). The words "in writing" apply, of course, only to consent, and not to instigation and request. *Griffith* v. *Hughes* (1892) 3 Ch. 105; approved in *re Somerset* (1894) 1 Ch. at p. 265, and *Mara* v. *Browne* (1895) 2 Ch. at p. 92.

"**The High Court may, if it thinks fit.**"—The discretion is a judicial discretion. Cf. observations of Romer, J., cited above.

"**Notwithstanding that the Beneficiary may be a Married Woman entitled for her Separate Use and restrained from Anticipation.**"—Before the Act of 1888 the Court had no power to impound the interest of a married woman restrained from anticipation. The Court will only exercise its jurisdiction to impound the interest in such a case with great caution, and bearing in mind that it is the duty of trustees to protect the married woman against herself. The relief was granted in the case of *Griffith* v. *Hughes* (1892) 3 Ch. 105, but refused in *Ricketts* v. *Ricketts*, 64 L.T. N.S. 263, *Bolton* v. *Curre* (1895) 1 Ch. 551, and *Mara* v. *Browne* (1895) 2 Ch. 69 (reversed on another point (1896) 1 Ch. 199).

"**By Way of Indemnity to the Trustee or Person claiming through him.**"—The right to impound as it existed before the Act of 1888, was primarily in favour of the innocent beneficiaries.

Sect. 45. It was only when the trustee had satisfied their claims that he was entitled to stand in their shoes and impound the interest of a concurring beneficiary to indemnify himself. Cf. judgment of Turner, L.J., in *Raby* v. *Ridehalgh*, 7 D.G.M. & G. at p. 109. The present section, however, deals with the rights of the trustees, and not with those of the innocent beneficiaries, unless these latter can be considered to be "persons claiming through" a trustee within the meaning of the section. Cf. *Leahy* v. *de Mullens* (1896) 1 Ir. R. 206, *ante*, p. 7, and *re Frith, Newton* v. *Rolfe* (1902) 1 Ch. 342, a case which deals with a creditor's right in suing a trustee to claim the benefit of the indemnity to which the trustee is entitled out of the estate. It seems doubtful, therefore, whether in favour of beneficiaries this section gives any additional right, either as against a married woman restrained from anticipation, or as against a beneficiary who has merely consented to a breach of trust, without otherwise concurring in it.

"**For impounding all or any Part of the Interest of the Beneficiary.**"—The section does not define the *extent* of the liability of a concurring beneficiary (cf. the dictum of Kay, J., cited above). It would therefore appear that the Court would still give effect to any principle limiting that liability recognised as existing before the passing of the Act. Whether any such principle existed limiting the liability of the share of the beneficiary to be impounded, as distinguished from the personal liability of the beneficiary to indemnify the trustee, is a question of some difficulty. The case of *Raby* v. *Ridehalgh*, 7 De G M. & G. 104, expressly limits the *personal* liability of a concurring beneficiary (which liability in earlier cases had been laid down in very general terms: cf. *Trafford* v. *Boehm*, 3 Atk. 440) to the extent to which such beneficiary had received capital or income under the breach of trust. The case has been cited as expressly limiting the liability of the *share of the beneficiary* in the same way. A possible explanation of the wording of the judgment in that case is suggested by A. L. Smith, L.J., in *Chillingworth* v. *Chambers* (1896) 1 Ch. at p. 709, viz. that the limited impounding there ordered was sufficient to indemnify the trustee. A careful consideration of the facts as reported would seem clearly to show that such was the case. The point was raised in argument in the case of *Sawyer* v. *Sawyer*, 28 C.D., pp. 601, 602, but as in that case the decision was that no charge was created, it is not an authority on the point. The decision of the Court of Appeal in *Chillingworth* v. *Chambers* (1896) 1 Ch. 685, in which case the question was very fully discussed, does not necessarily decide the point, for there the concurring beneficiary was also one of the trustees.

A possible view of the result of the authorities (a view which appears to have been adopted by Kay, L.J., in *Chillingworth* v. *Chambers, supra*), is that the rule as to the liability of a share to be impounded is different in the case of a concurring beneficiary who is also a trustee, to that which is applied

in the case of a concurring beneficiary who is not a trustee.
In the case of a beneficiary who is a trustee, *Chillingworth*
v. *Chambers, supra,* clearly decides that the whole share is
liable to be impounded, but when the principles from which
this result is obtained are examined, it appears doubtful
whether they can be extended to the case of a beneficiary not a
trustee. These principles, as stated in the judgment of North, J.,
in *Chillingworth* v. *Chambers, supra,* appear to be that where a
trustee beneficiary has concurred in a breach of trust, he is
bound (as is any trustee) to pay the shares of the innocent
beneficiaries in full. He cannot take anything out of the fund
for himself until this has been done. If when this has been
done no part of the fund remains to provide for his own share,
he cannot call upon his co-trustee to make good such share or
any part of it, for it is a very clearly established rule that a
beneficiary who has concurred in a breach of trust cannot call
upon the trustees to make good any loss which accrues to him
therefrom. In the result, therefore, the whole share is virtually
"impounded." But those principles do not apply to the case
of a beneficiary who is not a trustee. In such a case, notwithstanding the dicta of Lindley and A. L Smith, L.JJ., in *Chillingworth* v. *Chambers,* it appears to be still an open question
whether the Court can impound the interest of a beneficiary
to a greater extent than the amount of his personal liability
limited as stated above, and there appears to be no reported
cases in which such a course has been adopted.

As to the trustees' general right of indemnity in respect of
expenses properly incurred, see section 24, *supra.*

As to contribution between co-trustees generally, see also
Bahin v. *Hughes,* 31 C.D. 390; *Birks* v. *Micklethwait,* 33 Beav.
409, *Robinson* v. *Harkin* (1896) 2 Ch. 415; *Moxham* v. *Grant*
(1900) 1 Q.B. 88.

"Interest of the Beneficiary in the Trust Estate."—The
liability attaches not only to the original share of the beneficiary,
but also to shares to which he subsequently becomes entitled,
Evans v. *Benyon,* 37 C.D. 329; *Chillingworth* v *Chambers* (1896)
1 Ch. 685. The liability exists as against the assignee of the
share, *Bolton* v. *Curre* (1895) 1 Ch. 544.

Practice.—See p. 195, *infra.*
The power conferred by this Act can be invoked on behalf
of trustees defendants in an action, although they have not
counterclaimed, or served a third party notice, *re Holt, re
Rollason, Holt* v. *Holt* (1897) 2 Ch 525. It is within the com-
petence of the Court, on such a point being suggested by trustees
either to direct an inquiry, or to give leave to apply as to
enforcing the claim to impound. *Ib.,* and see *Molyneux* v.
Fletcher (1898) 1 Q.B. 648.

For definitions of "trustee" and "trust," see section 50,
infra.

Section 46.—The provisions of this Act with respect to the High Court shall, in their application to cases within the jurisdiction of a palatine court or county court, include that court, and the procedure under this Act in palatine courts and county courts shall be in accordance with the Acts and rules regulating the procedure of hose courts.

This section replaces section 21 of the Trustee Act, 1850 (13 & 14 Vict. c. 60), which section, as to part, was repealed by the Statute Law Revision Act, 1891, and as to the residue, by the present Act section 11 of the Court of Chancery (Lancaster) Act, 1854 (17 & 18 Vict. c. 82), and section 8 of the Palatine Court of Durham Act, 1889 (52 & 53 Vict. c. 47), which sections are repealed by the present Act. See section 51, and Schedule, *infra.*

"High Court."—"The expression 'High Court,' when used with reference to England or Ireland, shall mean Her Majesty's High Court of Justice in England or Ireland, as the case may be." Interpretation Act, 1889 (52 & 53 Vict. c. 63), section 13 (3.)

"Palatine Court."—See Chancery of Lancaster Act, 1890 (53 & 54 Vict. c. 23), and the Palatine Court of Durham Act, 1889 (52 & 53 Vict. c. 47); and see also Judicature Act, 1873 (36 & 37 Vict. c 66), sections 17 and 18.

"County Courts."—See County Courts Act, 1888 (51 & 52 Vict. c. 43), sections 67 and 68, which give jurisdiction to the County Court in cases where the trust estate or fund does not exceed £500 in amount or value; and see the County Court Rules, 1903, Order 38.

Part IV.

Miscellaneous and Supplemental.

Section 47.—(1.) All the powers and provisions contained in this Act with reference to the appointment of new trustees, and the discharge and retirement of trustees, are to apply to and include trustees for the purposes of the Settled Land Acts, 1882 to 1890, whether appointed by the Court or by the settlement, or under provisions contained in the settlement.

(2.) This section applies and is to have effect with respect to an appointment or a discharge and retirement of trustees taking place before as well as after the commencement of this Act.

(3.) This section is not to render invalid or prejudice any appointment or any discharge and retirement of trustees effected before the passing of this Act, otherwise than under the provisions of the Conveyancing and Law of Property Act, 1881.

The Conveyancing and Law of Property Act, 1881 (sections 31 and 32) contained provisions for the appointment, discharge, and retirement of trustees. In re *Wilcock*, 34 Ch. D. 508, North, J., doubted whether new trustees could be appointed under those sections for the purposes of the Settled Land Act, and this case was followed in re *Kane's Trusts*, 21 L R. Ir. 112. The Settled Land Act, 1890, section 17, provided that all the powers and provisions contained in the Conveyancing and Law of Property Act, 1881, with reference to the appointment of new trustees, and the discharge and retirement of trustees, were to apply to trustees for the purposes of the Settled Land Acts, 1882 to 1890. This section 17 contained subsections 2 and 3, identical in language with subsections 2 and 3 above. Sections 31 and 32 of the Conveyancing and Law of Property Act, 1881, and section 17 of the Settled Land Act, 1890, are repealed by section 51 of the present Act.

" All the Powers and Provisions contained in this Act."— See sections 10 to 12, and 25, 26, and 35 above.

The present section, unlike the repealed section 17 of the Settled Land Act, 1890, applies to appointments by the Court, as well as to those by individuals. Appointments of Settled Land Act trustees by the Court will usually be made under section 38 of the Settled Land Act, 1882, which is as follows:—

"(1) If at any time there are no trustees of a settlement within the definition in this Act, or where in any other case it is expedient, for purposes of this Act, that new trustees of a settlement be appointed, the Court may, if it thinks fit, on the application of the tenant for life, or of any other person having under the settlement an estate or interest in the settled land, in possession, remainder, or otherwise, or in the case of an infant of his testamentary or other guardian or next friend, appoint fit persons to be trustees under the settlement for purposes of this Act.

" (2) The persons so appointed, and the survivors and survivor of them, while continuing to be trustees or trustee, and, until the appointment of new trustees, the personal representatives or representative for the time being of the last

Sect. 47. surviving or continuing trustee, shall, for purposes of this Act,
—————— become and be the trustees or trustee of the settlement."

See also notes, p. 202, *infra*.

"Appointment of New Trustees."—As to the persons who
can properly be appointed trustees for the purposes of the
Settled Land Acts, it would appear that the general rules
applicable to the appointment of new trustees, and noted under
sections 10 and 25, *supra*, must be adhered to, for "the appointment of trustees for the purpose of the Settled Land Acts is
required to impose a check upon the extensive powers conferred
by the Act upon the tenant for life." Cotton, L.J., in *re Kemp's
Settled Estates*, 24 Ch. D. 485, 487. Thus in *Wheelright* v. *Walker*,
23 Ch. D. 752 (reported *sub nom, re Walker's Trusts*, 48 L.T. N S.
632 ; 31 W.R. 716), the Court refused to appoint the solicitor of
the tenant for life to be one of the trustees, where a person
interested in remainder objected. In *re Kemp's Settled Estates*,
24 Ch. D. 485, the Court of Appeal refused to appoint the
solicitor of the tenant for life to be one of the trustees. In a
special case, however, the Court will appoint as one of the
trustees the solicitor of the tenant for life, *re Marquis of Ailes-
bury* (1893) 2 Ch. 345, and although such an appointment will
only be made by the Court in exceptional cases, it will not, if
made by an individual donee of a power to appoint, be
necessarily invalid, *re Earl of Stamford* (1896) 1 Ch. 288. That
in no case can a tenant for life or a person who may become
tenant for life be appointed trustee of a settlement for the
purposes of the Settled Land Act, was laid down as a rule of
the Court by Pearson, J., in *re Harrop's Trusts*, 24 Ch. D. 717,
and this was followed in *re Thompson's Will*, 21 L.R. Ir. 109.
In *re Knowles's Settled Estates*, 27 Ch. D. 707, the Court objected
to appoint two brothers trustees, on the ground that there
should be two independent trustees. In exceptional circumstances the Court has appointed as Settled Land Act trustees
persons domiciled in Australia, *re Whitchurch* (1897) 1 Ch. 256.

Subsections 2 and 3.—The necessity for the introduction of
these subsections is not obvious. They were necessary in the
Settled Land Act, 1890, as the intention of that Act was to
declare that the Conveyancing and Law of Property Act, 1881,
should be deemed to have applied to the appointment of Settled
Land Act trustees from its commencement, whilst saving any
appointments made not in accordance with section 31 of that
Act. As section 17 of the Settled Land Act, 1890, was in
operation until its repeal by the present Act, there would
appear to be no reason for making the present section retrospective, unless it could be maintained that the revocation of
the subsection 2 of section 17 of the Settled Land Act, 1890,
removed the protection given to appointments made in accordance with the Act of 1881 prior to 1890. As against such a
contention, see section 38 of the Interpretation Act, 1889 (52
& 53 Vict. c. 63), p. 170, *infra*. Whether (assuming such a
contention is possible) the present subsection 2 could operate

retrospectively so as to avoid the difficulty, seems at least Sect. 47.
doubtful, for in effect it provides that the earlier provisions of
the present Act, as to appointment, discharge, and retirement of
trustees, are to apply, and to be held to have always applied,
to the appointment of Settled Land Act trustees. But those
earlier provisions are not themselves retrospective, and if the
same method of construction is applied as that adopted by
Halsbury, L.C., in *Smith* v. *Callender* (1901) A.C. 303, 304,
in constructing another Act, the result would appear to be that
these subsections do not give the protection desired.   The
questions thus raised are not likely to be of practical importance, but illustrate the confusion introduced by adopting in a
later Act the language of an earlier Act, passed in different
circumstances, and in a different state of the law.

For definition of "trustee," see section 50, *infra*.

Section 48.—Property vested in any person on Sect. 48
any trust or by way of mortgage shall not, in case
of that person becoming a convict within the mean- Trust estates
ing of the Forfeiture Act, 1870, vest in any such not affected
administrator as may be appointed under that Act, by trustee becoming a convict.
but shall remain in the trustee or mortgagee, or
survive to his co-trustee or descend to his representative as if he had not become a convict; provided
that this enactment shall not affect the title to the
property so far as relates to any beneficial interest
therein of any such trustee or mortgagee.

This section replaces sections 46 and 47 of the Trustee
Act, 1850 (13 & 14 Vict. c. 60), which sections are repealed by
the present Act.   See section 51, and Schedule, *infra*.
By an Act 4 and 5 Will. 4. c. 23, after a recital to the effect
that "great inconvenience had been found to result to persons
beneficially entitled to real or personal property by the escheat-
ing or forfeiture thereof to His Majesty, to corporations, to
lords of manors and others, in consequence of the death without
heirs, or the conviction for treason or felony of a trustee in
whom or in whose name the same is vested," it is provided as
follows· section 3, "And be it further enacted that no land,
chattels, or stock vested in any person upon any trust or by
way of mortgage, or any profits thereof, shall escheat or be
forfeited to His Majesty, his heirs, or successors, or to any
corporation, lord of a manor, or other person, by reason of the
attainder or conviction for any offence of such trustee or
mortgagee, but shall remain in such trustee or mortgagee, or
survive to his co-trustee, or descend or vest in his representative,
as if no such attainder or conviction had taken place;" and
section 5, "Provided always, and be it hereby enacted that

Sect. 48. nothing contained in this Act shall prevent the escheat or forfeiture of any land, chattels, or stock vested in any such trustee or mortgagee, so far as relates to any beneficial interest therein of any such trustee or mortgagee, but such land, chattels, or stock, so far as relates to any such beneficial interest, shall be recoverable in the same manner as if this Act had not passed."

The Trustee Act, 1850, by section 1 repealed the above two sections of 4 and 5 Will. 4. c. 23, and by sections 46 and 47 replaced them, with verbal amendments.

The Trustee Extension Act, 1852, by section 8 gave power to the Court, by order, to appoint a new trustee in the place of a convict, with an added proviso that "such order shall have the same effect as to lands as if the convict trustee had been free from any disability, and had duly executed a conveyance or assignment of his estate and interest in the same."

The Forfeiture Act, 1870 (33 & 34 Vict. c. 23), by section 1 generally abolishes forfeiture and escheat except in cases of outlawry; by section 6 defines "convict" as meaning any person against whom, after the passing of that Act, judgment of death or of penal servitude shall have been pronounced or recorded by any Court of competent jurisdiction in England, Wales, or Ireland, upon any charge of treason or felony; by section 8 provides that no convict, subject to the operation of that Act, shall be capable of alienating any property; by sections 9 and 10 for the vesting of the convict's property in an administrator appointed by the Court; and by other sections for the administration of the property by the administrator.

In *re Levy and Debenture Corporation's Contract*, 38 S.J. 530, North, J., in the course of his judgment said : "Before 4 and 5 Will. 4. c. 23, the inconveniences recited in the preamble to that statute were felt. The matter was then dealt with by the Trustee Act, 1850, section 46, and the Trustee Extension Act, 1852, section 8, which looks as if the author of that Act thought that a convict was under some disability. But under section 1 of the Trustee Extension Act, 1852, it has been held that 'as if free from disability' applies to a person under no disability at all. Section 48 of the Trustee Act, 1893, repeals those Acts, but follows out the lines of the old Acts. It is said, however, that the Forfeiture Act of 1870 applies, and that the property is vested in the convict's administrator. In my opinion, if it had been intended to change the well-established practice, the Act would have expressly said so. Other persons who might be trustees of the same property would not have been ignored if the Act had been intended to relate to them. Moreover, by other sections of the Act absolute power is given to the administrator to convey or mortgage. It is simply outrageous to suppose that the Legislature authorised the administrator to pay the costs of the prosecution, to make allowances for the support of the convict's family, and to make good amounts of which people have been defrauded by the convict, out of property of which the convict was a trustee. I must read the Act as a rational Act, and not as one providing for the maintenance of the convict out of the trust estate."

The result, therefore, appears to be that the present section, and the corresponding sections replaced by it, are merely declaratory of the law, since apart from their provisions a trustee who is made a convict was, and is, under no disability as regards the trust estate.

As to the power of the Court to replace a felon trustee, see section 25, *supra*, and notes thereto; and as to replacing such a trustee without the assistance of the Court, see section 10, *supra*, and notes thereto.

For definitions of "property," "mortgage," "mortgagee," and "trustee," see section 50, *infra*.

Section 49.—This Act, and every order purporting to be made under this Act, shall be a complete indemnity to the Banks of England and Ireland, and to all persons for any acts done pursuant thereto; and it shall not be necessary for the Bank or for any person to inquire concerning the propriety of the order, or whether the Court by which it was made had jurisdiction to make the same.

Provisions indemnifying the Banks of England and Ireland were contained in the Irish Trustee Relief Act (11 & 12 Vict. c. 68), in the further Trustee Relief Act (12 & 13 Vict. c. 74), and in section 20 of the Trustee Act, 1850 (13 & 14 Vict. c. 60). The present section replaces these and section 7 of the Trustee Extension Act, 1852 (15 & 16 Vict. c. 55), which latter section was similar in form and effect to the present section, except that it was limited to acts done pursuant to the Trustee Act, 1850, and the Trustee Extension Act, 1852.

This section applies in particular to the case of transfers directed under sections 35 and 42 of this Act. See notes to subsections 3 and 4 of section 35, *supra*, pp. 136, 137.

As to the making of an order being, in certain cases, conclusive evidence of the facts on the allegation of which it is founded, see section 40, *supra*.

Section 50.—In this Act, unless the context otherwise requires,—

The expression "bankrupt" includes, in Ireland, insolvent:

The expression "contingent right," as applied to land, includes a contingent or executory interest, a possibility coupled with an interest, whether the

Sect. 48.

Sect. 49.

Indemnity.

Sect. 50.

Definitions.

M

object of the gift or limitation of the interest, or possibility is or is not ascertained, also a right of entry, whether immediate or future, and whether vested or contingent :

The expressions "convey" and "conveyance" applied to any person include the execution by that person of every necessary or suitable assurance for conveying, assigning, appointing, surrendering, or otherwise transferring or disposing of land whereof he is seised or possessed, or wherein he is entitled to a contingent right, either for his whole estate or for any less estate, together with the performance of all formalities required by law to the validity of the conveyance, including the acts to be performed by married women and tenants in tail in accordance with the provisions of the Acts for abolition of fines and recoveries in England and Ireland respectively, and also including surrenders and other acts which a tenant of customary or copyhold lands can himself perform preparatory to or in aid of a complete assurance of the customary or copyhold land :

The expression "devisee ' includes the heir of a devisee and the devisee of an heir, and any person who may claim right by devolution of title of a similar description :

The expression "instrument" includes Act of Parliament :

The expression "land" includes manors and lordships, and reputed manors and lordships, and incorporeal as well as corporeal hereditaments, and any interest therein, and also an undivided share of land :

The expressions "mortgage" and "mortgagee" include and relate to every estate and interest regarded in equity as merely a security for money, and every person deriving title under the original mortgagee :

The expressions "pay" and "payment" as applied in relation to stocks and securities, and in connection with the expression "into court," include the deposit or transfer of the same in or into court :

The expression "possessed" applies to receipt of income of, and to any vested estate less than a life estate, legal or equitable, in possession or in expectancy, in, any land:

The expression "property" includes real and personal property, and any estate and interest in any property, real or personal, and any debt, and any thing in action, and any other right or interest, whether in possession or not:

The expression "rights" includes estates and interests:

The expression "securities" includes stocks, funds, and shares; and, so far as relates to payments into Court, has the same meaning as in the Court of Chancery (Funds) Act, 1872:

The expression "stock" includes fully paid up shares; and, so far as relates to vesting orders made by the Court under this Act, includes any fund, annuity, or security transferable in books kept by any company or society, or by instrument of transfer either alone or accompanied by other formalities, and any share or interest therein:

The expression "transfer," in relation to stock, includes the performance and execution of every deed, power of attorney, act, and thing on the part of the transferor to effect and complete the title in the transferee:

The expression "trust" does not include the duties incident to an estate conveyed by way of mortgage; but with this exception the expressions "trust" and "trustee" include implied and constructive trusts, and cases where the trustee has a beneficial interest in the trust property, and the duties incident to the office of personal representative of a deceased person.

This section is not a "definition clause." It ought rather to be called an "expounding clause": Chitty, J., in re *Merchant's Trusts and New British Iron Co*, 38 S.J. 253. That the effect of a clause such as the present is to leave to the word interpreted its ordinary meaning, as well as the added meaning, see remarks of Selborne, L.C., in *Robinson* v. *Local Board of Barton*

Sect. 50. *Eccles*, 8 App. Cas. at p. 801, and of Esher, M.R. in *Bodger* v. *Harrison* (1893) 1 Q.B. at p. 167.

It must be remembered that the provisions of the Interpretation Act, 1889 (52 & 53 Vict. c. 63), apply to the present Act, and contain definitions of the expressions "land," "Bank of England," "Bank of Ireland," "India," "municipal borough," "High Court," "Rules of Court," "person," "writing," "felony," "county court," "short title," and "commencement."

"**Bankrupt.**"—This expression is used in section 25 (Appointment of New Trustees).

"**Contingent Right.**"—This phrase occurs in sections 26, 27, 30, and 33, and in the definition of "conveyance" in this section. This definition is taken from the Trustee Act, 1850 (13 & 14 Vict. c. 60), section 2. It includes rights which, together with "a future interest," are enumerated in section 6 of the Real Property Act, 1845 (8 & 9 Vict. c. 106), and thereby made capable of disposition by deed. Although under the last-mentioned Act a right of entry for forfeiture was held not to be included in the expression "a right of entry" (see remarks of Jessel, M.R., in *Jenkins* v. *Jones*, 9 Q.B.D. at p. 131), there appears to be no reason for so restricting the meaning of the phrase in the present Act.

All rights of unborn and unascertained persons are necessarily contingent rights.

As to the distinction between a *spes successionis* and a contingent estate or interest, see *Clowes* v. *Hilliard*, 4 Ch. D. 413, and *re Parsons, Stockley* v. *Parsons*, 45 Ch. D. 51. Since, however, the expression "contingent right" is applied in section 27 to the rights of unborn persons (see note, "Unborn persons," to section 27, *supra*, p. 112), it would seem clear that the phrase, as used in the present Act, is sufficiently wide to include a mere *spes successionis*.

For definition of "land" and "rights," see *supra*.

"**Convey and Conveyance.**"—This definition combines the separate definitions of conveyance and assignment in the Trustee Act, 1850 (13 & 14 Vict c. 60), section 2.

The words occur in sections 12, 16, 18, 26, 29, 31, 32, 33, 34, and 38.

Where an order is made vesting, or appointing a person to convey, the estate of an infant tenant in tail in possession, the effect is to bar the estate tail and remainders over. *Powell* v. *Matthews*, 1 Jur. N.S. 973; *re Montagu, Faber* v. *Montagu* (1896) 1 Ch. 549.

The meaning of the phrase "convey and conveyance," as applied to copyholds, was discussed in *Rowley* v. *Adams*, 14 Beav. 130.

For definitions of "land," "possessed," and "contingent right," see *supra*.

"**Devisee.**"—The definition of "devisee" in the Trustee Act, 1850 (13 & 14 Vict. c. 60), section 2, is as follows: "The word 'devisee' shall, in addition to its ordinary signification, mean the heir of a devisee and the devisee of an heir, and generally any person claiming an interest in the lands of a deceased person, not as heir of such deceased person, but by a title dependent solely upon the operation of the laws concerning devise and descent." The alteration in the language of the definition is presumably intended to include a personal representative of a devisee, and a personal representative of an heir of a deceased trustee, dying before section 30 of the Conveyancing and Law of Property Act, 1881, came into operation.

The present definition is not expressly restricted to land, but the sections in which the word "devisee" occurs only deal with land.

For definition of "rights," see, *supra*, p. 163.

"Instrument."—The expression "instrument," as used in the Conveyancing and Law of Property Act, 1881 (44 & 45 Vict. c. 41), is expressed by section 2 of that Act to include "deed, will, enclosure award, and Act of Parliament." The word in its ordinary signification includes deed, will, and codicil.

The word occurs in sections 1, 3, 4, 5, 10, 11, 13, 17, 18, 21, 22, 24, 37, and 44.

"Land."—The word "land" as used in the Trustee Act, 1850 (13 & 14 Vict. c. 60), is defined by section 2 of that Act to include "manors, messuages, tenements, and hereditaments, corporeal and incorporeal, of every tenure and description, whatever may be the estate or interest therein." By virtue of section 2 of the Conveyancing and Law of Property Act, 1881 (44 & 45 Vict. c. 41), the expression "land" in that Act included "land of any tenure and tenements and hereditaments corporeal and incorporeal, and houses and other buildings, and an undivided share of land," and the expression "manor" in that Act included "lordship and reputed manor or lordship." Section 3 of the Interpretation Act, 1889 (52 & 53 Vict. c. 63), provides that in any Act passed after the year 1850 the expression "land" shall, unless the contrary intention appears, include "messuages, tenements and hereditaments, houses and buildings of any tenure."

By virtue of the definition clauses in the Interpretation Act, 1889, and the present Act, the expression "land" in the present Act has therefore a widely extended meaning; it will include, *e.g*, a right of way (see *Jones* v. *Watts*, 43 Ch. D. 574), a rent-charge (see *re Harrison*, Seton, 6th edit., p. 1213), and leaseholds (see *re Rathbone*, 2 Ch. D. 483). In framing vesting orders under the Act it must be remembered that the word "land," if used in such vesting order, may not have the same extended meaning, and the addition of the other apt words may be necessary (see *re Harrison*, cited above).

The word "land" occurs in sections 6, 12, 26 to 34, 36, 38, 39, 40, 41, and 44.

"Mortgage and Mortgagee."—This definition is virtually

identical with that contained in section 2 of the Trustee Act, 1850 (13 & 14 Vict. c. 60). See re *Underwood*, 3 K. & J. 475; *Lawrence* v. *Galsworthy*, 3 Jur. N.S. 1049.

These words occur in sections 5, 6, 9, 12, 19, 29, 30, 40, and 48, and in the definition of "trust."

"**Pay and Payments.**"—As to payment into Court, see section 42.

For definitions of "stocks," "securities," and "transfer," see *supra*, p. 163.

"**Possessed.**"—In the Trustee Act, 1850 (13 & 14 Vict. c. 60), when vested freehold estates are being dealt with, the expression "seized of" is employed (see definition of "seized" in section 2 of that Act); when vested leasehold estates are being dealt with, the expression "possessed of" is employed (see definition of "possessed" in section 2 of that Act); when contingent interests are being dealt with, the expression "entitled to" is employed.

In the present Act there is no definition of the word "seized," which is only used in the definition of "convey" in the present section. In sections 26, 27, 28, and 30 the word "seized" is replaced by the expression "entitled to," which expression is not defined in the present Act, and is apparently applicable to freehold and leasehold estates and interests, whether in possession or reversion, and whether vested or contingent.

The word "possessed" is retained in the present Act, but the definition of it contained in section 2 of the Trustee Act, 1850, is amended by the addition of the words "receipt of income." The effect of this addition appears to be to make the expression applicable to freeholds as well as leaseholds. The expression "receipt of income" is presumably borrowed from section 2, subsection (iii.) of the Conveyancing and Law of Property Act, 1881 (44 & 45 Vict. c. 41). Why it was thought necessary to introduce these words is by no means clear, especially as the expression "possessed of" is not used in the present Act in any section taken from the Conveyancing and Law of Property Act, 1881, but is only used in sections taken from the Trustee Act, 1850.

The result appears to be that the accurate language of the Trustee Act, 1850, has been abandoned in favour of language which is by no means clear or accurate. Thus the word "possessed" in the present Act applies to vested interests in possession or reversion in leaseholds, but only to receipt of income of freeholds.

The expression "possessed of" occurs in sections 26, 27, 28, and 30, and in the definition of "convey," *supra*, p. 162. The word "possession" is used in its ordinary restricted sense in section 29, and in the definition of "property," *supra*.

For definition of "land," see *supra*, p. 162.

"**Property.**"—The earlier part of this definition is identical with that in the Conveyancing and Law of Property Act, 1881

(44 & 45 Vict. c. 41), section 2. The words "whether in possession or not" occur in the definition in the Conveyancing Act, 1882 (45 & 46 Vict. c. 39), section 1. The word "property" is used in sections 5, 8, 10, 11, 12, 13, 17, 18, 20, 21, 37, and 48.

"Rights."—This word occurs in sections 31 and 32.

"Securities."—Section 3 of the Court of Chancery Funds Act, 1872 (35 & 36 Vict. c. 44), contains the following definition of "securities" as used in that Act: "The term 'securities' includes Government securities and any security of any Foreign State, any part of Her Majesty's Dominions out of the United Kingdom, or any body corporate, or company, or standing in books kept by any body corporate or any person in the United Kingdom, and all stocks, funds, and effects."

The word "securities" used in the Conveyancing and Law of Property Act, 1881 (44 & 45 Vict. c. 41), was expressed by section 2 of that Act to include "stocks, funds, and shares"

The word "securities" occurs in sections 1, 2, 5, 19, 20, 24, and 42.

For definitions of "stock" and "payment," see *supra*, pp. 162, 163.

"Stock."—The expression "stock" as used in the Trust Investment Act, 1889 (52 & 53 Vict. c. 32), was expressed by section 9 of that Act to include fully paid-up shares. The expression as used in the Trustee Act, 1850 (13 & 14 Vict. c. 60), was expressed by section 2 of that Act to mean any fund, annuity, or security transferable in books kept by any company or society established or to be established, or transferable by deed alone, or by deed accompanied by other formalities, and any share or interest therein.

The definition of "stock" in the Trustee Act, 1850, was held to include shares in a limited company whether fully paid up or not, *re New Zealand Trust and Loan Company* (1893) 1 Ch. 403; *re Gregson* (1893) 3 Ch. 233; and the word in the present Act, so far as relates to vesting orders, has doubtless the same effect.

Section 10 of the Merchant Shipping Act, 1855 (18 & 19 Vict. c. 91), provides that any shares registered under the Merchant Shipping Act, 1854, should be deemed to be included in the word "stock" as expressed by the Trustee Act, 1850. Although this extended meaning is not given to the word by the present definition, this is done by the provisions of section 35, subsection 6, *supra*, p 131.

The word "stock" occurs in sections 1, 2, 5, and 12, where it will include only fully paid-up shares, and in sections 35, 36, and 39, where it will include shares whether fully paid up or not. The word also occurs in the definition of "transfer," *supra*.

Sect. 50.

"**Transfer.**"—The language of this definition is taken from the definition of "transfer" in section 2 of the Trustee Act, 1850 (13 & 14 Vict. c. 60), and from section 6 of the Trustee Extension Act (15 & 16 Vict. c. 55).

The expression is used in relation to "stock" in sections 35 and 42, and in the definition of "payment," *supra*, p. 162.

For definitions of "pay" and "stock," see *supra*, pp. 162, 163.

"**Trust and Trustee.**"—The present definition is virtually identical with that contained in section 2 of the Trustee Act, 1850 (13 & 14 Vict. c. 60). No such definition was contained in the Conveyancing and Law of Property Act, 1881 (44 & 45 Vict c. 41). For the definition the Trustee Act, 1888, see p. 4, *supra*. As pointed out in the notes to the several sections, some provisions of the Act apply only to particular classes of trustees; thus sections 1 to 9 deal only with trustees for investment purposes, see note, "A trustee . . . may invest," *ante*, p. 18; sections 10 to 12 do not, it is submitted, apply to constructive trustees, nor to executors or administrators, see note, "A trustee," *ante*, p. 50; sections 13 and 17 to 19 apply only to trustees under instruments, see notes, "A trustee," *ante*, pp. 68, 77, 79, 81; section 16 deals only with bare trustees, and section 25 expressly excludes executors and administrators.

As to Mortgages.—In consequence of the reference in 4 & 5 Will. 4. c. 23 to section 8 of Lord St. Leonards's Trustee Act (11 Geo. 4. and 1 Will. 4. c. 60), a doubt was raised whether the word "trustee" in the last-mentioned Act did not include a mortgagee. This doubt was only set at rest by the passing of a supplementary Act, 1 & 2 Vict. c 69. See *Spunner* v. *Walsh*, 10 Ir. Eq. Reps. 214. It was presumably to avoid any such doubt as to the meaning of the word "trustee," as used in the Trustee Act, 1850, that the exception of "the duties incident to an estate conveyed by way of mortgage" was inserted in the definitions of "trust" in section 2 of that Act. Upon general principles of law, so long as merely an equity of redemption remains in the mortgagor, the mortgagee is not a trustee for him, *Warner* v. *Jacob*, 20 C.D. 220, but when the mortgage moneys have been repaid by the mortgagor, together with interest and costs, the mortgagee is trustee of the property for the mortgagor, *re Brooke and Fremlin* (1898) 1 Ch. 647. In cases in which the present definition applies the evidence of the payment off must be complete before the Court will hold such a mortgagee to be a trustee. Thus where a mortgage of real estate was made to two persons not trustees, one of whom afterwards went abroad, and the property was sold by the mortgagor, and so much of the purchase-money as was payable to the mortgagees was invested in their joint names, it was held that the Court had no jurisdiction, upon a petition presented under the Trustee Act, 1850, by the mortgagor and the mortgagee within the jurisdiction, in the absence of the other mortgagee, to make an order vesting in the purchaser the estate of the absent mortgagee, *re Osborn's Mortgage Trust*, 12 Eq 392.

In a similar case, where the mortgagees were trustees of the money lent, the absent trustee mortgagee was held to be a trustee of the legal estate vested in him by the mortgage, *re Walker*, 3 Ch. D. 209. A deed may, of course, be so framed that it will operate as a trust for sale and conversion, and not merely as a mortgage deed, and in such case the mortgagee may be a trustee within the Act, *re Underwood*, 3 K. & J. 745, but a security, in the form of a trust for sale but in substance a mortgage, does not create a trust within the meaning of the Statute of Limitations (3 & 4 Will 4. c. 27), nor, presumably, within the meaning of this Act, *Locking* v. *Parker*, 8 Ch. 30. Where a mortgagee has sold under his power of sale, and has paid himself his debt and costs out of the purchase-money, he is a trustee of the surplus remaining in his hands, *Locking* v. *Parker* (cited above); *Charles* v. *Jones*, 35 Ch. D. 544; *Thorne* v. *Heard* (1894) 1 Ch. 599, (1895) A.C. 498. It is submitted that such a mortgagee is a trustee of such surplus moneys within the meaning of the present Act. Where the mortgage security and the mortgage debt become vested in different persons, *e g.* in the heir and the personal representative of a deceased mortgagee, the person in whom the security is vested may be held a trustee of the security for the other person, *re Skitter*, 4 W.R. 791.

The language of the definition appears to have no application to the estate or duties of the mortgagor, *London and County Banking Co.* v. *Goddard* (1897) 1 Ch. 642, in which case North, J., made the following comment: "Now it is said that by section 50, the interpretation clause, the expression 'trust' does not include the duties incident to an estate conveyed by way of mortgage. This is the old definition of trust from the time of the earliest Trustee Act—a definition well understood in Courts of Equity. I have always understood it to refer to the principle that during the continuance of a mortgage there is no relationship of trustee and *cestui que trust* between mortgagor and mortgagee. It is quite clear that if lands in mortgage are sold by the mortgagee, there may be surplus proceeds, of which the mortgagee becomes trustee; or after the money has been paid off, if the land had not been reconveyed, there might be a trust of it in the mortgagee. In my opinion this definition relates exclusively to an estate conveyed by way of mortgage, while that mortgage security continues to exist as such. Again, the provision is that a trust does not include the duties incident to the estate. It does not say that no trust shall be created in addition to those incidental duties. I do not see any expression to the effect that a vesting declaration is not applicable to property on mortgage where the instrument of charge contains an express trust. If there is the relationship of trustee and *cestui que trust* established, there is no reason why the parties should not have the full benefit of the enactment. In my opinion this limitation of the word 'trust' does not apply where, in a deed of charge, there is an express declaration that the mortgagor will hold the

Sect. 50.

legal estate on trust." So in a case where a mortgagor had covenanted to surrender copyholds and had received the mortgage money, he was held to be a trustee for the mortgagee. *In re Crowe's Mortgage*, 13 Eq. 26, followed In *re D. Jones & Company's Mortgage Trusts* (1888) W.N. 217.

In several recent cases it has been held that a married woman mortgagee is, after receipt of the mortgage money, a bare trustee of the land for the mortgagor within the meaning of section 16 of the present Act, *re Brooke and Fremlin's Contract* (1898) 1 Ch. 647; *re Howgate and Osborn's Contract* (1902) 1 Ch. 456; *re West and Hardy's Contract* (1904) 1 Ch. 145. Although these cases seem to have been decided without reference to the definition of trustee contained in the Act, it is submitted that they are authorities for the proposition that a mortgagee who has been paid off is a trustee within the meaning of the Act.

As to Constructive Trusts.—A vendor after contract for sale is regarded in equity as trustee of the property for the purchaser. For the purpose of vesting orders under the Act, an important distinction appears to exist between the cases of sales of land and sales of personalty. This will be found fully discussed in the notes to sections 30 and 31, *supra*, pp. 118–121.

Executors and administrators are, by virtue of this definition, included in the term "trustee," and the duties incident to their offices in the term "trust." This raises a question which will be found discussed in the notes to section 10, *supra*, p. 50, whether a power is given by the Act to appoint new trustees to perform the duties of an executor. See notes to section 25, *supra*, p. 102

For definitions of "mortgage," and "property," see *supra*.

Sect. 51.

Repeal.

Section 51.—The Acts mentioned in the schedule to this Act are hereby repealed except as to Scotland to the extent mentioned in the third column of that schedule.

As to the effect of a repealing section such as this, see the Interpretation Act, 1889 (52 & 53 Vict. c. 63), section 11, which is as follows: (1) "Where an Act passed after the year 1850, whether before or after the commencement of this Act, repeals a repealing enactment, it shall not be construed as reviving any enactment previously repealed, unless words are added reviving that enactment. (2) Where an Act passed after the year 1850, whether before or after the commencement of this Act, repeals wholly or partially any former enactment and substitutes provisions for the enactment repealed, the repealed enactment shall remain in force until the substituted provisions come into operation." Section 38 is as follows: (1) "Where this Act or any Act passed after the commencement of this Act repeals and re-enacts, with or without modification, any provisions of a former Act, references in any other Act to the provisions so repealed shall, unless the contrary intention appears, be construed as references to the provisions so re-enacted. (2) Where this Act or any Act passed after the commencement of this Act repeals any other enactment, then, unless the contrary intention appears, the repeal shall not (a) revive anything not in force or existing at the time at which the repeal takes effect; or (b) affect the previous operation of any enactment so repealed or anything duly done or suffered under any enactment so repealed; or (c) affect any right, privilege, obligation, or liability acquired, accrued, or incurred under any enactment so repealed; or (d) affect any penalty, forfeiture, or punishment incurred in respect of any offence committed against any enactment so repealed; or (e) affect any investigation, legal proceeding, or remedy in respect of any such right, privilege, obligation, liability, penalty, forfeiture, or punishment as aforesaid; and any such investigation, legal proceeding, or remedy may be instituted, continued, or enforced, and any such penalty, forfeiture, or punishment may be imposed, as if the repealing Act had not been passed."

"**Except as to Scotland.**"—The exception as to Scotland is of course due to the fact that the present Act does not "extend to Scotland." See section 52 and notes thereon, *infra*.

Section 52.—This Act does not extend to Scotland.

The Act applies to England and Ireland. As to the Isle of Man and Channel Islands, see *supra*, p. 21.

Since the Act does not apply to Scotland, the Acts and sections of Acts repealed by it are only repealed "except as to Scotland." See section 51.

Where the Act is merely declaratory of the law, the law thus declared may be treated as applicable in the case of Scottish trusts. See dictum of Lord Macnaghten in *Wyman* v. *Paterson* (1900) A.C. at pp 280, 281.

As to the jurisdiction of the High Court in England and in Ireland to make vesting orders affecting land in any part (except Scotland) of His Majesty's Dominions, see section 41, *supra*, and section 2 of the Trustee Act, 1893, Amendment Act, 1894, *infra*.

In *re Trubee's Trusts* (1892) 3 Ch. 55, a vesting order was made under the Trustee Act, 1850, of property settled by a Scottish will. Generally as to the jurisdiction of the English Courts in the matter of Scottish trusts, see *Ewing* v. *Orr-Ewing*, 9 A.C. 34; Howden on Trusts, Trustees, and Trustee Acts in Scotland, 1893 edit., pp. 368–384; and as to what decides the question whether a trust is English, Scottish, or Irish, see the last-cited authority, and cf. *Chapman* v. *Browne* (1902) 1 Ch. 785, 799.

Section 53.—This Act may be cited as the Trustee Act, 1893.

Section 54.—This Act shall come into operation on the first day of January one thousand eight hundred and ninety-four.

Some sections, however, have a retrospective effect. See section 5 (Enlargement of Express Powers of Investment), section 8 (Loans and Investments by Trustees), section 9 (Improper Investments), section 12 (Vesting Declarations), section 17 (Power to authorise Receipt of Money), section 45 (Indemnity by Beneficiary), section 47 (Settled Land Act Trustees).

SCHEDULE.

Session and Chapter	Title or Short Title	Extent of Repeal.
36 Geo. 3 c. 52	The Legacy Duty Act, 1796	Section thirty-two
9 & 10 Vict. c. 101	The Public Money Drainage Act, 1846	Section thirty-seven
10 & 11 Vict c. 32	The Landed Property Improvement (Ireland) Act, 1847	Section fifty-three.
10 & 11 Vict. c 96	An Act for better securing trust funds, and for the relief of trustees	The whole Act
11 & 12 Vict. c. 68	An Act for extending to Ireland an Act passed in the last session of Parliament, entitled "An Act for better securing trust funds, and for the relief of trustees"	The whole Act.
12 & 13 Vict. c. 74	An Act for the further relief of trustees	The whole Act.
13 & 14 Vict. c. 60	The Trustee Act, 1850	Sections seven to nineteen, twenty-two to twenty-five, twenty-nine, thirty-two to thirty-six, forty-six, forty-seven, forty-nine, fifty-four and fifty-five; also the residue of the Act except so far as relates to the Court exercising jurisdiction in lunacy in Ireland

Session and Chapter.	Title or Short Title.	Extent of Repeal.
15 & 16 Vict. c. 55	The Trustee Act, 1852	Sections one to five, eight, and nine; also the residue of the Act except so far as relates to the Court exercising jurisdiction in lunacy in Ireland.
17 & 18 Vict. c. 82	The Court of Chancery of Lancaster Act, 1854	Section eleven.
18 & 19 Vict. c. 91	The Merchant Shipping Act Amendment Act, 1855	Section ten, except so far as relates to the Court exercising jurisdiction in lunacy in Ireland.
20 & 21 Vict. c. 60	The Irish Bankrupt and Insolvent Act, 1857	Section three hundred and twenty-two.
22 & 23 Vict. c 35	The Law of Property Amendment Act, 1859	Sections twenty-six, thirty and thirty-one.
23 & 24 Vict. c 38	The Law of Property Amendment Act, 1860	Section nine.
25 & 26 Vict. c. 108	An Act to confirm certain sales, exchanges, partitions, and enfranchisements by trustees and others	The whole Act.
26 & 27 Vict. c. 73	An Act to give further facilities to the holders of Indian stock	Section four.
27 & 28 Vict. c. 114	The Improvement of Land Act, 1864	Section sixty so far as it relates to trustees; and section sixty-one
28 & 29 Vict. c. 78	The Mortgage Debenture Act, 1865	Section forty.
31 & 32 Vict. c. 40	The Partition Act, 1868	Section seven
33 & 34 Vict. c. 71	The National Debt Act, 1870	Section twenty-nine.
34 & 35 Vict. c. 27	The Debenture Stock Act, 1871	The whole Act.
37 & 38 Vict. c. 78	The Vendor and Purchaser Act, 1874	Sections three and six.
38 & 39 Vict. c. 83	The Local Loans Act, 1875	Sections twenty-one and twenty-seven.
40 & 41 Vict. c. 59	The Colonial Stock Act, 1877	Section twelve.
43 & 44 Vict. c 8	The Isle of Man Loans Act, 1880	Section seven, so far as it relates to trustees.
44 & 45 Vict. c. 41	The Conveyancing and Law of Property Act, 1881	Sections thirty-one to thirty-eight.

Schedule.

Session and Chapter.	Title or Short Title	Extent of Repeal.
45 & 46 Vict. c. 39	The Conveyancing Act, 1882	Section five.
46 & 47 Vict. c. 52	The Bankruptcy Act, 1883	Section one hundred and forty-seven.
51 & 52 Vict. c. 59	The Trustee Act, 1888	The whole Act, except sections one and eight.
52 & 53 Vict. c. 32	The Trust Investment Act, 1889	The whole Act, except sections one and seven.
52 & 53 Vict. c. 47	The Palatine Court of Durham Act, 1889	Section eight.
53 & 54 Vict. c. 5	The Lunacy Act, 1890	Section one hundred and forty.
53 & 54 Vict. c. 69	The Settled Land Act, 1890	Section seventeen.
55 & 56 Vict c. 13	The Conveyancing and Law of Property Act, 1892	Section six.

TRUSTEE ACT, 1893, AMENDMENT ACT, 1894.

57 VICT. C. 10.

An Act to amend the Trustee Act, 1893.

[18th June, 1894.]

BE it enacted by the Queen's most Excellent Majesty, by and with the advice and consent of the Lords Spiritual and Temporal, and Commons, in this present Parliament assembled, and by the authority of the same, as follows :—

Section 1.—In section thirty of the Trustee Act, 1893, the words "as heir, or under the will of a deceased person, for payment of whose debts the judgment was given or order made" shall be repealed.

Sect. 1.

Amendment of 56 & 57 Vict. c. 53. s 30.

See notes to section 30 of the Trustee Act, 1893, p. 117, *supra*.

Section 2.—The powers conferred on the High Court in England by section forty-one of the Trustee Act, 1893, to make vesting orders as to all land and personal estate in Her Majesty's dominions except Scotland, are hereby also given to and may be exercised by the High Court in Ireland.

Sect. 2.

Extension to Ireland of 56 & 57 Vict. c 53 s 41.

See notes to section 41 of the Trustee Act, 1893, p 143, *supra*.

Section 3.—In section forty-four of the Trustee Act, 1893, after the word "trustee" in the first two places where it occurs shall be inserted the words "or other person."

Sect. 3.

Amendment of 56 & 57 Vict. c. 53. s 44

See notes to section 44 of the Trustee Act, 1893, p. 150, *supra*.

Sect. 4.

Liability of
trustee in
case of
change of
character of
investment.

Section 4.—A trustee shall not be liable for breach of trust by reason only of his continuing to hold an investment which has ceased to be an investment authorised by the instrument of trust or by the general law.

The immediate object of this enactment was, it is believed, to set at rest any doubts as to the propriety of the retention by trustees of investments described in section 1, subsection (*g*) of the Trustee Act, 1893. The language of the present section is wide, and would apparently cover the case of investments which from any cause whatever have ceased to be investments authorised.

The subject of the duty of trustees as to the retention of investments is not one with which the Legislature has ever dealt as a whole, nor one upon which any clear general principle has ever been pronounced by the Court. Both the Legislature and the Court have from time to time laid down rules for ascertaining the propriety of new investments, but these rules are not expressly made applicable to the retention of existing securities. It would indeed appear obvious that where an investment is one which might be properly made at the moment, it is one which may be properly retained. When, however, the investment is not one which could be properly made at the moment, the question arises whether it can be properly retained. There is no principle that in the absence of direction to the contrary a trustee is bound to realise investments which are not such investments as might properly be made at the moment. Such an obligation would appear to arise only in one of the following ways: (1) under an express direction to convert, (2) under such a direction implied in the fact that the trusts are declared by will of a residuary personalty given as one fund for persons in succession, or (3) where the security of the fund demands such a course. Where there is an express direction to convert into money and invest, it must of course be strictly complied with, though if the trustees are given a discretion as to the time of sale, the Court will not interfere with its exercise, *re Hargreaves* (1901) 2 Ch. 547, *n.* Where there is no such express direction, but only such a direction implied in the limitation of the beneficial interest in residuary personalty to persons in succession, it is the duty of trustees, with all convenient speed, to get in and invest on trustee securities any existing investments of a risky, fluctuating, or wasting nature, but not necessarily all investments which are not of a nature authorised for the investment of trust moneys. *Howe* v. *Lord Dartmouth*, 7 Ves. 137. Where the trust is for persons in succession, but is declared of specific property, and not of an undefined fund (cf. *Pickering* v. *Pickering*, 4 Myl. & Cr. 289), or is declared by deed and not by will (*In re Van Straubenzee, Boustead* v. *Cooper* (1901) 2 Ch. 779), and where the trusts are not for persons in succession (*e.g.* a trust for an infant absolutely), there is no implied direction to convert and invest, and the trustee would not be justified in changing the investment except for the purpose of preserving the property from loss. It would appear, therefore, that it is only in the case of a certain class of trusts that the present section can be required.

It may be well to consider particular instances in which the question of the liability of trustees may arise by reason of an investment ceasing to be an investment authorised. (1) A change in the law, by virtue of which certain investments at present authorised should cease to be so authorised. This case is perhaps not likely to occur, as the present tendency is rather to enlarge than to restrict the range of investment. (2) A change in the circumstances which originally had to be considered in making the investment, e.g. a change in the rate of dividend of the ordinary stock in the case of investments authorised by the Trustee Act, 1893, section 1, subsection (l), or in population in the case of investments authorised by the Trustee Act, 1893, section 1, subsections (m) and (n). Having regard to the language of the subsections referred to, it is submitted that, apart from the present section, no liability would accrue from the retention of such an investment in the event suggested. (3) A fall in the value of a mortgage security. This is the case which is likely to be of greater frequency and importance than any other here suggested. It would appear however that, apart from this section, there was no obligation on trustees to call in a mortgage merely because the value of the security had fallen below the limit necessary for a new investment of trust moneys, re Medland, 41 C D. 476; re Chapman (1896) 2 Ch. 763. In all the above three cases it is submitted that trustees are still bound, as before the passing of this Act, to use reasonable care and discretion in considering whether or not a change of investment is desirable, and will not be protected by the present sections if they have failed to use such care and discretion. (4) Change in the nature of the investment through no act of the trustee. Where a loan to a partnership is authorised by the trust instrument, it is submitted that any change in the membership of the partnership will now, as before the passing of this Act, necessitate the calling in of the loan. Cf. re Tucker (1894) 1 Ch. 724; see also Smith v. Patrick (1901) A.C. 282. So too on the reconstruction of a company, and the issue of shares in the new in exchange for the shares in the old company, it is submitted that this Act would not justify the trustees in accepting and retaining the new shares without the sanction of the Court. Cf. re Morrison (1901) 1 Ch. 701; re New (1901) 2 Ch. 534; re Smith (1902) 2 Ch. 667. (5) Change in the nature of the investment due to the foreclosure of a mortgage. Doubtless, where the trustees have no power to invest in the purchase of land, foreclosure of a mortgage should, if possible, be avoided. It may, however, become inevitable, and in such a case the retention of the land might be a "continuing to hold an investment" within the meaning of the section. Cf. the

N

Sect. 4. reasoning of Buckley, J., in *re Smith* (1902) 2 Ch. 667. It is submitted that where the trustees in their discretion considered a retention of the land unsold to be beneficial to all parties interested, the section would operate to free them from liability in so doing. Cf. *re Tollemache* (1903) 1 Ch. 457. (5) Expiration of a period limited by the instrument. Where an instrument authorises the retention of an investment for a limited time only, it would seem clear that this section would not justify a retention beyond that period. Such a case indeed is not within the section if (as is suggested is the right construction) the word "authorised" means "authorised to be made," and not "authorised to be retained."

It was held by Kekewich, J., in *re Chapman, Cocks v. Chapman* (1896) 1 Ch. 323 (reversed by the Court of Appeal on another point (1896) 2 Ch. 763), that the section is not retrospective, viz. that it does not apply to the retention of an investment before the 18th June, 1894.

"A Trustee."—There is no definition of the word "trustee" in the present Act. It must presumably be given its widest meaning, so as to embrace the case of any person who might be made liable for breach of trust in the Courts of England or Ireland. The Act is not expressed not to extend to Scotland, but it is submitted that it has only the same scope as the principal Act, see p. 171, *supra*.

"Liable."—Cf. the language of section 8 of the Trustee Act, 1893, in which the word "chargeable" is used, and the remarks of Kekewich, J., on the distinction between these words in *re Chapman* (1896) 1 Ch. 323; cf. also section 3 of the Judicial Trustees Act, 1896, which gives protection in certain cases in which "a trustee is, or may be, personally liable for any breach of trust."

"Continuing to hold."—As to the general duty of trustees as to retention of investments, see note above, p. 176. As to the retention of redeemable stock, see section 2, subsection 3 of the Trustee Act, 1893.

"Ceased to be an Investment authorised."—It is submitted that this phrase must mean ceased to be an investment of the nature authorised "to be made" (and not "to be retained"), for any other construction would lead to very strange results, and further, in the majority of cases neither the instrument nor the general law would be found to afford any directions as to "retention" of investments. As to the various ways in which the event here contemplated may occur, see the note above. As to exemption from liability under section 3 of the Judicial Trustees Act, 1896, in the case of the neglect by an executor to get in an unsecured debt in reliance on a direction to retain existing investments, see *re Grindey, Clews v. Grindey* (1898) 2 Ch. 593.

That the usual power given to trustees for sale to postpone sale is merely a power of management, and does not give a discretion to retain a reversionary interest unsold, so as to deprive the tenant for life of income arising from the proceeds, see *Bowlls* v. *Bebb* (1900) 2 Ch. 107; and *ante*, p. 33.

Section 5.—This Act may be cited as the Trustee Act, 1893, Amendment Act, 1894.

Sect 4.

Sect. 5.

Short title.

JUDICIAL TRUSTEES ACT, 1896.

59 & 60 VICT. C. 35.

An Act to provide for the Appointment of Judicial Trustees and otherwise to amend the Law respecting the Administration of Trusts and the Liability of Trustees.

[14th August, 1896.]

This Act was the outcome of the report, dated 5th May, 1895, of a special committee of the House of Commons appointed on the 18th February in that year " to inquire into the liabilities to which persons are exposed under the present law as to the administration of trusts, and whether any future legislative provision might be made for securing adequate administration of trusts without the necessity of subjecting private trustees and executors to the risks which they now run." The committee recommended that the Court should have power to relieve a trustee from liability in case of certain breaches of trust, and also power to give sanction beforehand to departure from the terms of the trust in special cases. The former of these recommendations is carried into effect by the provisions of section 3 of the present Act, but the Act contains no provision for giving effect to the latter. (See note, " Or may be liable," to section 3, *infra.*) The committee further reported that " a case has been made out in favour of the establishment of a system under which private trusts can be administered, if so desired, by and under the control of some official or judicial authority, which should also have the custody of funds." After considering three methods in which this proposal might be carried out, viz (1) by the establishment of a public trustee, as in New Zealand, (2) by appointment of an officer of the Court—a modification of the present system of administration by the Court, and (3) the creation of a trustee similar to the judicial factor of the Scots Law, the committee recommended the adoption of the last of the three suggestions. Section 1 of the Act provides for the appointment of such a trustee, and the rules made under the provisions of section 4 of the Act provide for the administration of the trusts by him.

The machinery provided by the Act for the administration of trusts has hitherto been very little used.

BE it enacted by the Queen's most Excellent Majesty, by and with the advice and consent of the Lords Spiritual and Temporal, and Commons, in this present Parliament assembled, and by the authority of the same, as follows :—

Section 1.—(1.) Where application is made to the Court by or on behalf of the person creating or intending to create a trust, or by or on behalf of a trustee or beneficiary, the Court may, in its discretion, appoint a person (in this Act called a judicial trustee) to be a trustee of that trust, either jointly with any other person or as sole trustee, and, if sufficient cause is shown, in place of all or any existing trustees.

Sect. 1.

Power of Court on application to appoint judicial trustee.

(2.) The administration of the property of a deceased person, whether a testator or intestate, shall be a trust, and the executor or administrator a trustee, within the meaning of this Act.

(3.) Any fit and proper person nominated for the purpose in the application may be appointed a judicial trustee, and, in the absence of such nomination, or if the Court is not satisfied of the fitness of a person so nominated, an official of the Court may be appointed, and in any case a judicial trustee shall be subject to the control and supervision of the Court as an officer thereof.

(4.) The Court may, either on request or without request, give to a judicial trustee any general or special directions in regard to the trust or the administration thereof.

(5.) There may be paid to a judicial trustee out of the trust property such remuneration, not exceeding the prescribed limits, as the Court may assign in each case, subject to any rules under this Act respecting the application of such remuneration where the judicial trustee is an official of the Court, and the remuneration so assigned to any judicial trustee shall, save as the Court may for special reasons otherwise order, cover all his work and personal outlay.

(6.) Once in every year the accounts of every

Sect. 1. trust of which a judicial trustee has been appointed
shall be audited, and a report thereon made to the
Court by the prescribed persons, and, in any case
where the Court shall so direct, an inquiry into the
administration by a judicial trustee of any trust, or
into any dealing or transaction of a judicial trustee,
shall be made in the prescribed manner.

"Where Application is made to the Court."—As to the mode
of application, see Judicial Trustee Rules, 1897, 2, 3, 4, p 205,
infra. As to the Courts having jurisdiction, see section 2, *infra*,
and rules 29, 30, 31. As to the powers of the master, see
rule 27.

"Person creating or intending to create a Trust."—When
the creation of the trust is completed, the only persons who can
make application are the trustees and beneficiaries.

Even if the expression "person intending to create a trust,"
having regard to the provisions of subsection 2, be construed
as including a testator, it is unlikely that the Court would,
in the lifetime of a testator, appoint a trustee or executor of a
will. The proper course to be adopted by a testator desirous of
having his estate administered by a judicial trustee, would be to
appoint executors, and direct them to apply to the Court for the
appointment of themselves, or others, as judicial trustees.

"Or by or on behalf of a Trustee or Beneficiary."—In the
case of the administration of the estate of a deceased testator or
intestate, the persons authorised to make application appear to
be an executor, an administrator, a legatee or devisee, an heir,
or the statutory next of kin, but presumably not a creditor of
the deceased.

"The Court may in its Discretion."—The jurisdiction
conferred by the section is purely discretionary, *re Ratcliff*
(1898) 2 Ch. 352; *re Chisholm, Legal and Reversionary Society
v. Knight*, 43 Sol. Journal, p. 43.

"Appoint a Person . . . to be a Trustee."—As to vesting
the property, see rule 6. As to the persons whom the Court
will appoint, see subsection 3 and rule 5.

"A Judicial Trustee."—The "judicial trustee" is a creation
of the present Act. Cf. the "judicial factor" of the law of
Scotland, and see general note on the present Act, *supra*.

"Either jointly with any other Person or as Sole Trustee."—
The appointment of a judicial trustee to act jointly with a
private trustee would be likely to lead to inconvenience, and
possibly confusion. It was pronounced undesirable by Kekewich, J., in *re Martin* (1900) W.N. 129. As to the appointment
of a sole ordinary trustee by the Court, see note to section 25
of the Trustee Act, 1893, *supra*, p. 100.

"**If Sufficient Cause is shown in Place of all or any Existing Trustees.**"—The Trustee Act, 1850, which first gave power to the Court by order to appoint new trustees, was held not to authorise the removal of a trustee against his will, although the power was expressed to be "to make an order appointing a new trustee or new trustees either in substitution for or in addition to any existing trustee or trustees." *Re Blanchard*, 3 De G.F. & J. 131. Accordingly, as already pointed out (p. 96, *supra*), the Court has only power to remove a trustee against his will, on petition or summons under section 25 of the Trustee Act, 1893, in certain specified cases, viz. where the trustee is a felon, a lunatic, or a bankrupt, but in the generality of cases a trustee can only be removed against his will in an action commenced by writ, under the general jurisdiction of the Court. *Letterstedt* v. *Broers*, 9 A.C. 371, at p. 385; *re Martin's Trust*, 34 C.D. 621. It remains to be seen what construction the Court will put upon the present section, but it is submitted that the intention of the section is to give the Court jurisdiction to remove a trustee where cause is shown which would be sufficient to justify the removal of a trustee in an action, and that it will not be necessary to show such cause as would be required to enable his removal under section 25 of the Act of 1893, and this construction appears to have been adopted by Kekewich, J., in *re Ratcliff*, *supra*. See dictum at foot of p. 355 of the report. As against this view it may be urged that so serious a step as the removal of a trustee should not be taken upon mere affidavit evidence, in proceedings instituted by petition or summons.

"**Executor or Administrator.**"—Cf. notes to Trustee Act, 1893, sections 10 and 25, *ante*, pp. 50 and 102. *Re Ratcliff* (1898) 2 Ch. 352, is a case in which an application was unsuccessfully made for the appointment of a judicial trustee to act with or in place of a sole executrix. In that case Kekewich, J., in commenting on the Act, said, "The Court can, under this Act, do what it could not do before—remove an executor." It seems clear that the section is intended to give the Court this power. Rule 5 makes provision for the appointment of an executor or administrator to be a judicial trustee for the purpose of the collection and distribution of the estate of a deceased person.

"**Any Fit and Proper Person.**"—Cf. notes to sections 10 and 25 of Trustee Act, 1893, *ante*, pp 57 and 99. See rule 5 removing restriction as to the appointment of certain persons trustees. By virtue of the Interpretation Act, 1889, "person" includes a corporation. The authors believe that in one or two cases corporations have been appointed judicial trustees under the Act on giving security. For an interesting account of the system in force in the Australian colonies under which trusts are administered by incorporated societies or companies, see Vol. 116 of the Law Times, p. 40.

"**An Official of the Court may be appointed.**"—The official

Sect. 1. solicitor is in ordinary cases to be the official appointed. See rule 7. For definition of official of the Court, see section 5 and rule 7.

Subsection 3 does not limit subsection 1, and thus in the event of the absence of nomination, or of the Court not being satisfied as to fitness, the Court is not limited in its choice of a trustee to officials of the Court. *Douglas* v. *Bolam* (1900) 2 Ch. 749.

"**Directions as to the Trust.**"—General provisions as to the administration of trusts by the judicial trustee are contained in rules 8 (statement of trust property), 9 (security to be furnished), 10 (bank account and custody of documents), 11 (payment of money into bank), 12, 13, 28 (obtaining direction from the Court), 14 to 16 (accounts and audit)

"**There may be paid . . . such Remuneration.**"—The Court has in exceptional cases allowed remuneration to ordinary trustees, *re Freeman's Trusts*, 37 C.D. 148; Lewin, 10th edit., 248

See rules 17 to 19.

"**Accounts shall be Audited.**"—See rules 14 to 16 The annual audit by the accountant of the Court does not exonerate a *curator bonis* under the law of Scotland from liability in respect of an investment improperly made, *Hutton* v. *Annan* (1898) A.C. 289, and it is apprehended that the audit provided for by the Trustee Act and Rules would not give protection to a judicial trustee in a similar case.

"**Inquiry into Administration.**"—See rule 22.

Sect. 2.

Court to exercise jurisdiction.

Section 2.—The jurisdiction of the Court under this Act may be exercised by the High Court, and as respects trusts within its jurisdiction by a palatine court, and (subject to the prescribed definition of the jurisdiction) by any County Court judge to whom such jurisdiction may be assigned under this Act.

"**High Court.**"—See Judicial Trustee Rules, 1897 Rules 2, 3, and 4 (p 205, *infra*) as to the mode of application to the Court, and Rule 29 (p 218, *infra*) as to District Registries.

"**Palatine Court.**"—See rules 30 and 34 (pp. 219, 221, *infra*).

"**County Court.**"—See rules 31 and 34 (pp. 219, 221, *infra*).

Sect. 3.

Jurisdiction of Court in cases of breach of trust.

Section 3.—(1.) If it appears to the Court that a trustee, whether appointed under this Act or not, is or may be personally liable for any breach of trust, whether the transaction alleged to be a breach of trust occurred before or after the passing of this Act, but

has acted honestly and reasonably, and ought fairly
to be excused for the breach of trust and for omitting
to obtain the directions of the Court in the matter in
which he committed such breach, then the Court may
relieve the trustee either wholly or partly from
personal liability for the same.

(2.) This section shall come into operation at the
passing of this Act.

This section may best be introduced in the words of Farwell,
J., in *re Lord de Clifford's Estate* (1900) 2 Ch. 707: "The
Legislature has given to the Court a dispensing power under
section 3, subsection 1 of the Judicial Trustees Act, 1896, in
cases where a breach of trust has been established; that is to
say, the Court, having found that a breach of trust has been
committed, can relieve the trustee from personal liability if he
'has acted honestly and reasonably, and ought fairly to be
excused for the breach of trust.' Now relief against the
stringent rules of the common law in cases of forfeiture and
the like was an old head of equity, which was applied on
a thoroughly intelligible principle. The forfeiture being intended to secure the payment of money or the performance of
a contract, equity gave no relief unless it could secure the
payment of the money or the performance of the contract in
favour of the person entitled to enforce the forfeiture, and it
granted relief on the ground that it thereby gave effect to the real
contract between the parties. No such principle is applicable
to the present case, in which equity is called upon to give relief
against its own decree. The Courts of Equity have established
certain rules imposing liability on a trustee, although honest,
and the Legislature has now given the same Courts power to
grant relief against the consequences of a breach of those rules
There is nothing analogous in this to the principle underlying
the relief against forfeiture at common law, and there is in fact
no principle which can serve as a guide. I have merely to
find as a fact that the trustee has acted honestly and reasonably,
and ought fairly to be excused, and then I have power to grant
relief. It is obvious that the exercise of such a jurisdiction is
beset with great difficulty, and requires great caution. I must
bear in mind on the one hand that this relief is granted at the
expense of the *cestui que trust*, and on the other that the trustee
assumes an onerous post without reward, and the real difficulty
is to say what is fair and right as between the beneficiary who
entrusts his money to the trustee and the trustee who acts
gratuitously on his behalf."

"Trustee."—There is no definition of trustee in the Act.
The word must presumably be given its widest meaning, so as
to include all persons who may be liable as having committed a
breach of trust, *e.g.* directors of a company. Cf. note, "Trustee,"

Sect. 3. p. 178, *supra.* (It must be remembered, however, that by virtue of section 6 the Act does not apply to the trustees of charities, and only applies to English as apart from Scotch or Irish trustees.) The word includes an executor, see section 1 subsection 2, and *re Kay, Mosley* v. *Kay* (1897) 2 Ch. 518.

"**Or may be.**"—These words are not to be taken as meaning "or may become," and as applying to a contemplated breach of trust. The section is not intended to give the Court power to exercise its authority by anticipation, and to excuse a trustee from liability for a breach of trust contemplated. *Per* Kekewich, J., *re Tollemache* (1903) 1 Ch 457, 466. The words "or may be" point rather to doubtful questions of construction. *Per* Lindley, M.R , *re Grindey, Clews* v. *Grindey* (1898) 2 Ch. 593, 598. See general note on the Act, p. 180, *supra.*

"**Breach of Trust.**"—This includes a devastavit by an executor, *re Kay, Mosley* v. *Kay* (1897) 2 Ch. 518.

"**Has acted honestly and reasonably.**"—The burden of proof lies on the trustee claiming relief, *re Stuart, Smith* v. *Stuart* (1897) 2 Ch. 583 No general rule can be laid down as to the application of the section, but it will be applied "freely and fairly," *re Turner, Barker* v *Ivimey* (1897) 1 Ch. 536. "A narrow construction ought not to be put upon the section, having regard to the general object in view, which is plain, namely, the relief of trustees who have acted reasonably. 'Reasonably' must mean reasonably as trustees." *Per* Chitty, L.J , *In re Grindey, Clews* v. *Grindey* (1898) 2 Ch. 593, 601. The mere fact that a trustee has acted in the same way with his own money is not sufficient to excuse him for actions resulting in loss to the trust fund, *per* Farwell, J., *In re Lord de Clifford's Estate* (1900) 2 Ch. 707, 716, and failure to exercise the same caution in administering a trust fund as in dealing with his own money would seem to disentitle him to relief, *re Stuart, Smith* v. *Stuart* (1897) 2 Ch. 583.

Relief under this section has been refused in the following cases on the ground that the trustee had not acted "reasonably," viz. (1) *Wynne* v. *Tempest* (1897) W.N. 43, a case in which the trustee left trust moneys in the hands of his co-trustee, a solicitor, instead of seeing that they were paid into the bank of the trustee's account; (2) *re Turner, Barker* v. *Ivimey* (1897) 1 Ch. 536, a case in which a trustee had made a mortgage investment without taking the precautions prescribed by section 8 of the Trustee Act, 1893 ; (3) *re Stuart, Smith* v. *Stuart* (1897) 2 Ch. 583, a case similar to the last cited; (4) *Chapman* v. *Browne* (1902) 1 Ch. 785, a case in which trust funds were invested on a third sub-mortgage of lands in Ireland; (5) *In re Second East Dulwich Building Society*, 68 L.J. Ch. 196, 79 L.T. 726, a case in which a trustee, by accepting without inquiry what his co-trustee told him, made it possible for the co-trustee to misappropriate part of the trust fund.

Relief has been granted in the following cases, viz. (1) *re Kay,*
Mosley v. *Kay* (1897) 2 Ch. 518, a case in which an executor paid
a legacy and instalments of an annuity out of an estate which he
believed to be a very large one, but which on the establishment
of an adverse claim turned out to be insolvent. The relief was
restricted, however, to the payments made before issue of the writ
in the action establishing the adverse claim.   (2) *Re Grindey,*
Clews v. *Grindey* (1898) 2 Ch. 593, a case in which an executor
and trustee, relying on a direction to retain existing investments,
failed to call in an unsecured debt.   (3) *Perrins* v. *Bellamy*
(1899) 1 Ch 797, a case in which a trustee acted on the mistaken
advice of his solicitor that he had a power of sale.   (4) *Re Lord*
de Clifford's Estate (1900) 2 Ch. 707, a case in which trust
moneys were paid to the solicitor of the trust on his assurance
that they were required for the purposes of administration.

"**Omitting to obtain the Directions of the Court.**"—The
question whether in case of doubt application should be made
to the Court frequently resolves itself into a question of cost.
It is apprehended that although the Court has granted relief
under this section in a case in which a trustee did not apply to
the Court for directions as to calling in an unsecured debt of
£166, *re Grindey, Clews* v. *Grindey* (1898) 2 Ch 593, relief would
probably not be granted in a case such as that of *re Beddoe*
(1893) 1 Ch. 547, in which expensive litigation is embarked
upon on the advice of counsel without previous application to
the Court.   The trustee must in each case exercise his discretion.
Cf. the remarks of Lindley, M.R., and Rigby, L.J., in *Perrins*
v. *Bellamy* (1899) 1 Ch. 797, 801.

"**The Court may relieve.**"—The power is discretionary. The
Court may grant relief though the Act is not specially pleaded,
but where the section is relied on as a defence it should be
pleaded, *Singlehurst* v. *Tapscott Steamship Co.* (1899) W.N. 133.
Relief may be given in an action for a common account, *re Lord*
de Clifford's Estate (1900) 2 Ch. 707. In such a case the relief
should be claimed when the order for accounts is made, *re*
Stuart, Smith v. *Stuart* (1897) 2 Ch. 583.

Section 4.—(1.) Rules may be made for carrying into effect this Act, and especially—
   (1) for requiring judicial trustees, who are not
     officials of the Court, to give security for the
     due application of any trust property under
     their control :

       See Judicial Trustee Rules, 1897. Rule 9, p. 208, *infra.*

   (2) respecting the safety of the trust property,
     and the custody thereof :

       See rule 10.

(3) respecting the remuneration of judicial trustees and for fixing and regulating the fees to be taken under this Act so as to cover the expenses of the administration of this Act, and respecting the payment of such remuneration and fees out of the trust property, and, where the judicial trustee is an official of the Court, respecting the application of the remuneration and fees payable to him :

See rules 17 to 19.

(4) for dispensing with formal proof of facts in proper cases :

See rule 13.

(5) for facilitating the discharge by the Court of administrative duties under this Act without judicial proceedings, and otherwise regulating procedure under this Act and making it simple and inexpensive .

See rules 27, 28, and rule of March, 1899.

(6) for assigning jurisdiction under this Act to County Court judges and defining such jurisdiction :

See rule 31.

(7) respecting the suspension or removal of any judicial trustee, and the succession of another person to the office of any judicial trustee who may cease to hold office, and the vesting in such person of any trust property :

See rules 7, 20 to 24, and *Douglas* v. *Bolam* (1900) 2 Ch. 749.

(8) respecting the classes of trusts in which officials of the Court are not to be judicial trustees, or are to be so temporarily or conditionally :

See rule 26.

(9) respecting the procedure to be followed where the judicial trustee is executor or administrator:

See rule 25.

(10) for preventing the employment by judicial trustees of other persons at the expense of the trust, except in cases of strict necessity:

(11) for the filing and auditing of the accounts of any trust of which a judicial trustee has been appointed.

See rules 14 to 16.

(2.) The rules under this Act may be made by the Lord Chancellor, subject to the consent of the Treasury in matters relating to fees and to salaries and numbers of officers, and to the consent of the authority for making orders under the Solicitors Remuneration Act, 1881, in matters relating to the remuneration of solicitors. The rules shall be laid before Parliament and have the same force as if enacted in this Act, provided that if, within thirty days after such rules have been laid before either House of Parliament during which that House has sat, the House presents to Her Majesty an address against such rules or any of them, such rules or the rule specified in the address shall thenceforward be of no effect.

Rules have been made under this section—
August, 1897, Judicial Trustee Rules, 1897 (see p. 205, *infra*).
April, 1899, Judicial Trustee Rules, 1899 (see p. 222, *infra*).
April, 1900, Judicial Trustee Rules, 1900 (see p. 223, *infra*).

Section 5.—In this Act—

The expression "official of the Court" means the holder of such paid office in or connected with the Court as may be prescribed.

The expression "prescribed" means prescribed by rules under this Act.

Rule 7 of the Judicial Trustee Rules, 1897 (p. 207, *infra*), amongst other things prescribes, "(5) for the purpose of the

Sect. 5.   definition of 'official of the Court' in section 5 of the Act, any paid office in or connected with the Court shall be a prescribed office." For definition of "officer of the Court," see rule 33.

The expression "official of the Court" is used in section 1, subsections 3 and 5, and section 4, subsection 1 (1), (3), (8).

Sect. 6.

Short title, extent, and commencement of Act.

Section 6.—(1) This Act may be cited as the Judicial Trustees Act, 1896.

(2.) This Act shall not extend to any charity, whether subject to or exempted from the Charitable Trusts Acts, 1853 to 1894.

(3.) This Act shall not extend to Scotland or Ireland.

(4.) This Act, except as by this Act otherwise provided, shall come into operation on the first day of May, one thousand eight hundred and ninety-seven.

"Shall not extend to any Charity."—No such restriction is contained in the Trustee Act, 1893. See section 39 of that Act.

"Shall not extend to Scotland or Ireland."—The Trustee Act, 1893, extends to Ireland, but not to Scotland. The reason for the exclusion of Ireland from the present Act is presumably to be found in the Report of the Special Committee referred to in the general note on the present Act, p. 180, *supra*. The Committee reported that in Ireland no need was felt for any amendment of the law. As to the meaning of the phrase "extend to" used in this connection, see notes to section 52 of the Trustee Act, 1893, p. 163, *supra*, and see *Chapman* v. *Browne* (1902) 1 Ch. 785, in which case the applicability of section 3 of the present Act to an Irish settlement was discussed, but not decided.

"Except as in this Act otherwise provided."—This refers to section 3, subsection 2

COLONIAL STOCK ACT, 1900.

63 & 64 VICT. C. 62.

An Act to amend the Colonial Stock Acts, 1877 and 1892, and the Trustee Act, 1893.

[8th August, 1900.]

BE it enacted by the Queen's most Excellent Majesty, by and with the advice and consent of the Lords Spiritual and Temporal, and Commons, in this present Parliament assembled, and by the authority of the same, as follows :—

Section 2.—The securities in which a trustee may invest under the powers of the Trustee Act, 1893, shall include any Colonial Stock which is registered in the United Kingdom in accordance with the provisions of the Colonial Stock Acts, 1877 and 1892, as amended by this Act, and with respect to which there have been observed such conditions (if any) as the Treasury may by order notified in the London Gazette prescribe.

  The restrictions mentioned in section two subsection (2) of the Trustee Act, 1893, with respect to the stocks therein referred to shall apply to Colonial Stock. The Treasury shall keep a list of any Colonial Stocks in respect of which the provisions of this Act are for the time being complied with, and shall publish the list in the London and Edinburgh Gazettes, and in such other manner as may give the public full information on the subject.

Sect. 2.

Power for trustees to invest in Colonial Stock.

Short title.

Section 4.—This Act may be cited as the Colonial Stock Act, 1900, and the Colonial Stock Acts, 1877 and 1892, and this Act may be cited collectively as the Colonial Stock Acts, 1877 to 1900.

For list of the Colonial Stocks in respect of which the requirements of this Act have been complied with, see Supplementary Volume.

RULES OF THE SUPREME COURT
(TRUSTEE ACT), 1893.

ORDER LIV*b*.

PROCEEDINGS UNDER THE TRUSTEE ACT, 1893.

1. All proceedings in the High Court commenced O. 54b, r. 1. under the Trustee Act, 1893 (in this Order called "the Act"), shall be assigned to the Chancery Division of the Court.

These Rules (constituting Order LIV*b* of the Rules of the Supreme Court) regulate the procedure in applications under the Trustee Act, 1893.

"**All Proceedings . . . commenced under the Trustee Act, 1893.**"—The following is a list of proceedings under the Act:—
Applications for—
(*a*) Appointment of new trustees (section 25).
(*b*) Vesting order as to land (section 26).
(*c*) Releasing or vesting contingent rights in land of unborn persons (section 27).
(*d*) Vesting order in place of conveyance by infant mortgagee (section 28).
(*e*) Vesting order in place of conveyance by heir or devisee or personal representative of mortgagee (section 29).
(*f*) Vesting order consequential on judgment for sale or mortgage of land (section 30).
(*g*) Vesting order consequential on judgment for specific performance, partition, etc (section 31)
(*h*) Appointment of person to convey land or release contingent rights in land in lieu of vesting order (section 33).
(*i*) Vesting order as to stock and choses in action (section 35).
(*j*) Appointment of person to make transfer of stock in lieu of vesting order (section 35 (2))
(*k*) Vesting land, stock, or chose in action in trustees of charity or society (section 39).
(*l*) Payment into Court by trustees (section 42).
(*m*) Order for payment into Court by majority of trustees (section 42).

O. 54b, r. 1.   (*n*) Order on banker, broker, or depositary to pay or deliver moneys or securities to majority of trustees for the purpose of payment into Court (section 42).

(*o*) Sanction to sale of land reserving minerals, and *vice versâ* (section 44).

(*p*) Impounding interest of a beneficiary by way of indemnity for a breach of trust (section 45).

(*q*) Appointment of new trustees for the purposes of the Settled Land Acts (section 47).

(*r*) Payment out of Court.

O. 54b, r. 2.   **2. All applications under the Act may be made by petition except as otherwise provided under Order LV.**

.   "Applications under the Act."—See note to Rule 1, *supra*, p. 193.

"Made by Petition except as otherwise provided under Order LV."—The conjoint effect of this rule and Order LV., Rules 2 and 13a of the Rules of the Supreme Court (*infra*, p. 202) is that the following applications are made by petition :—

(1) Applications for vesting orders, except when consequential on the appointment of a new trustee, and except when a judgment or order has been given or made for the sale, conveyance, or transfer of any land or stock, or the suing for or recovering of any *chose in action; e.g* vesting orders in consequence of refusal of trustee to transfer to person beneficially entitled; vesting order in place of conveyance by infant mortgagee, or heir, devisee, or personal representative of mortgagee.

(2) Applications for release of contingent rights in land of unborn persons, except when consequential on the appointment of a new trustee, and except when a judgment or order has been given or made for the sale, conveyance, or transfer of any land.

(3) Applications for appointment of person to convey land or transfer stock, or release contingent right in land, except when consequential as aforesaid.

(4) Applications for order for payment into Court by majority of trustees.

(5) Applications for order on bankers, brokers, or depositaries for payment or transfer to majority of trustees for the purpose of lodgment in Court.

(6) Applications for payment out of Court where funds exceed £1000, and there has been no order declaring the rights of the parties, and the title does not depend merely upon proof of identity or birth, marriage, or death of any person.

(7) Application for leave to sell land reserving minerals, or *vice versâ*.

(8) Applications for impounding interest of a beneficiary by way of indemnity.   As to this, see *post*, p. 195.

The applications may doubtless be made in an action, thus,

payment out was made on further consideration in *Pullen* v. **O. 54b, r. 2.**
Isaacs (1895) W.N. 90, and the impounding of the interest of a ─────────
beneficiary is not usually made on an application expressly made
for the purpose, but usually in an action. Cf. *re Holt* (1897)
2 Ch. 525, and *infra*.

Payment into Court under section 42 (*ante*, p. 144) does not
involve an application to the Court (unless an order is required
under subsection 3 of section 42) but is made under rule 4
(*post*, p. 198).

Petitions.—*Form* For forms of petitions, see Daniell's
Chancery Forms For title, see rule 4*a*, *post*.

Petitioners.—Petition for vesting order of trust property,
or for release of contingent rights in trust land, or for appointment of person to convey trust land, or transfer trust stock, or
release contingent right in trust land, or payment out of funds.
See section 36 (1).

Petition for payment into Court by majority of trustees, or
for order on bankers, brokers, or depositaries for payment to
majority of trustees (see section 36 (1)), usually the majority
of trustees should petition.

Petition for leave to sell trust land apart from minerals, etc.
See section 36 (1), and rule 3, *infra*, p. 196.

Petition for impounding interest of a beneficiary by way of
indemnity. An application under this section hardly seems to
come within section 36 (1). The trustee should apply. In *re
Holt* (1897) 2 Ch. 525, it was argued that the powers of section 45
could only be enforced in an action, but it would seem open to
argument that such an application can be made by petition
under the rules. Usually the question of impounding arises in
an action by a beneficiary against a trustee. See as to this,
ante, p. 155.

Petition for vesting order as to mortgaged property, or for
appointment of person to convey or transfer mortgaged property,
or for sale of mortgaged land reserving minerals, etc. See section
36 (2).

Respondents. — Petitions relating to trust property by
persons beneficially interested should, as a general rule, be
served on the trustee or his representatives in whom the property has vested, and on any other beneficiaries interested in the
property. Service on the trustee or his representatives aforesaid is not necessary in the following cases, viz. · trustee
permanently abroad. *re Martin Pye*, 42 L T. 247; absconding
trustee, *Hyde* v. *Benbow* (1884) W N. 117, heir of trustee
permanently abroad, *re Stanley* (1893) W.N. 30; *re Greenwood*,
27 C.D. 359; trustee of unsound mind where no committee has
been appointed, *re East*, 8 Ch. 735; trustee refusing to convey,
re Crowe, 13 Eq. 26; *re Baxter*, 2 Sm. & Giff., App. V.; infant
heir; there is a conflict of authority, four decisions holding
service unnecessary, *re Tweedy*, 9 W.R. 398; *re Willan*, 9 W.R.
689; *re Davies* (1889) W.N. 215; *re Little*, 7 Eq. 323; and four
holding the contrary, *re Jones*, 22 W.R. 837; *re Adams* (1887)

O. 54b, r. 2. W.N. 175; *re Russell* (1866) W.N. 125; *re Cooper*, 9 W.R. 531. Probably the latest decision, that of Chitty, J., in *re Davies, supra*, where the attention of the Court was drawn to the conflict of authority, will be followed in future and service dispensed with. See also cases as to service of summonses for appointment of new trustees and vesting orders, *post*, p. 203. As to dispensing such service on other beneficiaries, see *post*, p. 203.

Petitions relating to trust property by trustees should, as a general rule, be served on the beneficiaries (see *post*, p. 203).

Petitions for *orders* for payment into Court by majority of trustees should be served on the minority of trustees, *re Bryant* (1868) W.N. 123, and the beneficiaries.

Petitions for orders on bankers, brokers, or depositaries for payment to majority of trustees should be served on the bankers, brokers, or depositaries, the minority of trustees, and the beneficiaries.

Petitions for leave to sell trust land apart from minerals, etc. (see rule 3, *infra*).

Petitions for impounding interest of a *cestui que trust* should be served on the beneficiary in question.

Petitions for payment out of Court (see rule 4, *infra*, and notes, p. 204).

Petitions for vesting orders, or orders appointing persons to convey mortgaged property, should, as a general rule, be served on the person upon whom the mortgaged property has devolved. This has been held unnecessary in the case of an infant, *re Willan*, 9 W.R. 689, but see the conflict of authority on this point, *supra*, p. 195, and in the case of a mortgagor of copyholds who covenanted to surrender but refused to do so, *re Crowe's Mortgage*, 13 Eq. 26, and see cases, *supra*, p. 195.

Petitions for sale of mortgaged land apart from minerals (see rule 3, *infra*).

Service.—The petition must state in a footnote the names of the persons to be served (O. 52, r 16), mentioning the respondents' names, *Meyrick v. Lawes* (1877) W.N. 223. As to the time to elapse between service and hearing, see O. 52, r. 17. Where an infant is named respondent and served, though unnecessarily, a guardian *ad litem* must be appointed and appear, or the petition amended by striking out the footnote stating the intention to serve the infant, *re Tweedy*, 9 W.R. 398. As to tendering 30s. to a respondent on a petition, and giving him notice that in case of his appearance his costs will be objected to, see O. 65, r. 27 (19).

Evidence.—The evidence may be given by affidavit (O. 38, r. 1).

O. 54b, r. 3.   3. An application under section forty-four of the Act may be made by the trustees authorised to dispose of the land as in the said section mentioned.

"**An Application under Section 44.**"—The application is by O. 54b, r. 3.
petition (see *ante*, p. 194). The necessity for this rule is not ——————
obvious; an application under section 44 would appear to be an
application concerning land subject to a trust, or subject to a
mortgage, as the case may be, and therefore to be within
section 36. The rule was made before the Amending Act was
passed extending the provisions of the section so as to include
mortgages, hence it only provides for the case of trust property.
For forms of petitions, see Daniell's Chancery Forms, p. 1091.
As to title of petition, see rule 4a, *infra*.

Petitioners.—In the case of trust property, having regard to
this rule, the trustees should be petitioners, though it is submitted that the application might be made on the application
of any person beneficially interested under section 36, subsection 1.

The beneficiaries may be co-petitioners jointly with the
trustees, *re Palmer*, 13 Eq. 408.

In the case of mortgaged property it is conceived that under
section 36 (2) any person beneficially interested in either the
equity of redemption or the mortgage money can apply. In
practice the mortgagee is invariably the petitioner. The mortgagee can petition, whether or not in possession, and although
he have commenced an action for foreclosure, *re Wilkinson*, 13
Eq. 634. In that case the petition was not entituled in the
cause, but in the matter of the 25 & 26 Vict. c. 108.

Respondents.—In the case of trust property, if not made
co-petitioners, all beneficiaries should, if possible, be made respondents. The authorities are, however, in conflict on the point.
Beneficiaries were held necessary parties in *re Palmer*, 13 Eq.
408; *re Hirst*, 45 C.D. 263; and in *re Woodcock*, 37 Sol. J. 250;
and in *re Hardstaff* (1899) W.N. 256, service was directed on
all beneficiaries "having regard to the state of the authorities."
In *re Wynn*, 16 Eq. 237, no beneficiaries were parties, nor in
re Wadsworth, 63 L.T. 217. In *re Pryse*, 10 Eq. 531; *re Nagle*,
6 C.D 104, and *re Powell*, 23 W.R. 151, the power of sale was
vested in trustees with the consent of the tenant for life, and it
was held that the remaindermen were not necessary parties.
Remaindermen were required to be served in *re Woodcock*, *supra*,
and *re Hardstaff*, *supra*, and the present practice may be taken
to be as above stated. Where one of the beneficiaries is out of
the jurisdiction, service on him may be dispensed with, even
though he be known to object to the application, *re Skinner*
(1896) W.N. 68. As to dispensing with service on beneficiaries,
see *post*, p. 203.

In the case of mortgaged property, a petition by mortgagees
must be served on the mortgagor, *re Hirst*, 43 C.D. 263, and the
reasoning of that case also applies to subsequent encumbrancers,
though it was held in *re Beaumont*, 12 Eq. 86, that subsequent
encumbrancers need not be served.

Service.—See *ante*, p. 196.

Evidence.—The evidence may be given by affidavit (O 38,
r. 1). An order may be made in favour of a mortgagee,

O. 54b, r. 3 notwithstanding the opposition of a later mortgagee or the
————— mortgagor, *re Wilkinson, supra.*

Form of Order.—See Seton, 1748 ; *re Willway,* 32 L.J. Ch.
226 ; *re Thomas,* 40 Sol. J. 98.

O. 54b, r. 4.   **4. (1.)** Where a trustee desires to make a
————— lodgment in Court under section forty-two of the
Lodgment Act he shall make and file an affidavit intituled
under in the matter of the trust (described so as to
section 42 be distinguishable) and of the Act, and setting
forth—

> (*a*) A short description of the trust and of the
> instrument creating it.
>
> (*b*) The names of the persons interested in and
> entitled to the money or securities, and
> their places of residence to the best of his
> knowledge and belief.
>
> (*c*) His submission to answer all such inquiries
> relating to the application of the money
> or securities paid into Court, as the Court
> or Judge may make or direct.
>
> (*d*) The place where he is to be served with any
> petition, summons, or order or notice of
> any proceeding relating to the money or
> securities.

Provided that if the fund consists of money or
securities being, or being part of, or representing a
legacy or residue to which an infant or person
beyond seas is absolutely entitled, and on which the
trustee has paid the legacy duty, or on which no
duty is chargeable, the trustee may make the lodgment (without an affidavit) on production of the
Inland Revenue certificate in manner prescribed by
the Supreme Court Funds Rules for the time being
in force.

(2.) Where the lodgment in Court is made on
affidavit—

> (*a*) the person who has made the lodgment
> shall forthwith give notice thereof, by
> prepaid letter through the post, to the
> several persons whose names and places
> of residence are stated in his affidavit as

interested in or entitled to the money or <u>O. 54b, r. 4.</u>
securities lodged in Court;

(*b*) no petition or summons relating to the money or securities shall be answered or issued unless the petitioner or applicant has named therein a place where he may be served with any petition or summons, or notice of any proceeding or order relating to the money or securities or the dividends thereof;

(*c*) service of any application in respect of the money or securities shall be made on such persons as the Court or Judge may direct.

"**Lodgment . . . under Section 42.**"—This means, under subsection 1 only of that section, cases in which no order is requisite. Where an order is requisite under subsection 3 of section 42, the application is by petition (see *ante*, p. 194).

"**Affidavit.**"—The affidavit must have a printed schedule. Supreme Court Funds Rules, rule 41, *infra*, p. 200. It should be sworn by all the trustees, but the affidavit of one of two trustees has been held sufficient, *Anon*, 1 Jur. N.S. 974. The amount to be lodged should be expressed in words, not figures, *re Watts*, 24 W.R. 701.

"**Description of the Trust and of the Instrument creating it.**"—In the Trustee Relief Act, 1847, the words "shortly describing the instrument creating the trust" appeared in the body of the enactment, and, it would seem, limited the enactment not only to persons who were trustees, but to trustees of trusts created by instrument. Cf. *Matthew v. Northern Assurance Co.*, 9 C.D. 80, at p. 87. There is no such implied limit in section 42 of the Act of 1893, which relies on the definition in section 50 for the inclusion of executors, and which definition also includes implied and constructive trusts. It is conceived that the terms of this rule cannot limit the provisions of the Act.

"**Money or Securities.**"—Section 42 of the Act authorises the payment into Court of money or securities. See the definition of securities applicable to that section, *ante*, p. 167. From this it would appear that shares in foreign companies and shares not fully paid up are securities within the meaning of the Act. Form 16 of the Appendix of forms under the Supreme Court Funds Rules, 1894, has a note, "describe securities, if any, which must be such as the paymaster can properly accept." The practice would appear to be that all kinds of securities may be lodged except those of any company

O. 54b, r. 4. not established in the United Kingdom, and that all shares must be fully paid up and free from any liability. (Annual Practice, Vol. II., note to rule 30 of Supreme Court Funds Rules, 1894.) It is further stated in the same note that securities coming within the exception may be ordered to be placed in a box and so lodged under Practice Masters Rules (22). That rule, however, appears to have no bearing on lodgment in Court under the Trustee Act. It seems a matter for consideration how far the note to Form 16 of the Supreme Court Funds Rules can limit the express provisions of the section.

"**The Place where he is to be served.**"—These words do not dispense with the necessity for personal service on the trustee of a petition or summons dealing with the fund, but if personal service cannot be effected, service at the address for service given in the affidavit may be ordered, *exparte Baugham*, 16 Jur. 325; *re Lawrence*, 14 W.R. 93; see 42 Sol. J. 517.

"**Lodgment (without an Affidavit).**"—The Supreme Court Funds Rules provide (r. 41) as follows:—

Lodgments under the Trustee Act, 1893.

41. Where a legal personal representative desires to lodge funds in Court, under the Trustee Act, 1893, without an affidavit, he shall leave with the paymaster a request, signed by him or his solicitor, with a certificate of the Commissioners of Inland Revenue; such request and certificate to be in the Form No. 16 in the Appendix to these Rules, with such variations as may be necessary, or, as regards such certificate, in such other form as shall from time to time be adopted by the said Commissioners, with the consent of the Lords Commissioners of Her Majesty's Treasury. The money or securities so lodged shall be placed to the credit mentioned in such request.

When a trustee or other person desires to lodge funds in Court in the Chancery Division under the Trustee Act, 1893, upon an affidavit, he shall annex to such affidavit a schedule in the same printed form as the lodgment schedule to an order, setting forth—

(*a*) His own name and address:

(*b*) The amount and description of the funds proposed to be lodged in Court:

(*c*) The ledger credit in the matter of the particular trust to which the funds are to be placed:

(*d*) A statement whether legacy or estate or succession duty (if chargeable) or any part thereof has or has not been paid:

(*e*) A statement whether the money or the dividends on the securities so to be lodged in Court, and all accumulations of dividends thereon, are desired to be invested in any and what description of Government securities, or whether it is deemed unnecessary so to invest the same.

An office copy of such schedule is to be left with the paymaster.

And see rule 30 and form 16.   O. 54b, r. 4.

"**Forthwith give Notice thereof.**"—This renders obsolete
re Graham (1891) 1 Ch. 151.

"**Service of any Application.**"—The judges of the Chancery
Division in January, 1894, gave the following directions as to
service :—

We, the undersigned judges of the Chancery Division of
the High Court of Justice, direct that all applications dealing
with funds lodged in Court on affidavit under the Trustee Act,
1893, or under the repealed Trustee Relief Acts, be in ordinary
cases served upon the trustees and the person named in the
trustee's affidavit as interested in or entitled to the money or
securities. When a special direction is required, it should be so
stated on the petition or summons, and the petition should, when
presented, be referred to Chambers for such direction to be
given before it is answered for hearing in Court.

JOSEPH W. CHITTY, J.
FORD NORTH, J.
JAMES STIRLING, J.
ARTHUR KEKEWICH, J.
ROBERT ROMER, J.

The directions only apply to funds lodged on affidavit. In
the case of funds lodged without affidavit, under the proviso to
rule 4 (1) the trustee is not served.

For the old practice as to service; and generally, under the
repealed Trustee Relief Acts, see Morgan's Chancery Acts,
6th edit., pp. 50–61.

4A. Applications to deal with funds lodged in   O. 54b,
Court under the Act shall be intituled in the same   r. 4a.
manner as the affidavit or request on which the
funds were lodged. All other applications under   Application
the Act, not made in any pending cause or matter,   under Act,
                                                       how intituled.
shall be intituled in the matter of the trust (described
so as to be distinguishable) and of the Act. Every   Sections, when
petition or summons for a vesting order, or the   to be remem-
                                                       bered in
appointment of a person to convey, shall state the   petition or
section or sections of the Act under which it is   summons.
proposed that the order shall be made.

This rule was added in February, 1895. Rules of Supreme
Court (5).

"**In the same Manner as the Affidavit.**"—See rule 4 (1).

"**All other Applications under the Act.**"—See notes to
rule 1, *ante*, p. 193.

O. 54b, r. 4a.   "**Vesting Order or Appointment of a Person to convey.**" —This requirement is in accordance with the previous practice (see *re Moss*, 37 C.D. 513).

"**All other Applications . . . shall be entituled.**"—An application for an order vesting land registered under the Land Transfer Acts, 1875 and 1897, must, if the course of applying for rectification of the register (see *ante*, p. 111) is adopted, be also entituled in the matter of the Land Transfer Acts, 1875 and 1897.

An application for the appointment of new trustees for the purposes of the Settled Land Acts will usually be made under those Acts (see *ante*, p. 157). Where new trustees are required for the general purposes of the settlement as well as for the purposes of the Acts, it is conceived the appointment could be made under sections 25 and 47 of the Trustee Act, 1893, on a summons entituled in the matter of the Trustee Act alone, but it will be safer to also entitule such a summons in the matter of the Settled Land Acts.

O. 54b, r. 5.   5. Order LV., Rule 13A, is hereby repealed, and the following rule shall be substituted therefor :—

Application by summons under Trustee Act, 1893

Appointment of new trustees and vesting order

Vesting order

13A. Any of the following applications under the Trustee Act, 1893, may be made by summons :—

(*a*) An application for the appointment of a new trustee with or without a vesting or other consequential order.

(*b*) An application for a vesting order or other order consequential on the appointment of a new trustee, whether the appointment is made by the Court or a Judge, or out of Court.

Vesting order on sale, etc.

(*c*) An application for a vesting or other consequential order in any case where a judgment or order has been given or made for the sale, conveyance, or transfer of any land or stock [or the suing for or recovering any close in action].

Payment out of Court.

(*d*) An application relating to a fund paid into Court in any case [coming within the provisions of rule 2 of this Order].

The words in brackets were substituted for the words, "where the money or securities in Court does not or do not exceed £1000 or £1000 nominal value," by the Rules of the Supreme Court, February, 1895, rule 6.

O. 54b, r. 5.

Under paragraph (d), *supra*, the following applications are made by summons:—

(*a*) Applications for payment or transfer to any person of any cash or securities in Court in any case where there has been a judgment or order declaring the rights, or where the title depends only upon proof of the identity or the birth, marriage, or death of any person (O. 55, r. 2 (1)).

(*b*) Applications for payment or transfer to any person of any cash or securities in Court where the cash does not exceed £1000 or the securities do not exceed £1000 nominal value (O. 55, r. 2 (2)).

(*c*) Applications for payment to any person of the dividend or interest on any securities in Court whether to a separate account or otherwise (O. 55, r. 2 (3)).

(*d*) Applications relating to a fund paid into Court as to the guardianship, maintenance, and advancement of infants (O. 55, r. 2 (12).

(*e*) Such other applications relating to a fund in Court as the judge may think fit to dispose of at Chambers (O. 55, r 2 (18)).

Under this last heading the judge has power to dispose in Chambers of such parts of the matters brought before him on petition as he thinks can be more conveniently disposed of in Chambers, *re Tweedy*, 28 C.D. 529.

"Summons."—*I.e.* either originating summons, or, if in a pending cause or matter, ordinary summons. For forms of summonses, see Daniell's Chancery Forms. For title, see rule 4a, *ante*, p 201.

Applicants.—See section 36 (1) of the Trustee Act, 1893, but the trustees are not the proper persons to apply for payment out of funds in Court.

Respondents—Applications by beneficiaries for the appointment of a new trustee or for a vesting order should, as a general rule, be served on the trustee or his representatives in whom the property has vested, and on any other beneficiaries interested in the property. Service on the trustee or his representatives aforesaid is not necessary in the cases mentioned on p. 195, *ante*. To the authorities there cited may be added the following: *re Bignold*, 7 Ch. 223, appointment of new trustee in place of trustee permanently abroad; the like application where the trustee was of unsound mind, and no committee had been appointed, *re Green*, 10 Ch. 272; the like application where the trustee had absconded, *re Harford*, 13 C.D. 135; the like application where the trustee was from physical infirmity incapable of acting, *re Weston* (1898) W.N. 151.

If a committee of a lunatic trustee has been appointed, he should be served, as he may have a claim for costs, *re Saumarez*, 8 De G.M. & G. 390.

Service on beneficiaries may also be dispensed with in some cases. The judge exercises his discretion according to the circumstances of each case, and satisfies himself that there is a fair

O. 54b, r. 5. hearing of all possible contentions as to the persons to be appointed trustees and otherwise. *Practice note* (1901, W.N. 85). Thus in *re Smyth*, 2 De G & Sm. 781, service was dispensed with on *cestuis que trust* under settlements of shares in the trust estate of which new trustees were being appointed, the trustees of such settlements alone being served; and see *re Blanchard*, 3 De G.F. & J. 131, at p. 137; *re Lightbody*, 52 L.T. 40, *re Wilson*, 31 C.D. 522, where service was dispensed with on a *cestui que trust* who was abroad.

The proposed new trustee ought not to be served or appear for the mere purpose of consenting to act, *re Draper*, 2 W.R. 440.

Applications by trustees should as a rule be served on the beneficiaries, but such service may be in some cases dispensed with as above mentioned.

Summons relating to funds lodged in Court on affidavit should be served in accordance with the judge's directions dated January, 1894 (see *ante*, p. 201). In the case of applications dealing only with payment of income, a special direction should be asked for, dispensing (in accordance with the old practice, *re Marner*, 3 Eq. 432) with service on remaindermen.

Summonses relating to a legacy or share of residue paid in without an affidavit are not served on the trustee (see *ante*, p. 201).

Service.—The ordinary practice as to service of summonses applies. Order 65, r. 27 (19) as to tendering 30s. to a respondent *on a petition* and giving him notice that if he appears his costs will be objected to, does not apply to a respondent on a summons.

Evidence.—The evidence may be given by affidavit (O. 38, r. 1). On a summons for the appointment of new trustees there must be an affidavit of fitness of the new trustee, and his written consent to act must be produced.

O. 54b, r. 6.

Repeal

6. The following rules are hereby repealed :—

Order LII. Rules 19, 20, 21, 22;

Order LV. Rule 2 (4), (5), (8).

Chancery Funds Amended Orders, 1874.

Orders 5, 6, 7, 8, 9, and 10.

O. 54b, r. 7.

Citation.

7. These rules may be cited as the "Rules of the Supreme Court (Trustee Act), 1893," and each rule may be cited separately according to the heading thereof with reference to the Rules of the Supreme Court, 1883. They shall come into operation on the first day of January, 1894.

JUDICIAL TRUSTEE RULES.

RULES UNDER THE JUDICIAL TRUSTEES ACT, 1896.

1.—The following rules may be cited as the Judicial Trustee Rules, 1897, and shall apply as far as practicable to all matters and proceedings under the Judicial Trustees Act, 1896 (in these rules called the Act).

Appointment of Judicial Trustee.

2.—An application to the Court to appoint a judicial trustee shall be in the Chancery Division, and—

    (*a*) if not made in a pending cause or matter, shall be made by originating summons; and

    (*b*) if made in a pending cause or matter, shall be made as part of the relief claimed, or by summons in the cause or matter.

3.—(1.) The summons shall be served,—

    (*a*) where the application is made by or on behalf of a trustee, on the other trustee (if any); and

    (*b*) where the application is made by or on behalf of a beneficiary, on the trustees (if any),

and in either case on such (if any) of the beneficiaries as the Court directs.

(2.) Where the application is made by or on behalf of a person creating or intending to create a trust, the summons, subject to any direction of the Court, need not be served on any person.

Rule 3.

(3.) The Court may give any directions it thinks fit, either dispensing with the service of the summons on any person on whom it is required to be served under this rule, or requiring the service of the summons on any person on whom it is not required to be served under this rule.

Rule 4.

Statement to be supplied on application.

4.—(1.) Where an application is made for the appointment of a judicial trustee by originating summons, the applicant must, when he takes out the summons, supply for the use of the Court a written statement signed by him containing the following particulars so far as he can gain information with regard to them :—

(a) A short description of the trust and instrument by which it is, or is to be, created, and of the relation which the applicant bears to the trust;

(b) If a person is nominated as judicial trustee, the name and address of the person nominated, and short particulars of the reasons which lead to his nomination;

(o) If a person is nominated as judicial trustee, a statement whether it is proposed that the person nominated should be remunerated or not;

(d) Short particulars of the trust property, with an approximate estimate of its income, and capital value;

(e) Short particulars of the incumbrances (if any) affecting the trust property;

(f) A statement whether it is proposed that the judicial trustee should be a sole trustee or should act jointly with other trustees;

(g) Particulars as to the persons who are in possession of the documents relating to the trust;

(h) The names and addresses of the beneficiaries and short particulars of their respective interests;

(*i*) Any exceptional circumstances specially affecting the administration of the trust.

(2.) An affidavit by the applicant verifying the statement shall be sufficient *primâ facie* evidence of the particulars contained in the statement.

(3.) Where the applicant cannot gain the information necessary for making the required statement on any point, he must mention the fact in his statement.

5.—(1.) The Court shall not be precluded by any existing practice as to the appointment of trustees from appointing any person to be a judicial trustee by reason of that person being a beneficiary, or a relation or husband or wife of a beneficiary, or a solicitor to the trust or to the trustee, or to any beneficiary, or a married woman, or standing in any special position with regard to the trust.

(2.) A person may be appointed to be a judicial trustee of a trust although he is already a trustee of the trust.

6. On the appointment of any person to be judicial trustee the Court shall make such vesting or other orders and exercise such other powers as may be necessary for vesting the trust property in the judicial trustee either as sole trustee or jointly with other trustees as the case requires.

Appointment of Official of Court to be Judicial Trustee.

7.—(1.) Where an official of the Court is appointed judicial trustee, the official solicitor of the Court shall (subject to the provisions hereinafter contained in rules twenty-nine, thirty, and thirty-one) be so appointed, unless, for special reasons, the Court directs that some other official of the Court should be so appointed.

(2.) Any official of the Court appointed to be a judicial trustee shall, on his ceasing to hold office,

[margin: Rule 4]

[margin: Rule 5. Removal of restriction as to appointment of certain persons to be trustees.]

[margin: Rule 6. Vesting orders.]

[margin: Rule 7. Official judicial trustee.]

Rule 7.

cease to be such a trustee without any formal resignation.

(3.) Where an official of the Court is judicial trustee, any trust property vested in or held by him shall be vested in and held by him under his official title and not in his own name.

(4.) Where an official of the Court appointed to be a judicial trustee of a trust dies, or ceases to hold office, his successor in office shall, unless the Court otherwise directs, become judicial trustee of the trust without any order of the Court or formal appointment, and the trust property shall, without any conveyance, assignment, or transfer, in such a case become vested in the successor as it was vested in his predecessor in office.

(5.) For the purpose of the definition of " official of the Court," in section five of the Act, any paid office in or connected with the Court shall be a prescribed office.

Administration of the Trust.

Rule 8.

Statement of trust property

8.—(1.) A judicial trustee must, unless in any case the Court considers that it is unnecessary, as soon as may be after his appointment, furnish the Court with a complete statement of the trust property, accompanied with an approximate estimate of the income and capital value of each item.

(2.) It shall be the duty of the judicial trustee to give such information to the Court as may be necessary for the purpose of keeping the statement of the trust property correct for the time being.

Rule 9.

Security.

9.—(1.) A judicial trustee, if not an official of the Court, must give security to the Court for the due application of the trust property, unless the Court dispenses with security under this rule.

(2.) The Court may, on the appointment of a judicial trustee, or at any time during his continuance in office as judicial trustee, dispense with security on the application either of the person who is to be appointed or is judicial trustee, or of any person appearing to the Court to be interested in the trust, and shall do so where a judicial trustee is appointed on the application of a person creating or intending to create a trust, and that person desires that security should be dispensed with, unless for special reasons the Court consider that security is in such a case necessary or desirable.

(3.) The security must be given, either by recognisance, bond, or otherwise, as the Court directs, and with such sureties as the Court approves.

(4.) If the Court is satisfied that sufficient provision is made for the safety of the capital of the trust property, the amount of the security shall, in ordinary cases, be an amount exceeding by twenty per centum the income of the trust property as estimated by the Court.

(5.) The Court may at any time require that the amount or nature of the security given by a judicial trustee under this rule be varied, or that security be given where it has previously been dispensed with, and a judicial trustee shall comply with any such requirement.

(6.) It shall be a condition of every recognisance, bond, or other form of security given under this rule that the judicial trustee shall give immediate notice to the Court of the death or insolvency of any of his sureties.

(7.) Any recognisance, bond, or other form of security given for the purpose of this rule may be vacated in such manner and subject to such conditions as the Court may direct.

(8.) Where security is not dispensed with, the appointment of a person to be judicial trustee shall not take effect. until he has given the security required by the Court under this rule.

(9.) Any premium payable by a judicial trustee to any guarantee company on account of his security may, if the Court so directs, be paid out of the trust property.

10.—(1.) When a judicial trustee is appointed, a separate account for receipts and payments on behalf of the trust must be kept in the name of the trustees at some bank approved by the Court.

(2.) All title deeds and all certificates and other documents which are evidence of the title of the trustee to any of the trust property shall be deposited either with that bank or in such other custody as the Court directs.

(3.) The deeds or documents must be deposited in the names of the trustees, and the judicial trustee must give notice to the body or person with whom the deeds or documents are so deposited not to deliver any of them over to any person except on a request signed by the judicial trustee and countersigned by the officer of the Court, and also to allow any person authorised by the officer of the Court in writing to inspect them during business hours.

(4.) The judicial trustee must deposit with the Court a list of all deeds or documents deposited in any custody in pursuance of this rule, and must give information to the Court from time to time of any variation to be made in the list.

(5.) The judicial trustee must, if at any time directed by the Court, give an order to the bank at which the trust account is kept, not to pay at any one time any sum over a specified amount out of the trust account except on an order countersigned by the officer of the Court.

(6.) Any payments on account of the income of the trust property may be provided for by means of a standing order to the bank at which the trust account is kept.

(7.) The Court may give such directions to the judicial trustee as may, in the opinion of the Court, be necessary or expedient for carrying this rule into effect, and for securing the safety of the trust property.

(8.) Where an official of the Court is judicial trustee, the Court may direct that, instead of a separate account of the receipts and payments on behalf of the trust being kept at some bank approved by the Court, all receipts on behalf of the trust may be dealt with, and all payments on behalf of the trust may be made, in such manner, and subject to such regulations as to the accounts to be kept of the receipts and payments and the procedure to be followed in dealing therewith, as the Treasury direct.

Rule 10.

11.—A judicial trustee must pay all money coming into his hands on account of his trust without delay to the trust account at the bank, and if he keeps any such money in his hands for a longer time than the Court considers necessary, shall be liable to pay interest upon it at such rate not exceeding five per centum as the Court may fix for the time during which the money remains in his hands.

Rule 11.

Judicial trustee not to keep money in his hands

12.—(1.) A judicial trustee may at any time request the Court to give him directions as to the trust or its administration.

(2.) The request must be accompanied by a statement of the facts with regard to which directions are required, and by the fee required under these rules in respect of a communication from the Court with regard to the administration of the trust.

(3.) The Court may require the trustee or any other person to attend at Chambers if it appears that such an attendance is necessary or convenient for the purpose of obtaining any information or explanation required for properly giving directions, or for the purpose of explaining the nature of the directions.

Rule 12.

Directions to judicial trustees

13.—The Court, if satisfied that there is no reasonable doubt of any fact which affects the administration of a trust by a judicial trustee, may give directions to the judicial trustee to act without formal proof of the fact.

Rule 13.

Power to dispense with formal evidence.

Accounts and Audit.

14.—(1.) The Court shall give directions to a judicial trustee as to the date to which the accounts of the trust are to be made up in each year, and shall fix in each year the time after that date within which the accounts are to be delivered to it for audit.

(2.) The accounts shall in ordinary cases be audited by the officer of the Court, but the Court, if it considers that the accounts are likely to involve questions of difficulty, may refer them to a professional accountant for report, and order the payment to him of such amount in respect of his report as the Court may fix.

15.—(1.) The accounts of any trust of which there is a judicial trustee, with a note of any corrections made upon the audit, shall be filed as the Court directs.

(2.) The judicial trustee shall send a copy of the accounts, or, if the Court thinks fit, of a summary of the accounts, of the trust to such beneficiaries or other persons as the Court thinks proper.

(3.) The Court may, if it thinks fit, having regard to the nature of the relation of the applicant to the trust, allow any person applying to inspect the filed accounts so to inspect them on giving reasonable notice to the officer of the Court.

16.—A judicial trustee shall, unless the Court otherwise directs, be allowed on the audit of his accounts deductions made on account of his remuneration and allowances under these rules and also on account of the fees paid by him under these rules, but shall not be allowed any deduction on account of the expenses of professional assistance, or his own work, or personal outlay, unless the deduction has been authorised by the Court in pursuance of the Act, or the Court is satisfied that the deduction is justified by the strict necessity of the case.

Remuneration and Allowances.

17.—(1.) Where a judicial trustee is to be remunerated, the remuneration to be paid to him shall be fixed by the Court, and may be altered by the Court from time to time.

(2.) In fixing the remuneration, regard shall be had to the duties entailed upon the judicial trustee by the trust.

(3.) The Court may make, if it thinks fit, special allowances to judicial trustees for the following matters, to be paid out of the trust property :—

    (*a*) for the statement of trust property prepared by a judicial trustee on his appointment, an allowance not exceeding ten guineas ;

    (*b*) for realising and re-investing trust property, where the property is realised for the purpose of re-investment, an allowance not exceeding one and a half per centum on the amount realised and re-invested ;

    (*c*) for realising or investing trust property in any other case, an allowance not exceeding one per centum on the amount realised or invested.

(4.) The Court may also in any year make a special allowance to a judicial trustee, if satisfied that in that year more trouble has been thrown upon the trustee by reason of exceptional circumstances than would ordinarily be involved in the administration of the trust.

(5.) Where a trustee is remunerated, any allowance under this rule may be paid in addition to his remuneration.

(6.) Any remuneration or allowance payable to a judicial trustee shall be paid or allowed to him at such times and in such manner as the Court directs.

18.—Where an official of the Court is appointed to be a judicial trustee, any remuneration, allowances, or other payments payable to him on account of his services as trustee shall be paid, accounted for, and applied in such manner as the Treasury direct.

Rule 19.

Forfeiture of remuneration.

19.—(1.) If the Court is satisfied that a judicial trustee has failed to comply with the Act, or with these rules, or with any direction of the Court or officer of the Court made in accordance with the Act or these rules, or has otherwise misconducted himself in relation to the trust, the Court may order that the whole or any part of the remuneration of the trustee be forfeited.

(2.) This rule shall not affect any liability of the judicial trustee for breach of trust or to be removed or suspended.

(3.) A judicial trustee shall have an opportunity of being heard by the Court, before any order is made for the forfeiture of his remuneration or any part of it.

Removal and Suspension of Judicial Trustee.

Rule 20.

Suspension of judicial trustee.

20.—(1.) The Court may at any time, either without any application or on the application of any person appearing to the Court to be interested in the trust, suspend a judicial trustee, if the Court considers that it is expedient to do so in the interests of the trust, and a judicial trustee while suspended shall not have power to act as trustee.

(2.) When a judicial trustee is suspended, the Court shall cause notice to be given to such of the persons appearing to the Court to be interested in the trust as the Court directs, and also to the persons having the custody of the trust property, and shall give any other directions which appear necessary for securing the safety of the trust property.

Rule 21.

Removal of judicial trustee.

21.—(1.) The Court may, either without any application or on the application of any person appearing to the Court to be interested in the trust, remove a judicial trustee if the Court considers that it is expedient to do so in the interests of the trust.

(2.) Any application to remove a judicial trustee must be made by summons.

(3.) A judicial trustee shall not be removed by

the Court without an application for the purpose, **Rule 21.** except after notice has been given to him by the Court of the grounds on which it is proposed to remove him, and of the time and place at which the matter will be heard.

(4.) The Court shall cause a copy of the notice to the trustee to be sent to such of the persons appearing to the Court to be interested in the trust as the Court directs, and the same procedure shall be followed in the matter so far as possible as on a summons to remove a judicial trustee.

22.—Where an inquiry into the administration by **Rule 22.** a judicial trustee of any trust, or into any dealing or transaction of a judicial trustee is ordered, the inquiry *Inquiry into conduct of* shall, unless the Court otherwise directs, be conducted *judicial trustee.* by the officer of the Court, and he shall have the same powers in relation thereto as he has in relation to any other inquiry directed by the Court.

Resignation and Discontinuance of Judicial Trustee.

23.—(1.) If a judicial trustee desires to be dis- **Rule 23.** charged from his trust, he must give notice to the Court, stating at the same time what arrangements *Resignation of judicial* it is proposed to make with regard to the appoint- *trustee.* ment of a successor.

(2.) The Court shall give facilities for the appointment on a proper application of an official of the Court to be judicial trustee in place of a judicial trustee who desires to be discharged, in cases where no fit and proper person appears available for the office, or where the Court considers that such an appointment is convenient or expedient in the interests of the trust.

24.—(1.) Where there is a judicial trustee of a **Rule 24.** trust, the Court may at any time, on the application made by summons of any person appearing to the *Discontinu-ance of* Court to be interested in the trust, order that there *judicial* shall cease to be a judicial trustee of the trust, *trustee.*

Rule 24.   whether the person who is judicial trustee continues as trustee or not.

(2.) If the Court is satisfied that all the persons appearing to the Court to be interested in the trust concur in an application under this rule, the Court shall accede to the application, and in any case shall ascertain as far as may be the wishes of those appearing to the Court to be interested in the trust with regard to the application.

(3.) Where an order is made under this rule, the Court shall make all such orders as may be necessary for carrying it into effect, and where in pursuance of any such order a new trustee is appointed in the place of an official of the Court, shall make all such vesting or other orders and exercise all such other powers as may be necessary for vesting the trust property in the new trustee either as sole trustee or jointly with other trustees as the case requires.

Special Trusts.

Rule 25.

Executors and administrators.

25.—(1.) Any person who is an executor or administrator may be appointed a judicial trustee for the purpose of the collection and distribution of the estate of a deceased person in the same manner and subject to the same provisions as in the case of an ordinary trust.

(2.) Where an administrator has given an administration bond, he need not give security as a judicial trustee under these rules unless the Court directs that he is to do so.

Rule 26.

Special trusts.

26.—(1.) An official of the Court shall not be appointed or act as judicial trustee for any persons in their capacity as members or debenture holders of, or being in any other relation to, any incorporated or unincorporated company, or any club.

(2.) Where the circumstances of any trust of which an official of the Court is a judicial trustee, or of which it is proposed to appoint an official of the Court to be a judicial trustee, involve the carrying on of any trade or business, special intimation of the fact shall be given to the Court either by the judicial trustee or by the person making the application for the appointment of the judicial trustee, as the case may be, and the Court shall specially consider the facts of the case with a view to determining whether the official of the Court should continue or be appointed as judicial trustee, and whether any special condition should be made or directions given with a view to ensuring the proper supervision of the trade or business.

Rule 26.

Exercise of the Powers of the Court.

27.—For the purpose of the Act or these rules the officer of the Court may exercise any power which may be exercised by the Court (including the power of making an order for the appointment of a judicial trustee or making any vesting order), and may perform any duty to be performed by the Court, and may hear and investigate any matter which may be heard or investigated by the Court, subject in any case to the right of any party to bring any particular point before the Judge.

Rule 27.

Exercise of powers of Court

28.—(1.) It shall not be necessary to take out a summons for any purpose under the Act or these rules, except in cases where a summons is required by these rules, or where the Court directs a summons to be taken out.

(2.) Where a judicial trustee desires to make any application or request to the Court, or to communicate with the Court as to the administration of his trust, he may do so by letter addressed to the officer of the Court without any further formality.

(3.) The Court may give any direction to a judicial trustee with regard to the administration of his trust by letter signed by the officer of the Court, and addressed to the trustee without drawing up any order or formal document.

Rule 28.

Communication between judicial trustee and Court.

(4.) For the purpose of the attendance at chambers of the judicial trustee or any other person connected with the trust for purposes relating to the administration of the trust, the officer of the Court may make such appointments as he thinks fit by letter without the service of formal notices.

(5.) Any document may be supplied for the use of the Court by leaving it with, or sending it by post to, the officer of the Court.

District Registries.

29.—(1.) An originating summons under these rules, for the purpose of an application to appoint a judicial trustee, may be sealed and issued in a district registry, and appearances thereon shall be entered in that registry.

(2.) Where a judicial trustee of a trust is appointed on an originating summons taken out in a district registry, or an application in any cause or matter pending in a district registry, all proceedings with respect to the trust and the administration thereof under the Act or these rules shall, unless the Court otherwise directs, be taken in the district registry.

(3.) Where proceedings under the Act or these rules are taken in the district registry, the official of the Court to be appointed judicial trustee where an official of the Court is to be so appointed, shall not be the official solicitor, unless the Court for special reasons otherwise directs.

(4) For the purpose of the Act and these rules the Court may transfer any trust of which there is a judicial trustee from a district registry to London, or from London to a district registry, or from one district registry to another district registry, according as it appears convenient for the administration of the trust.

Palatine Courts.

30.—(1.) These rules shall apply to a Palatine Court as respects trusts within the jurisdiction of such Court, subject to such modifications (if any) as may be made by rules of that Court for the purpose of making these rules properly applicable having regard to any special practice of the Court, or the duties of the officers attached to the Court.

(2.) Where proceedings under the Act or these rules are taken in the Palatine Court, the official of the Court to be appointed judicial trustee where an official of the Court is to be so appointed, shall not be the official solicitor, unless the Palatine Court for special reasons otherwise directs.

Rule 30.

Palatine Courts.

County Courts.

31.—(1). For the purpose of the Act and these rules the jurisdiction of the County Court judge shall extend to any trust in which the trust property does not exceed in value five hundred pounds, as if that jurisdiction had been given under section sixty-seven of the County Courts Act, 1888, but that jurisdiction shall be exercised only in a Metropolitan County Court, or in a County Court for the time being having bankruptcy jurisdiction.

(2.) Where the district of any County Court (other than a Metropolitan County Court) or any part of such a district is attached for the purpose of bankruptcy jurisdiction to some Court other than the County Court of the district, that district or part shall be attached to the same Court for the purpose of jurisdiction under the Act and these rules.

(3.) Where proceedings under the Act or these rules are taken in the County Court, the official of the Court to be appointed judicial trustee, where an official of the Court is to be so appointed, shall not be the official solicitor, unless the Court for special reasons otherwise directs.

Rule 31.

County Court jurisdiction.

Rule 31.

(4.) In the application of these rules to the County Court a petition shall be substituted for a summons, whether an ordinary or an originating summons.

(5.) For the purposes of this rule the expression "Metropolitan County Court" means any of the County Courts mentioned in the third schedule of the Bankruptcy Act, 1883.

Fees.

Rule 32.

Fees.

32.—(1.) The fees mentioned in the schedule to these rules shall be paid in respect of the matters therein mentioned.

(2.) The fees paid by a judicial trustee may be deducted out of the income of the trust property unless the Court otherwise directs.

(3.) Any fees payable under these rules may be remitted by post, and may be so remitted in any manner except by means of postage stamps or coin.

(4.) All fees payable under these rules in the High Court, Palatine Court, or County Court shall, except as provided by these rules, be subject to similar provisions as to payment, account, and application as other fees payable in those Courts respectively.

Officer of the Court.

Rule 33.

Meaning of "officer of Court."

33.—In these rules the expression "officer of the Court" means—

(a) as regards proceedings in the High Court other than proceedings in a district registry, the Chancery Master; that is to say, the Master attached to the chambers of the Judge of the Chancery Division to whom the matter is assigned; and

(b) as regards proceedings in a district registry, any registrar of that registry; and

(c) as regards proceedings in a Palatine Court, **Rule 33.**
any registrar of that Court;

(d) as regards proceedings in the County Court,
the registrar of the County Court.

Supplemental.

34.—These rules shall be construed, so far as they **Rule 34.**
relate to the High Court, as one with the Rules of
the Supreme Court, 1883, and any rules amending *Rules to be construed as*
those rules, so far as they relate to a Palatine Court, *part of the*
as one with the rules of that Court, and so far as *general rules of Court*
they relate to the County Court, as one with the
County Court Rules, 1889, and any rules amending
those rules.

35.—The Interpretation Act, 1889, shall apply **Rule 35.**
for the purpose of the interpretation of these rules
as it applies for the purpose of the interpretation of *Application of Interpretation Act*
an Act of Parliament.

August 31, 1897.

Halsbury, C.

SCHEDULE.

Fees.

	£	s.	d.
The following fees shall be payable under these rules:—			
1. In respect of any thing or matter for which a fee is provided under the orders in force for the time being with regard to Supreme Court, Palatine Court, or County Court fees, as the case may be.	The fee so provided.		
In respect of any communication from the Court with regard to the administration of the trust ...	0	2	6
For filing the statement of the trust property ...	0	10	0
For filing any alteration in the statement	0	5	0
For filing the accounts of the trust	0	5	0
For filing any other document relating to the trust	0	2	6
For auditing the accounts of the trust when audited by the officer of the Court, for every 100l. or fraction of 100l. of the gross amount received as income of the trust without deducting any payments	0	2	6

On the audit of the accounts of the trust where they are referred to a professional accountant for report.	A fee equal to the amount paid to the accountant.

					£ s. d.
On the inspection of filed accounts for each hour or part of an hour occupied					0 2 6
Not exceeding on one day					0 10 0

ADDITIONAL RULE DATED 27th APRIL, 1899, UNDER JUDICIAL TRUSTEE ACT, 1896.

Where an official of the Court is judicial trustee it shall be lawful for the Bank of England and Bank of Ireland, and for any other corporation, company, or public body (all of which other bodies are hereinafter included in the term "company"), to open and keep accounts of stocks, shares, annuities, and securities (all of which are hereinafter included in the term "stock") in the name of such official under his official *title* without naming him, and the dividends on such stock may from time to time be received, and such stock, or any part thereof, may from time to time be transferred by the person for the time being holding such office without any order or direction of the Court as if the same stood in his own name.   And without any order or direction of the Court such official may, by letter of attorney, authorise the Bank of England, or the Bank of Ireland, or all or any of their proper officers, to sell and transfer all or any part of the stock from time to time standing in the books of the said banks on such account, and to receive the dividends due and to become due thereon.   And where, according to the practice of any company (other than the said banks) such stock is accustomed to be sold and transferred, or the dividends to be received by letter of attorney, such official may authorise such company, or the proper officer or officers thereof, *or any other person*, to sell and transfer all or any part of the stock from time to time standing in the books of such company on such account, and to receive the dividends due and to become due thereon. And notwithstanding section 20 of 29 & 30 Vict. c. 39, no request of the Treasury shall be necessary to authorise any such account of Government stocks and annuities to be opened, and no order in writing of the Treasury shall be necessary for the sale or transfer of any such Government stocks or annuities.

This rule shall be read with the Judicial Trustees Rules, 1897.

The 27th of April, 1899.

THE JUDICIAL TRUSTEE RULE (APRIL), 1900.
DATED 21st MAY, 1900.

Notwithstanding anything in these Rules contained, where an official of the Court is sole judicial trustee, the trust funds and the title deeds, certificates, and other documents which are evidence of the title of the trustee to any of the trust property, and all receipts on behalf of the trust, shall be dealt with, and all payments on behalf of the trust shall be made, and accounts shall be kept, in such manner and subject to such regulations as the Treasury may direct.

This rule shall be construed as one with the Judicial Trustee Rules, 1897.

Dated the 21st of May, 1900.

NOTE.—This rule was signed in confirmation of the rule signed and declared urgent on the 9th of April, 1900.

APPENDIX A.

(See p. 21, *ante*.)

IN making an investment on real security trustees must consider—

1. The physical nature of the property. (*a*) *The property should be permanent in nature and value.*—"The object of trustees must ever be to make a permanent investment, that is, one which will be maintained for a considerable period, and which will not only during that period yield the stipulated income, but will ultimately, and whenever required, realise the full sum advanced." *Per* Kekewich, J., *re Somerset* (1894) 1 Ch. 231.

Primâ facie trustees ought not to lend on property of a wasting character, such as mines, quarries, or brickfields, which from their nature necessarily involve a diminution of the substance of the security. Nor ought they to lend on property, the value of which is speculative, or liable to considerable fluctuation, or the value of which depends on some accidental circumstance, such as an hotel, or other licensed premises.

In reference to a loan on a brickfield, the following remarks were made in *re Whiteley*, 33 C D. 347 "I have not adverted to the fact that in a brickfield you are constantly exhausting the security. . . . I agree it would require the trustee to exercise more caution in lending the money when the security is on that which from its very nature necessarily involves a diminution of the substance of the security" (*per* Cotton, L.J. 33 C.D, at p. 352). "As an abstract proposition I am not prepared to say that a freehold brickfield cannot be a real security within the meaning of the power. It would clearly be a real security within the power if the value of the land, apart from the particular trade carried on upon it, was sufficient to secure the sum advanced; but where the value of the land, apart from the particular trade of brickmaking carried on upon it, is nothing like the sum advanced, the whole aspect of the case changes. The value of such a brickfield as a security for money lent on it in excess of the value of the land as land depends on the trade of brickmaking, and on the probability of a purchaser being found to buy and work the brickfield in the event of the mortgage money being called in. This depends on the state of the brickmaking trade and on the profits which can be made by selling bricks made in the field in question. Moreover, a lender of money on such a security must exercise unusual

Q

vigilance in seeing that he does not allow the money to remain uncalled in longer than is safe. A security of so hazardous a nature as this is not a proper security for trust money; it is not in truth a real security for any sum beyond the value of the land as land" (*per* Lindley, L J., in *re Whiteley*, *supra*). "The investment is not (a proper real security). Its value mainly depends on the success of a speculative and fluctuating business, a business for which it is difficult to find customers, a business largely depending on the energy and solvency of those working it, a business of necessity of precarious duration, which cannot be carried on without such an excavation and destruction of the soil as must eventually leave what remains nearly useless for agricultural and other purposes It is said that the trustees could call in or realise the security before any serious depreciation of the property took place. I do not think trustees are justified in investing trust funds in any property where active and exceptional vigilance and diligence is requisite on their part to anticipate and prevent a loss to their *cestuis que trust*" (*per* Lopes, L.J., in *re Whiteley*, *supra*).

The principle of *Learoyd* v. *Whiteley*, *supra*, extends to all premises devoted to trade. Trustees *primâ facie* cannot regard premises devoted to trade as proper investments. In a case (*Stickney* v. *Sewell*, 1 Cr. & My. 8) relating to a loan on a windmill, it was said: "One of the witnesses states as a cause that raised the value, that there was only one other windmill there in 1815, whereas now there are three. You cannot say that it is a proper investment which derives its value from the accidental absence of competition in trade." And in *Stretton* v. *Ashmall*, 3 Drew. 9 · "Now that property appears to be principally of a nature for carrying on trade, and I observe for that reason alone, it is property liable to great fluctuation in value." And in *Sheffield Building Society* v *Aizlewood*, 44 C.D. 412: "The property (a colliery) was of a speculative description, and dependent for its value on the course of trade. Such property would not, according to *Learoyd* v. *Whiteley*, have formed a proper subject for an advance by trustees of an ordinary will or settlement." And in *re Somerset* (1894) 1 Ch. 231 . "*Learoyd* v. *Whiteley* is a warning to trustees that land devoted to trade may not be regarded as a proper security at all."

With reference to a loan on a colliery, it has been said (*Sheffield Building Society* v. *Aizlewood*, *supra*): "It is said the advance . . . was not made on such security [freehold, copyhold, or leasehold estates], but on the security of the colliery carried on by Mr. Joseph. In fact, however, the properties were held under leases, and constituted leasehold estate. The leases included minerals which were to be worked and got by the lessees. The property offered as security was therefore to some extent of a wasting nature, and its value was affected by its being used for the purposes of the colliery business carried on by Joseph. Those were matters fit and proper to be considered in determining what amount should be advanced on the security of the leasehold property; but, in my judgment, it cannot be

said that the society was precluded, by reason of the evidence of
these circumstances, from making any advance, however small,
on mortgage of it." In that case the mortgagees were trustees
of a building society, and it was held that trustees of a building
society may properly make advances on classes of securities
forbidden to ordinary trustees, and that they are not under an
obligation to avoid investments attended with hazard.

Referring to a loan on licensed premises, it has been said:
"The value of an hotel is necessarily of a very speculative
character, and may, like the property in the case of *Stickney* v.
Sewell, supra, arise from accident. It was a security which
trustees were not justified in taking" *Budge* v. *Gummow,* 7
Ch. 719.

(*b*) *The property should be income-producing.*—*Primâ facie*
trustees ought not to lend on the security of property which, in
the event of the mortgagor not being able to pay, cannot readily
be made available to yield income to pay the interest on the
mortgage. No express limits as to the proportion between the
amount of the interest and the income of the security have ever
been laid down. It is conceived, notwithstanding the *dictum*
of Kekewich, J., below cited, that, *as a general rule,* the interest
should not exceed two-thirds of the income. In reference to
this point, the following observations were made in *re Whiteley,
supra.* "Trustees are bound to preserve the money for those
entitled to the corpus in remainder, and they are bound to
invest it in such a way as will produce a reasonable income for
those enjoying the income for the present" (*per* Cotton, L.J.)
And in *Smethurst* v. *Hastings,* 30 C.D. 490, referring to a loan
on unfinished houses, unlet, and on a building estate of which
the roads and drainage were in a defective condition: "Can it
be said that any prudent man . . . would venture his money to
the extent of more than half the estimated value of the property,
when that property consisted of houses, recently built, unoccupied,
not wholly finished, *producing no fixed certain rents.* . . . The
investment upon mortgage of houses, which would not be
immediately occupied, and from which rents were not secured,
nor receivable, was a breach of the duties of the trustees" (*per*
Bacon, V.C.). See, too, *Mara* v. *Browne* (1895) 2 Ch. 69, *per*
North, J. And in *re Somerset* (1894) 1 Ch. 231· "The object
of trustees must ever be to make a permanent investment, that is
one which will be maintained for a considerable period, and
which will not only during that period yield the stipulated
income, but will ultimately . . . realise the full sum advanced.
Trustees must regard any advice given to them from this double
point of view, and cannot be absolved from liability for loss
arising from a particular transaction by showing that their
advance was within the allowed limits as regards capital if they
were exceeded as regards income, and the income was insufficient to pay the stipulated interest. I express myself thus,
because the limits stated with reference to capital have not been
specifically applied to income; and I am not sure that, as regards
income, some larger latitude might not safely be permitted"

(*per* Kekewich, J.). And in *Chapman* v. *Browne* (1902) 1 Ch. 785 : "Our Courts have always considered it a matter of importance to be borne in mind by a trustee contemplating an advance of trust money on security of realty . . . that the security should be one, which, in case of the mortgagor not being able to pay, could readily be made available to yield income to pay the interest which might be required by a tenant for life, or possibly for the maintenance of some infant *cestui que trust*."

(c) *The property should be readily marketable.*—Primâ facie trustees ought not to lend on property which will not readily, and whenever required, realise the full sum advanced.

In reference to this point, the following observations were made in *re Whiteley, supra* : "The value of such a brickfield as a security for money lent on it in excess of the value of the land as land depends on the trade of brickmaking, and on the probability of a purchaser being found to buy and work the brickfield in the event of the mortgage money being called in. This depends on the state of the brickmaking trade and on the profits which can be made by selling bricks made in the field in question" (*per* Cotton, L.J.). And in the same case in the House of Lords (*Learoyd* v. *Whiteley, supra*) : "A security of a peculiarly hazardous character . . . the value of the buildings and fixed machinery depended entirely on the mortgagees being able to find a purchaser for it as a going concern for the manufacture of bricks" (*per* Lord Fitzgerald) And in *Smethurst* v. *Hastings*, 30 C.D. 490 . "The houses were unfit for the investment of trust funds—that being only in course of erection, or recently erected, they were of merely speculative value, *not of readily marketable value*, and that their selling value was less than the several sums advanced" (*per* Bacon, V.C.).

2. The estate or interest in the property of the mortgagor. (a) *Its possible duration.*—The estate may be freehold or less than freehold. Freehold estates are for life, in tail, or in fee simple. Estates less than freehold are for years, at will, or at sufferance.

Estates less than freehold are not real property, *Townend* v. *Townend*, 1 Giff. 201, at p. 211. There is, however, a *dictum* of Jessel, M.R., in *re Chennell*, 8 C.D 492, to the effect that a mortgage of leaseholds for a long term at a peppercorn rent without onerous covenants would be a "real security." In the later case of *re Boyd's Settled Estates*, 14 C.D. 626, the same judge said that, as a general rule, long terms of years do not answer the description of real securities. And see *Leigh* v. *Leigh* (1886) W.N, 191, where Stirling, J., held that a long term was not a real security. See now section 5 of the 1893 Act, *ante*, p. 34.

A life interest, or lease for lives (*Lander* v. *Weston*, 3 Drew. 389), is not a proper, though, it is conceived, it is an authorised, security. This is so although the security also comprises a policy of life assurance on the *cestui que vie*. *Lander* v. *Weston, supra*.

A tenant in tail cannot create a mortgage valid against the remaindermen, except by an enrolled deed, creating a fee simple, either absolute or base.

Life leaseholds, perpetually renewable, have been held a not improper security. It is the common tenure of land in Ireland, and differs very little from a fee simple. *Macleod v. Annesley*, 16 Beav. 600. See, however, a decision of Shadwell, V.C, to the contrary, mentioned by Jessel, M.R., in *re Boyd*, 14 C.D. 627. It is conceived that the risk of failure to renew within due time brings the security within the observations in *re Whiteley*, cited *ante*, p. 225, as to the impropriety of lending on securities requiring active and exceptional vigilance to anticipate and prevent loss.

An estate in fee simple may be absolute, qualified (or base), or conditional. Fee simple absolute is the ordinary unqualified estate limited to a man and his heirs, and is understood to be intended by the term fee simple without any more. A "qualified" or "base fee" is where a qualification is annexed to the estate, so that it must determine whenever the qualification is at an end; *e.g.* a grant to "A. and his heirs, tenants of the Manor of Dale," is a base fee (Co. Litt. 27*a*). A more familiar instance of a base fee is the estate created by a tenant in tail barring his issue by an enrolled deed, but failing to create a fee simple absolute, for want of the concurrence of the protector of the settlement. A conditional fee at the common law was a fee restrained to some particular heirs exclusive of others. Such estates were converted by the statute *De donis* into estates tail. They are only now met with in copyholds to which the statute *De donis* has no application. Whether a base fee could be a proper security for trust moneys must, it is conceived, depend on the nature of the qualification attached to the estate. *Primâ facie*, to lend on an estate capable of determination, would be hazardous, and therefore an improper act on the part of a trustee, unless, indeed, the qualification attached to the estate be so remote as to be practically negligible

A fee simple absolute may be subject to a condition. Such an estate is created by a grant of land for building purposes, limiting a fee farm rent-charge, and subject to covenants for building and a condition for re-entry. Whether land so held can be a proper security for trust money must, it is conceived, depend on the amount of the rent, as compared with the income of the land from which it issues (see *Macleod v. Annesley*, 16 Beav. 600), and the nature of the covenants, or events, giving rise to the right of re-entry. It is conceived that where the rent is amply secured, and where the covenants are not onerous, and are of such a character that relief from forfeiture for breach thereof could be obtained under the Conveyancing Acts, trustees would not be precluded from lending. But where the rent is large and the security for it slender, or where there exist covenants or conditions, from forfeiture for breach of which no relief could be obtained, trustees would not be justified in lending.

(*b*) *Its time of enjoyment.*—The mortgagor's estate may be in possession or in expectancy. *Primâ facie* trustees should only lend on estates in possession.

An estate in expectancy may be either expectant on a term of years, or on a life estate, or estate tail.

A reversion expectant on a term of years is only in a somewhat qualified sense a reversion; the right to immediate possession is postponed, but the reversioner remains seised of the immediate freehold. Thus, in the ordinary case of a lease for years at a rent, the right to the rent is annexed to the reversion; and the receipt of the rent is, in fact, only a mode of enjoyment by the reversioner of the present profits of the land. A loan on the security of an estate in fee simple absolute, in land or buildings, subject to a long lease reserving a ground rent, is a proper trustee investment. *Vickery* v. *Evans*, 33 Beav. 376; and see *re Peyton*, 7 Eq. 463. As to the amount which can properly be lent on such a security, see *ante*, p. 44.

A reversion expectant on a lease for life *at a rent* would, it is conceived, also form a proper authorised security.

A reversion expectant on a particular estate out of which no rent is limited, though, undoubtedly, an authorised security (see *re Turner* (1897) 1 Ch. 536), is not a proper security for trustees; it is not income-producing, it is not freely marketable, and its value is extremely speculative.

(c) *Its nature.*—The mortgagor's estate may be either legal or equitable, and may be either joint, in common, or several, and may be or not be subject to incumbrances.

Trustees cannot safely invest on the security of an equitable mortgage (*Chapman* v. *Browne* (1902) 1 Ch. 783), whether the legal estate remain vested in a prior legal mortgagee (*Drosier* v. *Brereton*, 15 Beav. at p. 226; *Robinson* v. *Robinson*, 1 De G.M. & G. 247; *Lockhart* v. *Reilly*, De G. & J. 464; *Sheffield B.S.* v. *Aizlewood*, 44 C.D. 412, at p. 459), or in the mortgagor (*Norris* v. *Wright*, 14 Beav. at p. 308; *Swaffield* v. *Nelson*, 1876, W.N. 255), and although the deeds be deposited with the mortgagee, and the mortgagor undertake to execute a legal mortgage when called on (*Swaffield* v. *Nelson*, *supra*), nor accept any title where the legal estate is outstanding, except when the title is such that under no circumstances can the acquisition of the legal estate become necessary for its protection.

A mortgage of the undivided interest of a joint tenant or tenant in common, though undoubtedly "real security" (*re Turner* (1897) 1 Ch. 536), cannot be considered a desirable form of investment for trustees. Such an interest is not readily marketable; the control of the trustee over the property is not absolutely in his own hands; it is not desirable that trust moneys should in any way become complicated with the rights and interests of other persons; and the risk of becoming involved in a long and expensive partition action cannot be ignored.

3. **The market value of the property and amount of loan.**— See notes to section 8 of the Trustee Act, 1893, *ante*, p. 42.

4. The form of the security. (a) *The security should vest in the mortgagee the legal estate.*—The necessity of acquiring the legal estate has already been referred to, *ante,* p. 230 A legal sub-mortgage is unobjectionable. *Smethurst* v. *Hastings,* 30 C.D. 490.

The question arises, whether a registered charge, under the Land Transfer Acts, is a proper security for trust money. It is conceived that it is not. A registered charge does not confer the legal estate, and, although for many purposes a registered charge is free from the risks attaching to an ordinary equitable mortgage, yet, for some purposes, the possession of the legal estate is of vital importance. It is pointed out (Brickdale and Sheldon on the Land Transfer Acts, p. 35) that if the mortgagee wish to enter on the land, or if he obtain foreclosure, the legal estate would still be of use, and would be difficult to obtain. The recent case of *Capital and Counties Bank, Limited* v. *Rhodes* (1903) 1 Ch. 631, illustrates the importance of the legal estate in the case of a security on a reversion expectant on a term of years. The right of re-entry for breach of covenant passed with the reversion. Had the plaintiffs in that case merely had a registered charge, they would not have been in a position to enforce the covenants and conditions in the lease. See also *infra,* as to ejectment. Cf. 48 Sol. J. 451.

(b) *The security should vest in the mortgagee sole control over the property.*—A loan on a contributory mortgage, in the names of the trustees and other persons jointly, or (where there is no contribution of mortgage money) a loan on the security of a mortgage in the names of themselves and a stranger, is a breach of trust. *Webb* v. *Jonas,* 39 C.D. 660.

"Trustees are bound to invest on a mortgage where they have the entire control in their own hands, and where they can exercise their own discretion for the benefit of their *cestuis que trust,* and not where they are bound to consult others, or where, if they do not consult others, they are bound to act for the benefit of others as well as for themselves." *Per Kekewich, J.,* in *Webb* v. *Jonas,* 39 C.D. at p. 668 See also *Stokes* v. *Prance* (1898) 1 Ch. 212; *re Massingberd,* 63 L.T. 297.

(c) *The security should be enforceable by sale*—It is not a breach of trust for a trustee to take a mortgage not containing, or conferring, a power of sale. *Farrar* v. *Barraclough,* 2 Sm. & G. 231. Nevertheless, trustees should insist on having either the statutory or an express power.

(d) *The security should be enforceable by ejectment and fore-closure.*—The security ought to be such as to be capable of being enforced by ejectment and by foreclosure. *Mant* v. *Leith,* 15 Beav. 524. A mortgage of the undertaking of a railway company pursuant to the Companies Clauses Act, 1845, does not comply with these requirements. *Mant* v. *Leith, supra; Mortimore* v. *Mortimore,* 4 De G. & J. 472. As to road bonds, see *Holgate* v. *Jennings,* 24 Beav. 623; *Robinson* v. *Robinson,* 1 De G.M. & G. 247.

A registered charge under the Land Transfer Acts can be

enforced by foreclosure (see section 26 of the Act of 1875). Although section 25 of that Act confers a right to enter upon the land charged, it does not enable the mortgagee to eject a tenant, for the person in whom the legal estate is vested is a necessary party to an ejectment action. *Allen* v. *Woods*, 68 L.T. 143. Possibly, the proprietor of the charge could make the person in whom the legal estate is vested a defendant in the ejectment action, but it is stated (Annual Practice (1903), p. 275) that the practice is, in the K.B.D., to allow as defendants in the action only such persons as are in possession of the land. If this be so, the proprietor of the charge would first be compelled to get in the legal estate, pursuant to the covenants for title, and this might lead to great difficulty and expense. Cf. *Webb* v. *Jonas*, 39 C.D. at p. 668, as to securities which involve the bringing of additional parties before the Court on any proceedings affecting them.

(e) *The security should not prohibit the calling in of the mortgage money.*—Trustees are not justified in inserting a provision in a mortgage that it shall not be called in for a certain period. *Vickery* v. *Evans*, 33 Beav. 376; *Mant* v. *Leith*, 15 Beav. 524 "Under the powers in the Act of Parliament, the security (a railway mortgage) cannot be enforced, in the ordinary way, by ejectment or foreclosure; payment cannot be demanded for seven years, and can only be made available by a sale; and the parties in remainder may happen to become entitled to receive the money before the expiration of that time, and yet may be unable to realise it except by a forced sale, and possibly at a great disadvantage. Taking all the circumstances into consideration, I am of opinion that this was not a proper investment for the trustee to make." *Per* Romilly, M.R., *Mant* v. *Leith, supra..*

In *Vickery* v *Evans, supra,* the same judge said in a case where an ordinary mortgage contained a condition that the money should not be called in for five years. "This point was also referred to—that the money was lent on a condition that it should not be called in for five years, and as the mortgage deed is dated October, 1862, the plaintiff (reversioner) might be kept out of his money if the tenant for life were to die before the five years. I think the plaintiff would in that event be entitled either to have a transfer of the mortgage or to have the mortgage sold and the deficiency made up by the trustees, because he is entitled to payment at once."

(f) *The security should contain a covenant for payment.*— Trustees are bound to consider all the circumstances, including the means of the mortgagor.

"On the question how far, if at all, trustees may properly rely on the position of the borrower, there is, so far as I am aware, no authority. [But see *Sheffield B.S.* v. *Aizlewood, post,* p. 233]. Men of ordinary care and prudence managing their own affairs, would, no doubt, take this into consideration, and in the mercantile world it is frequently treated as equally important with the value of the security. It is impossible, I

think, to exclude it from the consideration of trustees, who are
bound to have regard to all the circumstances connected with
any proposed advance on security, and it would not be difficult
to put cases in which the solvency or insolvency of the borrower
would properly influence them in making an advance somewhat
in excess of the limits generally allowed, or declining the transaction altogether; but where the object is to make a permanent
investment of trust money on mortgage of real estate, it seems
to me wrong to advance a sum largely in excess of what is
otherwise right because it is believed that the borrower is now,
and it is anticipated that he will remain, capable of paying the
principal and interest or such part thereof as cannot be realised
from the security." *Per* Kekewich, J., in *re Somerset* (1894) 1
Ch. 231; and see *re Turner* (1897) 1 Ch 536, *per* Byrne, J.: "I
think if he (the trustee) was a businesslike man, he would not
before lending his money have been satisfied without some
further inquiry as to the means of the mortgagor."

The extent to which the personal security of the borrower
(or other collateral personal security) may be relied on is defined
by Stirling, J., in *Sheffield Building Society v. Aizlewood,* 44
C.D. at p. 451, a case of a building society authorised to lend
on freehold, copyhold, or leasehold estates, which it is conceived, on this particular point, applies equally to trustees
"It was not disputed in argument, and in my judgment,
properly, that a building society making an advance to a member
on the security of freehold, copyhold, or leasehold estate, might
take from him a personal covenant for payment of what might
be due from him to the society, and I think that the officers of
the society might, to a large extent, and for certain purposes,
rely on the solvency or the mortgagor. For example, an action
on the covenant of a solvent borrower affords an effectual and
comparatively speedy and inexpensive mode of recovering what
is due, and may be the means of avoiding the delay, costs, and
liability incident to remedies (such as foreclosure, sale, or entry
into possession) available only against the subject-matter of the
security. If the circumstances of the borrower are such that
his personal covenant is without value, the building society
may, in my opinion, secure a like advantage by means of the
personal guarantee of a third party or a charge on some readily
available pure personal estate. The benefit so obtained must,
however, be purely collateral, and the validity or propriety of
the transaction is to be tested as if no such ingredient entered
into it. If there be no freehold, copyhold, or leasehold estate
comprised in the security, or if the estate so comprised be merely
nominal or its value out of all proportion to the amount
advanced, the transaction is beyond the powers of the society,
and invalid. But where, as here, the borrower offers as security
such estate to a substantial extent, an advance is within the
powers conferred by the Act of 1874, and the question for the
officers of the society to determine is, what amount may be
properly advanced, and that question they must decide having
regard solely to the nature and value of the freehold, copyhold,

or leasehold estate offered to them, and without reference to the solvency of the borrower, or the worth of any personal estate he may be willing to throw in by way of security."

(g) *The security should not be a "stock mortgage."*—Trustees are not justified in lending on a stock mortgage. "It must not be a stock mortgage but mortgage in the ordinary way for securing certain fixed capital." *Per* Giffard, L.J., *Whitney* v. *Smith*, 4 Ch. 513.

(h) *Copyholds.*—In a mortgage of copyholds, trustees should not rely on a mere covenant to surrender, but a conditional surrender should be effected. The mortgagee is not usually admitted until he wishes to realise his security.

APPENDIX B.

TRUSTEE ACT, 1893.

56 & 57 VICT. C. 53.

An Act to consolidate Enactments relating to Trustees.
[22nd September, 1893]

BE it enacted by the Queen's most Excellent Majesty, by and with the advice and consent of the Lords Spiritual and Temporal, and Commons, in this present Parliament assembled, and by the authority of the same, as follows :—

PART I.

INVESTMENTS.

Section 1.—A trustee may, unless expressly forbidden by the instrument (if any) creating the trust, invest any trust funds in his hands, whether at the time in a state of investment or not, in manner following, that is to say—

Sect. 1.

Authorised investments.

    (*a.*) In any of the parliamentary stocks or public funds or Government securities of the United Kingdom :

    (*b.*) On real or heritable securities in Great Britain or Ireland :

    (*c.*) In the stock of the Bank of England or the Bank of Ireland :

    (*d.*) In India Three and a half per cent. stock and India Three per cent. stock, or in any other capital stock which may at any time hereafter be issued by the Secretary of State in Council of India under the authority of Act of Parliament, and charged on the revenues of India :

    (*e.*) In any securities the interest of which is for the time being guaranteed by Parliament :

    (*f.*) In consolidated stock created by the Metropolitan Board of Works, or by the London County Council, or in debenture stock created by the Receiver for the Metropolitan Police District :

    (*g.*) In the debenture or rentcharge, or guaranteed or preference stock of any railway company in Great Britain or Ireland incorporated by special Act of

Sect. 1.

Parliament, and havir̃g during each of the ten years last past before the datȝ of investment paid a dividend at the rate of not less than three per centum per annum on its ordinary stock:

(*h.*) In the stock of any railway or canal company in Great Britain or Ireland whose undertaking is leased in perpetuity or for a term of not less than two hundred years at a fixed rental to any such railway company as is mentioned in subsection (*g.*), either alone or jointly with any other railway company:

(*i.*) In the debenture stock of any railway company in India the interest on which is paid or guaranteed by the Secretary of State in Council of India:

(*j.*) In the "B" annuities of the Eastern Bengal, the East Indian, and the Scinde Punjaub and Delhi Railways, and any like annuities which may at any time hereafter be created on the purchase of any other railway by the Secretary of State in Council of India, and charged on the revenues of India, and which may be authorised by Act of Parliament to be accepted by trustees in lieu of any stock held by them in the purchased railway; also in deferred annuities comprised in the register of holders of annuity Class D. and annuities comprised in the register of annuitants Class C. of the East Indian Railway Company:

(*k.*) In the stock of any railway company in India upon which a fixed or minimum dividend in sterling is paid or guaranteed by the Secretary of State in Council of India, or upon the capital of which the interest is so guaranteed:

(*l.*) In the debenture or guaranteed or preference stock of any company in Great Britain or Ireland, established for the supply of water for profit, and incorporated by special Act of Parliament or by Royal Charter, and having during each of the ten years last past before the date of investment paid a dividend of not less than five pounds per centum on its ordinary stock:

(*m.*) In nominal or inscribed stock issued, or to be issued, by the corporation of any municipal borough having, according to the returns of the last census prior to the date of investment, a population exceeding fifty thousand, or by any county council, under the authority of any Act of Parliament or Provisional Order:

(*n.*) In nominal or inscribed stock issued or to be issued by any commissioners incorporated by Act of Parliament for the purpose of supplying water, and having a compulsory power of levying rates over an area having, according to the returns of the last census prior to the date of investment, a population exceeding fifty thousand, provided that during each of the ten years last past before the date of investment the rates levied by such commissioners shall not have exceeded eighty per centum of the amount authorised by law to be levied :

(*o*.) In any of the stocks, funds, or securities for the time being authorised for the investment of cash under the control or subject to the order of the High Court,

and may also from time to time vary any such investment.

Section 2.—(1.) A trustee may under the powers of this Act invest in any of the securities mentioned or referred to in section one of this Act, notwithstanding that the same may be redeemable, and that the price exceeds the redemption value.

(2.) Provided that a trustee may not under the powers of this Act purchase at a price exceeding its redemption value any stock mentioned or referred to in subsections (*g*.), (*i*), (*k*.), (*l*.), and (*m*) of section one, which is liable to be redeemed within fifteen years of the date of purchase at par or at some other fixed rate, or purchase any such stock as is mentioned or referred to in the subsections aforesaid, which is liable to be redeemed at par or at some other fixed rate, at a price exceeding fifteen per centum above par or such other fixed rate.

(3.) A trustee may retain until redemption any redeemable stock, fund, or security which may have been purchased in accordance with the powers of this Act.

Section 3.—Every power conferred by the preceding sections shall be exercised according to the discretion of the trustee, but subject to any consent required by the instrument, if any, creating the trust with respect to the investment of the trust funds.

Section 4.—The preceding sections shall apply as well to trusts created before as to trusts created after the passing of this Act, and the powers thereby conferred shall be in addition to the powers conferred by the instrument, if any, creating the trust.

Section 5.—(1.) A trustee having power to invest in real securities, unless expressly forbidden by the instrument creating the trust, may invest and shall be deemed to have always had power to invest—

(*a*) on mortgage of property held for an unexpired term of not less than two hundred years, and not subject to a reservation of rent greater than a shilling a year, or to any right of redemption or to any condition for re-entry, except for non-payment of rent; and

(*b*) on any charge, or upon mortgage of any charge, made under the Improvement of Land Act, 1864.

(2.) A trustee having power to invest in the mortgages or bonds of any railway company or of any other description of

Sect. 5. company may, unless the contrary is expressed in the instrument authorising the investment, invest in the debenture stock of a railway company or such other company as aforesaid.

(3.) A trustee having power to invest money in the debentures or debenture stock of any railway or other company may, unless the contrary is expressed in the instrument authorising the investment, invest in any nominal debentures or nominal debenture stock issued under the Local Loans Act, 1875.

(4.) A trustee having power to invest money in securities in the Isle of Man, or in securities of the government of a colony, may, unless the contrary is expressed in the instrument authorising the investment, invest in any securities of the Government of the Isle of Man, under the Isle of Man Loans Act, 1880.

(5.) A trustee having a general power to invest trust moneys in or upon the security of shares, stock, mortgages, bonds, or debentures of companies incorporated by or acting under the authority of an Act of Parliament, may invest in, or upon the security of, mortgage debentures duly issued under and in accordance with the provisions of the Mortgage Debenture Act, 1865.

Sect. 6.

Power to invest, notwithstanding drainage charges

Section 6.—A trustee having power to invest in the purchase of land or on mortgage of land may invest in the purchase, or on mortgage of any land, notwithstanding the same is charged with a rent under the powers of the Public Money Drainage Acts, 1846 to 1856, or the Landed Property Improvement (Ireland) Act, 1847, or by an absolute order made under the Improvement of Land Act, 1864, unless the terms of the trust expressly provide that the land to be purchased or taken in mortgage shall not be subject to any such prior charge.

Sect. 7.

Trustees not to convert inscribed stock into certificates to bearer

Section 7.—(1.) A trustee, unless authorised by the terms of his trust, shall not apply for or hold any certificate to bearer issued under the authority of any of the following Acts, that is to say—

(a) The India Stock Certificate Act, 1863;
(b) The National Debt Act, 1870;
(c) The Local Loans Act, 1875;
(d) The Colonial Stock Act, 1877.

(2.) Nothing in this section shall impose on the Bank of England or of Ireland, or on any person authorised to issue any such certificates, any obligation to inquire whether a person applying for such a certificate is or is not a trustee, or subject them to any liability in the event of their granting any such certificate to a trustee, nor invalidate any such certificate if granted.

Sect. 8.

Loans and investments

Section 8.—(1.) A trustee lending money on the security of any property on which he can lawfully lend shall not be chargeable with breach of trust by reason only of the proportion borne by the amount of the loan to the value of the property at

the time when the loan was made, provided that it appears to
the Court that in making the loan the trustee was acting upon
a report as to the value of the property made by a person whom
he reasonably believed to be an able practical surveyor or valuer
instructed and employed independently of any owner of the
property, whether such surveyor or valuer carried on business
in the locality where the property is situate or elsewhere, and
that the amount of the loan does not exceed two equal third
parts of the value of the property as stated in the report, and
that the loan was made under the advice of the surveyor or
valuer expressed in the report.

(2.) A trustee lending money on the security of any leasehold property shall not be chargeable with breach of trust only
upon the ground that in making such loan he dispensed either
wholly or partly with the production or investigation of the
lessor's title.

(3.) A trustee shall not be chargeable with breach of trust
only upon the ground that in effecting the purchase of or in
lending money upon the security of any property he has accepted
a shorter title than the title which a purchaser is, in the absence
of a special contract, entitled to require, if in the opinion of the
Court the title accepted be such as a person acting with prudence
and caution would have accepted.

(4.) This section applies to transfers of existing securities
as well as to new securities, and to investments made as well
before as after the commencement of this Act, except where an
action or other proceeding was pending with reference thereto
on the twenty-fourth day of December one thousand eight
hundred and eighty-eight.

Section 9.—(1.) Where a trustee improperly advances trust
money on a mortgage security which would at the time of the
investment be a proper investment in all respects for a smaller
sum than is actually advanced thereon the security shall be
deemed an authorised investment for the smaller sum, and the
trustee shall only be liable to make good the sum advanced in
excess thereof with interest.

(2.) This section applies to investments made as well before
as after the commencement of this Act except where an action
or other proceeding was pending with reference thereto on the
twenty-fourth day of December one thousand eight hundred
and eighty-eight.

PART II.

Various Powers and Duties of Trustees.

Appointment of New Trustees

Section 10.—(1.) Where a trustee, either original or substituted, and whether appointed by a Court or otherwise, is
dead, or remains out of the United Kingdom for more than

Margin notes:
Sect. 8.
by trustees not charge-able as breaches of trust.

Sect. 9.
Liability for loss by reason of improper investments.

Sect. 10.
Power of appointing new trustees.

Sect. 10. twelve months, or desires to be discharged from all or any of the trusts or powers reposed in or conferred on him, or refuses or is unfit to act therein, or is incapable of acting therein, then the person or persons nominated for the purpose of appointing new trustees by the instrument, if any, creating the trust, or if there is no such person, or no such person able and willing to act, then the surviving or continuing trustees or trustee for the time being, or the personal representatives of the last surviving or continuing trustee, may, by writing, appoint another person or other persons to be a trustee or trustees in the place of the trustee dead, remaining out of the United Kingdom, desiring to be discharged, refusing, or being unfit or being incapable, as aforesaid.

(2.) On the appointment of a new trustee for the whole or any part of trust property—

(a) the number of trustees may be increased; and

(b) a separate set of trustees may be appointed for any part of the trust property held on trusts distinct from those relating to any other part or parts of the trust property, notwithstanding that no new trustees or trustee are or is to be appointed for other parts of the trust property, and any existing trustee may be appointed or remain one of such separate set of trustees; or, if only one trustee was originally appointed, then one separate trustee may be so appointed for the first-mentioned part; and

(c) it shall not be obligatory to appoint more than one new trustee where only one trustee was originally appointed, or to fill up the original number of trustees where more than two trustees were originally appointed; but, except where only one trustee was originally appointed, a trustee shall not be discharged under this section from his trust unless there will be at least two trustees to perform the trust; and

(d) any assurance or thing requisite for vesting the trust property, or any part thereof, jointly in the persons who are the trustees, shall be executed or done.

(3.) Every new trustee so appointed, as well before as after all the trust property becomes by law, or by assurance, or otherwise, vested in him, shall have the same powers, authorities, and discretions, and may in all respects act, as if he had been originally appointed a trustee by the instrument, if any, creating the trust.

(4.) The provisions of this section relative to a trustee who is dead include the case of a person nominated trustee in a will but dying before the testator, and those relative to a continuing trustee include a refusing or retiring trustee, if willing to act in the execution of the provisions of this section.

(5.) This section applies only if and as far as a contrary intention is not expressed in the instrument, if any, creating the trust, and shall have effect subject to the terms of that instrument and to any provisions therein contained.

(6.) This section applies to trusts created either before or after the commencement of this Act.

Section 11.—(1.) Where there are more than two trustees, if one of them by deed declares that he is desirous of being discharged from the trust, and if his co-trustees and such other person, if any, as is empowered to appoint trustees, by deed consent to the discharge of the trustee, and to the vesting in the co-trustees alone of the trust property, then the trustee desirous of being discharged shall be deemed to have retired from the trust, and shall, by the deed, be discharged therefrom under this Act, without any new trustee being appointed in his place.

(2.) Any assurance or thing requisite for vesting the trust property in the continuing trustees alone shall be executed or done.

(3.) This section applies only if and as far as a contrary intention is not expressed in the instrument, if any, creating the trust, and shall have effect subject to the terms of that instrument and to any provisions therein contained.

(4.) This section applies to trusts created either before or after the commencement of this Act.

Section 12.—(1.) Where a deed by which a new trustee is appointed to perform any trust contains a declaration by the appointor to the effect that any estate or interest in any land subject to the trust, or in any chattel so subject, or the right to recover and receive any debt or other thing in action so subject, shall vest in the persons who by virtue of the deed become and are the trustees for performing the trust, that declaration shall, without any conveyance or assignment, operate to vest in those persons, as joint tenants, and for the purposes of the trust, that estate, interest, or right.

(2.) Where a deed by which a retiring trustee is discharged under this Act contains such a declaration as is in this section mentioned by the retiring and continuing trustees, and by the other person, if any empowered to appoint trustees, that declaration shall, without any conveyance or assignment, operate to vest in the continuing trustees alone, as joint tenants, and for the purposes of the trust, the estate, interest, or right to which the declaration relates.

(3.) This section does not extend to any legal estate or interest in copyhold or customary land, or to land conveyed by way of mortgage for securing money subject to the trust, or to any such share, stock, annuity, or property as is only transferable in books kept by a company or other body, or in manner directed by or under Act of Parliament.

(4.) For purposes of registration of the deed in any registry, the person or persons making the declaration shall be deemed the conveying party or parties, and the conveyance shall be deemed to be made by him or them under a power conferred by this Act.

R

Sect. 12. (5.) This section applies only to deeds executed after the thirty-first of December one thousand eight hundred and eighty-one.

Purchase and Sale.

Sect. 13.

Power of trustee for sale to sell by auction, &c.

Section 13.—(1) Where a trust for sale or a power of sale of property is vested in a trustee, he may sell or concur with any other person in selling all or any part of the property, either subject to prior charges or not, and either together or in lots, by public auction or by private contract, subject to any such conditions respecting title or evidence of title or other matter as the trustee thinks fit, with power to vary any contract for sale, and to buy in at any auction, or to rescind any contract for sale and to re-sell, without being answerable for any loss.

(2.) This section applies only if and as far as a contrary intention is not expressed in the instrument creating the trust or power, and shall have effect subject to the terms of that instrument and to the provisions therein contained.

(3.) This section applies only to a trust or power created by an instrument coming into operation after the thirty-first of December one thousand eight hundred and eighty-one.

Sect. 14.

Power to sell subject to depreciatory conditions.

Section 14.—(1.) No sale made by a trustee shall be impeached by any beneficiary upon the ground that any of the conditions subject to which the sale was made may have been unnecessarily depreciatory, unless it also appears that the consideration for the sale was thereby rendered inadequate.

(2.) No sale made by a trustee shall, after the execution of the conveyance, be impeached as against the purchaser upon the ground that any of the conditions subject to which the sale was made may have been unnecessarily depreciatory, unless it appears that the purchaser was acting in collusion with the trustee at the time when the contract for sale was made.

(3.) No purchaser, upon any sale made by a trustee, shall be at liberty to make any objection against the title upon the ground aforesaid.

(4.) This section applies only to sales made after the twenty-fourth day of December one thousand eight hundred and eighty-eight.

Sect. 15.

Power to sell.

Section 15.—A trustee who is either a vendor or a purchaser may sell or buy without excluding the application of section two of the Vendor and Purchaser Act, 1874.

Sect. 16.

Married woman as bare trustee may convey

Section 16.—When any freehold or copyhold hereditament is vested in a married woman as a bare trustee she may convey or surrender it as if she were a *feme sole*.

Various Powers and Liabilities.

Sect. 17.

Power to

Section 17.—(1.) A trustee may appoint a solicitor to be his agent to receive and give a discharge for any money or valuable consideration or property receivable by the trustee under the trust, by permitting the solicitor to have the custody of, and to produce, a deed containing any such receipt as is referred to in section fifty-six of the Conveyancing and Law of Property Act, 1881; and a trustee shall not be chargeable with breach of trust by reason only of his having made or concurred in making any such appointment; and the producing of any such deed by the solicitor shall have the same validity and effect under the said section as if the person appointing the solicitor had not been a trustee.

(2.) A trustee may appoint a banker or solicitor to be his agent to receive and give a discharge for any money payable to the trustee under or by virtue of a policy of assurance, by permitting the banker or solicitor to have the custody of and to produce the policy of assurance with a receipt signed by the trustee, and a trustee shall not be chargeable with a breach of trust by reason only of his having made or concurred in making any such appointment.

(3.) Nothing in this section shall exempt a trustee from any liability which he would have incurred if this Act had not been passed, in case he permits any such money, valuable consideration, or property to remain in the hands or under the control of the banker or solicitor for a period longer than is reasonably necessary to enable the banker or solicitor (as the case may be) to pay or transfer the same to the trustee.

(4.) This section applies only where the money or valuable consideration or property is received after the twenty-fourth day of December one thousand eight hundred and eighty-eight.

(5.) Nothing in this section shall authorise a trustee to do anything which he is in express terms forbidden to do, or to omit anything which he is in express terms directed to do, by the instrument creating the trust.

Section 18.—(1.) A trustee may insure against loss or damage by fire any building or other insurable property to any amount (including the amount of any insurance already on foot) not exceeding three equal fourth parts of the full value of such building or property, and pay the premiums for such insurance out of the income thereof or out of the income of any other property subject to the same trusts, without obtaining the consent of any person who may be entitled wholly or partly to such income.

(2.) This section does not apply to any building or property which a trustee is bound forthwith to convey absolutely to any beneficiary upon being requested to do so.

(3.) This section applies to trusts created either before or after the commencement of this Act, but nothing in this section shall authorise any trustee to do anything which he is in express terms forbidden to do, or to omit to do anything which he is in express terms directed to do, by the instrument creating the trust.

Sect. 17.

authorise receipt of money by banker or solicitor.

Sect. 18.

Power to insure building.

Sect. 19.

Power of
trustees of
renewable
leaseholds
to renew
and raise
money for
the purpose.

Section 19.—(1.) A trustee of any leaseholds for lives or years which are renewable from time to time, either under any covenant or contract, or by custom or usual practice, may, if he thinks fit, and shall, if thereto required by any person having any beneficial interest, present or future, or contingent, in the leaseholds, use his best endeavours to obtain from time to time a renewed lease of the same hereditaments on the accustomed and reasonable terms, and for that purpose may from time to time make or concur in making a surrender of the lease for the time being subsisting, and do all such other acts as are requisite : Provided that, where by the terms of the settlement or will the person in possession for his life or other limited interest is entitled to enjoy the same without any obligation to renew or to contribute to the expense of renewal, this section shall not apply unless the consent in writing of that person is obtained to the renewal on the part of the trustee.

(2.) If money is required to pay for the renewal, the trustee effecting the renewal may pay the same out of any money then in his hands in trust for the persons beneficially interested in the lands to be comprised in the renewed lease, and if he has not in his hands sufficient money for the purpose, he may raise the money required by mortgage of the hereditaments to be comprised in the renewed lease, or of any other hereditaments for the time being subject to the uses or trusts to which those hereditaments are subject, and no person advancing money upon a mortgage purporting to be under this power shall be bound to see that the money is wanted, or that no more is raised than is wanted for the purpose.

(3.) This section applies to trusts created either before or after the commencement of this Act, but nothing in this section shall authorise any trustee to do anything which he is in express terms forbidden to do, or to omit to do anything which he is in express terms directed to do, by the instrument creating the trust.

Section 20.—(1.) The receipt in writing of any trustee for any money, securities, or other personal property or effects payable, transferable, or deliverable to him under any trust or power shall be a sufficient discharge for the same, and shall effectually exonerate the person paying, transferring, or delivering the same from seeing to the application or being answerable for any loss or misapplication thereof.

(2.) This section applies to trusts created either before or after the commencement of this Act.

Section 21.—(1.) An executor or administrator may pay or allow any debt or claim on any evidence that he thinks sufficient.

(2.) An executor or administrator, or two or more trustees, acting together, or a sole acting trustee where by the instrument, if any, creating the trust a sole trustee is authorised to execute the trusts and powers thereof, may, if and as he or they may think fit, accept any composition or any security, real or personal, for any debt or for any property, real or personal, claimed, and may allow any time for payment for any debt, and may compromise, compound, abandon, submit to arbitration, or otherwise settle any debt, account, claim, or thing whatever relating to the testator's or intestate's estate or to the trust, and for any of those purposes may enter into, give, execute, and do such agreements, instruments of composition or arrangement, releases, and other things as to him or them seem expedient, without being responsible for any loss occasioned by any act or thing so done by him or them in good faith.

(3.) This section applies only if and as far as a contrary intention is not expressed in the instrument, if any, creating the trust, and shall have effect subject to the terms of that instrument, and to the provisions therein contained.

(4.) This section applies to executorships, administratorships, and trusts constituted or created either before or after the commencement of this Act.

Section 22.—(1.) Where a power or trust is given to or vested in two or more trustees jointly, then, unless the contrary is expressed in the instrument, if any, creating the power or trust, the same may be exercised or performed by the survivor or survivors of them for the time being.

(2.) This section applies only to trusts constituted after or created by instruments coming into operation after the thirty-first day of December one thousand eight hundred and eighty-one.

Section 23.—A trustee acting or paying money in good faith under or in pursuance of any power of attorney shall not be liable for any such act or payment by reason of the fact that at the time of the payment or act the person who gave the power of attorney was dead or had done some act to avoid the power, if this fact was not known to the trustee at the time of his so acting or paying.

Provided that nothing in this section shall affect the right of any person entitled to the money against the person to whom the payment is made, and that the person so entitled shall have the same remedy against the person to whom the payment is made as he would have had against the trustee.

Section 24.—A trustee shall, without prejudice to the provisions of the instrument, if any, creating the trust, be chargeable only for money and securities actually received by him notwithstanding his signing any receipt for the sake of conformity, and shall be answerable and accountable only for his own acts, receipts, neglects, or defaults, and not for those of any other trustee, nor for any banker, broker, or other person with whom any trust moneys, or securities may be deposited, nor for the insufficiency or deficiency of any securities, nor for any other loss, unless the same happens through his own wilful default; and may reimburse himself, or pay or discharge out of the trust premises, all expenses incurred in or about the execution of his trusts or powers.

PART III.

POWERS OF THE COURT.

Appointment of New Trustees and Vesting Orders.

Sect. 25.

Power of the Court to appoint new trustees.

Section 25.—(1.) The High Court may, whenever it is expedient to appoint a new trustee or new trustees, and it is found inexpedient, difficult, or impracticable so to do without the assistance of the Court, make an order for the appointment of a new trustee or new trustees either in substitution for or in addition to any existing trustee or trustees, or although there is no existing trustee. In particular and without prejudice to the generality of the foregoing provision, the Court may make an order for the appointment of a new trustee in substitution for a trustee who is convicted of felony, or is a bankrupt.

(2.) An order under this section, and any consequential vesting order or conveyance, shall not operate further or otherwise as a discharge to any former or continuing trustee than an appointment of new trustees under any power for that purpose contained in any instrument would have operated.

(3.) Nothing in this section shall give power to appoint an executor or administrator.

Sect. 26.

Vesting orders as to land.

Section 26.—In any of the following cases, namely :—

(i.) Where the High Court appoints or has appointed a new trustee; and

(ii.) Where a trustee entitled to or possessed of any land, or entitled to a contingent right therein, either solely or jointly with any other person,—
    (*a*) is an infant, or
    (*b*) is out of the jurisdiction of the High Court, or
    (*c*) cannot be found; and

(iii.) Where it is uncertain who was the survivor of two or more trustees jointly entitled to or possessed of any land; and

(iv.) Where, as to the last trustee known to have been entitled to or possessed of any land, it is uncertain whether he is living or dead; and

(v.) Where there is no heir or personal representative to a trustee who was entitled to or possessed of land and has died intestate as to that land, or where it is uncertain who is the heir or personal representative or devisee of a trustee who was entitled to or possessed of land and is dead; and

(vi.) Where a trustee jointly or solely entitled to or possessed of any land, or entitled to a contingent right therein, has been required, by or on behalf of a person entitled to require a conveyance of the land or a release of the right, to convey the land or to release the right, and has wilfully refused or neglected to convey the land or release the right for twenty-eight days after the date of the requirement;

the High Court may make an order (in this Act called a vesting order) vesting the land in any such person in any such manner and for any such estate as the Court may direct, or releasing or disposing of the contingent right to such person as the Court may direct.

Provided that—

    (*a*) Where the order is consequential on the appointment of a new trustee the land shall be vested for such estate as the Court may direct in the persons who on the appointment are the trustees; and

    (*b*) Where the order relates to a trustee entitled jointly with another person, and such trustee is out of the jurisdiction of the High Court or cannot be found, the land or right shall be vested in such other person, either alone or with some other person.

Section 27.—Where any land is subject to a contingent right in an unborn person or class of unborn persons who, on coming into existence would, in respect thereof, become entitled to or possessed of the land on any trust, the High Court may make an order releasing the land from the contingent right, or may make an order vesting in any person the estate to or of which the unborn person or class of unborn persons would, on coming into existence, be entitled or possessed in the land.

Section 28.—Where any person entitled to or possessed of land, or entitled to a contingent right in land, by way of security for money, is an infant, the High Court may make an order vesting or releasing or disposing of the land or right in like manner as in the case of an infant trustee.

Section 29—Where a mortgagee of land has died without having entered into the possession or into the receipt of the rents and profits thereof, and the money due in respect of the mortgage has been paid to a person entitled to receive the same, or that last-mentioned person consents to any order for the reconveyance of the land, then the High Court may make an order vesting the land in such person or persons in such manner and for such estate as the Court may direct in any of the following cases, namely:—

    (*a*) Where an heir or personal representative or devisee of the mortgagee is out of the jurisdiction of the High Court or cannot be found; and

    (*b*) Where an heir or personal representative or devisee of the mortgagee on demand made by or on behalf of a person entitled to require a conveyance of the land has stated in writing that he will not convey the same or does not convey the same for the space of twenty-eight days next after a proper deed for conveying the land has been tendered to him by or on behalf of the person so entitled; and

Sect. 29.

    (c) Where it is uncertain which of several devisees of the mortgagee was the survivor; and

    (d) Where it is uncertain as to the survivor of several devisees of the mortgagee or as to the heir or personal representative of the mortgagee whether he is living or dead; and

    (e) Where there is no heir or personal representative to a mortgagee who has died intestate as to the land, or where the mortgagee has died and it is uncertain who is his heir or personal representative or devisee.

Sect. 30.

Vesting order consequential on judgment for sale or mortgage of land.

Section 30.—Where any Court gives a judgment or makes an order directing the sale or mortgage of any land, every person who is entitled to or possessed of the land, or entitled to a contingent right therein as heir, or under the will of a deceased person for payment of whose debts the judgment was given or order made, and is a party to the action or proceeding in which the judgment or order is given or made or is otherwise bound by the judgment or order, shall be deemed to be so entitled or possessed, as the case may be, as a trustee within the meaning of this Act; and the High Court may, if it thinks expedient, make an order vesting the land or any part thereof for such estate as that Court thinks fit in the purchaser or mortgagee or in any other person.

Sect. 31.

Vesting order consequential on judgment for specific performance, &c

Section 31.—Where a judgment is given for the specific performance of a contract concerning any land, or for the partition, or sale in lieu of partition, or exchange, of any land, or generally where any judgment is given for the conveyance of any land either in cases arising out of the doctrine of election or otherwise, the High Court may declare that any of the parties to the action are trustees of the land or any part thereof within the meaning of this Act, or may declare that the interests of unborn persons who might claim under any party to the action, or under the will or voluntary settlement of any person deceased who was during his lifetime a party to the contract or transactions concerning which the judgment is given, are the interests of persons who, on coming into existence, would be trustees within the meaning of this Act, and thereupon the High Court may make a vesting order relating to the rights of those persons, born and unborn, as if they had been trustees.

Sect. 32.

Effect of vesting order.

Section 32.—A vesting order under any of the foregoing provisions shall in the case of a vesting order consequential on the appointment of a new trustee, have the same effect as if the persons who before the appointment were the trustees (if any) had duly executed all proper conveyances of the land for such estate as the High Court directs,   there is no such person, or no such person of full capacity, as if such person had existed and been of full capacity and had duly executed all proper conveyances of the land for such estate as the Court directs, and shall in every other case have the same effect as if

the trustee or other person or description or class of persons to Sect. 32.
whose rights or supposed rights the said provisions respectively
relate had been an ascertained and existing person of full
capacity, and had executed a conveyance or release to the effect
intended by the order.

Section 33.—In all cases where a vesting order can be made Sect. 33.
under any of the foregoing provisions, the High Court may, if
it is more convenient, appoint a person to convey the land or Power to
release the contingent right, and a conveyance or release by appoint
that person in conformity with the order shall have the same person to
effect as an order under the appropriate provision. convey.

Section 34.—(1.) Where an order vesting copyhold land in Sect. 34
any person is made under this Act with the consent of the lord
or lady of the manor, the land shall vest accordingly without Effect of
surrender or admittance. vesting order
(2.) Where an order is made under this Act appointing any as to copy-
person to convey any copyhold land, that person shall execute hold.
and do all assurances and things for completing the assurance
of the land; and the lord and lady of the manor and every
other person shall, subject to the customs of the manor and the
usual payments, be bound to make admittance to the land and
to do all other acts for completing the assurance thereof, as if
the persons in whose place an appointment is made were free
from disability and had executed and done those assurances and
things.

Section 35.—(1.) In any of the following cases, namely :— Sect. 35.
  (i.) Where the High Court appoints or has appointed a
      new trustee; and Vesting
  (ii.) Where a trustee entitled alone or jointly with another orders as to
      person to stock or to a chose in action— stock and
        (a) is an infant, or choses in
        (b) is out of the jurisdiction of the High Court, or action.
        (c) cannot be found; or
        (d) neglects or refuses to transfer stock or receive
            the dividends or income thereof, or to sue
            for or recover a chose in action, according
            to the direction of the person absolutely
            entitled thereto for twenty-eight days next
            after a request in writing has been made
            to him by the person so entitled; or
        (e) neglects or refuses to transfer stock or receive
            the dividends or income thereof, or to sue
            for or recover a chose in action for twenty-
            eight days next after an order of the High
            Court for that purpose has been served on
            him; or
  (iii.) Where it is uncertain whether a trustee entitled alone
      or jointly with another person to stock or to a chose
      in action is alive or dead,

Sect. 35.

the High Court may make an order vesting the right to transfer or call for a transfer of stock, or to receive the dividends or income thereof, or to sue for or recover a chose in action, in any such person as the Court may appoint:

Provided that—

(a) Where the order is consequential on the appointment by the Court of a new trustee, the right shall be vested in the persons who, on the appointment, are the trustees; and

(b) Where the person whose right is dealt with by the order was entitled jointly with another person, the right shall be vested in that last-mentioned person either alone or jointly with any other person whom the Court may appoint.

(2.) In all cases where a vesting order can be made under this section, the Court may, if it is more convenient, appoint some proper person to make or join in making the transfer.

(3) The person in whom the right to transfer or call for the transfer of any stock is vested by an order of the Court under this Act, may transfer the stock to himself or any other person, according to the order, and the Banks of England and Ireland and all other companies shall obey every order under this section according to its tenor.

(4.) After notice in writing of an order under this section it shall not be lawful for the Bank of England or of Ireland or any other company to transfer any stock to which the order relates or to pay any dividends thereon except in accordance with the order.

(5.) The High Court may make declarations and give directions concerning the manner in which the right to any stock or chose in action vested under the provisions of this Act is to be exercised.

(6.) The provisions of this Act as to vesting orders shall apply to shares in ships registered under the Acts relating to merchant shipping as if they were stock.

Sect. 36.

Persons entitled to apply for orders.

Section 36.—(1) An order under this Act for the appointment of a new trustee or concerning any land, stock, or chose in action subject to a trust, may be made on the application of any person beneficially interested in the land, stock, or chose in action, whether under disability or not, or on the application of any person duly appointed trustee thereof.

(2.) An order under this Act concerning any land, stock, or chose in action subject to a mortgage may be made on the application of any person beneficially interested in the equity of redemption, whether under disability or not, or of any person interested in the money secured by the mortgage.

Sect. 37.

Powers of new trustee appointed by Court.

Section 37.—Every trustee appointed by a Court of competent jurisdiction shall, as well before as after the trust property becomes by law, or by assurance, or otherwise, vested in him, have the same powers, authorities, and discretions, and may in all respects act as if he had been originally appointed a trustee by the instrument, if any, creating the trust.

Sect. 37.

Section 38.—The High Court may order the costs and expenses of and incident to any application for an order appointing a new trustee, or for a vesting order, or of and incident to any such order, or any conveyance or transfer in pursuance thereof, to be paid or raised out of the land or personal estate in respect whereof the same is made, or out of the income thereof, or to be borne and paid in such manner and by such persons as to the Court may seem just.

Sect. 38.

Power to charge costs on trust estate

Section 39.—The powers conferred by this Act as to vesting orders may be exercised for vesting any land, stock, or chose in action in any trustee of a charity or society over which the High Court would have jurisdiction upon action duly instituted, whether the appointment of the trustee was made by instrument under a power or by the High Court under its general or statutory jurisdiction.

Sect. 39.

Trustees of charities

Section 40.—Where a vesting order is made as to any land under this Act or under the Lunacy Act, 1890, or under any Act relating to lunacy in Ireland, founded on an allegation of the personal incapacity of a trustee or mortgagee, or on an allegation that a trustee or the heir or personal representative or devisee of a mortgagee is out of the jurisdiction of the High Court or cannot be found, or that it is uncertain which of several trustees or which of several devisees of a mortgagee was the survivor, or whether the last trustee or the heir or personal representative or last surviving devisee of a mortgagee is living or dead, or on an allegation that any trustee or mortgagee has died intestate without an heir or has died and it is not known who is his heir or personal representative or devisee, the fact that the order has been so made shall be conclusive evidence of the matter so alleged in any Court upon any question as to the validity of the order, but this section shall not prevent the High Court from directing a reconveyance or the payment of costs occasioned by any such order if improperly obtained.

Sect. 40.

Orders made upon certain allegations to be conclusive evidence.

Section 41.—The powers of the High Court in England to make vesting orders under this Act shall extend to all land and personal estate in Her Majesty's dominions, except Scotland.

Sect. 41.

Application of vesting order to land out of England.

Payment into Court by Trustees.

Section 42.—(1.) Trustees, or the majority of trustees, having in their hands or under their control money or securities belonging to a trust, may pay the same into the High Court; and the same shall, subject to rules of Court, be dealt with according to the orders of the High Court.

(2.) The receipt or certificate of the proper officer shall be

Sect. 42.

Payment into Court by trustees.

Sect. 42. a sufficient discharge to trustees for the money or securities so paid into Court.

(3.) Where any moneys or securities are vested in any persons as trustees, and the majority are desirous of paying the same into Court, but the concurrence of the other or others cannot be obtained, the High Court may order the payment into Court to be made by the majority without the concurrence of the other or others; and where any such moneys or securities are deposited with any banker, broker, or other depositary, the Court may order payment or delivery of the moneys or securities to the majority of the trustees for the purpose of payment into Court, and every transfer, payment, and delivery made in pursuance of any such order shall be valid and take effect as if the same had been made on the authority or by the act of all the persons entitled to the moneys and securities so transferred, paid, or delivered.

Miscellaneous.

Sect. 43.

Power to give judgment in absence of a trustee.

Section 43.—Where in an action the High Court is satisfied that diligent search has been made for any person who, in the character of trustee, is made a defendant in any action, to serve him with a process of the Court, and that he cannot be found, the Court may hear and determine the action and give judgment therein against that person in his character of a trustee, as if he had been duly served, or had entered an appearance in the action, and had also appeared by his counsel and solicitor at the hearing, but without prejudice to any interest he may have in the matters in question in the action in any other character.

Sect. 44.

Power to sanction sale of land or minerals separately

Section 44.—(1.) Where a trustee is for the time being authorised to dispose of land by way of sale, exchange, partition, or enfranchisement, the High Court may sanction his so disposing of the land with an exception or reservation of any minerals, and with or without rights and powers of or incidental to the working, getting, or carrying away of the minerals, or so disposing of the minerals, with or without the said rights or powers, separately from the residue of the land.

(2.) Any such trustee, with the said sanction previously obtained, may, unless forbidden by the instrument creating the trust or direction, from time to time, without any further application to the Court, so dispose of any such land or minerals.

(3.) Nothing in this section shall derogate from any power which a trustee may have under the Settled Land Acts, 1882 to 1890, or otherwise.

Sect. 45.

Power to make beneficiary

Section 45.—(1.) Where a trustee commits a breach of trust at the instigation or request or with the consent in writing of a beneficiary, the High Court may, if it thinks fit, and notwithstanding that the beneficiary may be a married woman entitled

for her separate use and restrained from anticipation, make $\quad$ Sect. 45.
such order as to the Court seems just, for impounding all or
any part of the interest f the beneficiary in the trust estate $\quad$ indemnify for
by way of indemnity to the trustee or person claiming $\quad$ breach of
through him. $\quad$ trust.

(2.) This section shall apply to breaches of trust committed
as well before as after the passing of this Act, but shall not
apply so as to prejudice any question in an action or other
proceeding which was pending on the twenty-fourth day of
December one thousand eight hundred and eighty-eight, and is
pending at the commencement of this Act.

Section 46.—The provisions of this Act with respect to the $\quad$ Sect. 46.
High Court shall, in their application to cases within the
jurisdiction of a Palatine Court or County Court, include that $\quad$ Jurisdiction
Court, and the procedure under this Act in Palatine Courts and $\quad$ of Palatine
County Courts shall be in accordance with the Acts and rules $\quad$ and County
regulating the procedure of those Courts. $\quad$ Courts.

PART IV.

MISCELLANEOUS AND SUPPLEMENTAL.

Section 47.—(1.) All the powers and provisions contained $\quad$ Sect. 47.
in this Act with reference to the appointment of new trustees,
and the discharge and retirement of trustees, are to apply to $\quad$ Application
and include trustees for the purposes of the Settled Land Acts, $\quad$ to trustees
1882 to 1890, whether appointed by the Court or by the $\quad$ under Settled
settlement, or under provisions contained in the settlement. $\quad$ Land Acts
$\qquad$ of provisions
(2.) This section applies and is to have effect with respect $\quad$ as to appoint-
to an appointment or a discharge and retirement of trustees $\quad$ ment of
taking place before as well as after the commencement of $\quad$ trustees.
this Act.

(3.) This section is not to render invalid or prejudice any
appointment or any discharge and retirement of trustees effected
before the passing of this Act, otherwise than under the
provisions of the Conveyancing and Law of Property Act,
1881.

Section 48—Property vested in any person on any trust or $\quad$ Sect. 48.
by way of mortgage shall not, in case of that person becoming
a convict within the meaning of the Forfeiture Act, 1870, vest $\quad$ Trust estates
in any such administrator as may be appointed under that Act, $\quad$ not affected
but shall remain in the trustee or mortgagee, or survive to his $\quad$ by trustee
co-trustee or descend to his representative as if he had not $\quad$ becoming a
become a convict; provided that this enactment shall not affect $\quad$ convict.
the title to the property so far as relates to any beneficial
interest therein of any such trustee or mortgagee.

Sect. 49.

Indemnity.

Section 49.—This Act, and every order purporting to be made under this Act, shall be a complete indemnity to the Banks of England and Ireland, and to all persons for any acts done pursuant thereto; and it shall not be necessary for the Bank or for any person to inquire concerning the propriety of the order, or whether the Court by which it was made had jurisdiction to make the same.

Sect. 50.

Definitions

Section 50.—In this Act, unless the context otherwise requires—

The expression " bankrupt " includes, in Ireland, insolvent:

The expression " contingent right," as applied to land, includes a contingent or executory interest, a possibility coupled with an interest, whether the object of the gift or limitation of the interest, or possibility is or is not ascertained, also a right of entry, whether immediate or future, and whether vested or contingent:

The expressions " convey " and " conveyance " applied to any person include the execution by that person of every necessary or suitable assurance for conveying, assigning appointing, surrendering, or otherwise transferring or disposing of land whereof he is seised or possessed, or wherein he is entitled to a contingent right, either for his whole estate or for any less estate, together with the performance of all formalities required by law to the validity of the conveyance, including the acts to be performed by married women and tenants in tail in accordance with the provisions of the Acts for abolition of fines and recoveries in England and Ireland respectively, and also including surrenders and other acts which a tenant of customary or copyhold lands can himself perform preparatory to or in aid of a complete assurance of the customary or copyhold land:

The expression " devisee " includes the heir of a devisee and the devisee of an heir, and any person who may claim right by devolution of title of a similar description:

The expression " instrument " includes Act of Parliament:

The expression " land " includes manors and lordships, and reputed manors and lordships, and incorporeal as well as corporeal hereditaments, and any interest therein, and also an undivided share of land:

The expressions " mortgage " and " mortgagee " include and relate to every estate and interest regarded in equity as merely a security for money, and every person deriving title under the original mortgagee:

The expressions " pay " and " payment " as applied in relation to stocks and securities, and in connection with the expression " into Court," include the deposit or transfer of the same in or into Court:

The expression " possessed " applies to receipt of income of, and to any vested estate less than a life estate, legal or equitable, in possession or in expectancy, in, any land:

The expression "property" includes real and personal property, and any estate or interest in any property, real or personal, and any debt, and any thing in action, and any other right or interest, whether in possession or not:

The expression "rights" includes estates and interests:

The expression "securities" includes stocks, funds, and shares; and so far as relates to payments into Court has the same meaning as in the Court of Chancery (Funds) Act, 1872:

The expression "stock" includes fully paid up shares; and, so far as relates to vesting orders made by the Court under this Act, includes any fund, annuity, or security transferable in books kept by any company or society, or by instrument of transfer either alone or accompanied by other formalities, and any share or interest therein:

The expression "transfer," in relation to stock, includes the performance and execution of every deed, power of attorney, act, and thing on the part of the transferor to effect and complete the title in the transferee:

The expression "trust" does not include the duties incident to an estate conveyed by way of mortgage; but with this exception the expressions "trust" and "trustee" include implied and constructive trusts, and cases where the trustee has a beneficial interest in the trust property, and the duties incident to the office of personal representative of a deceased person.

Section 51.—The Acts mentioned in the Schedule to this Act are hereby repealed except as to Scotland to the extent mentioned in the third column of that schedule.

Section 52.—This Act does not extend to Scotland.

Section 53.—This Act may be cited as the Trustee Act, 1893.

Section 54.—This Act shall come into operation on the first day of January one thousand eight hundred and ninety-four.

Sect. 50

Sect. 51.

Repeal.

Sect. 52.

Extent of Act.

Sect. 53.

Short title.

Sect. 54.

Commencement.

SCHEDULE.

Session and Chapter.	Title or Short Title.	Extent of Repeal.
36 Geo 3. c. 52	The Legacy Duty Act, 1796	Section thirty-two.
9 & 10 Vict. c. 101	The Public Money Drainage Act, 1846	Section thirty-seven.
10 & 11 Vict. c. 32	The Landed Property Improvement (Ireland) Act, 1847	Section fifty-three.
10 & 11 Vict. c. 96	An Act for better securing trust funds, and for the relief of trustees	The whole Act.
11 & 12 Vict. c. 68	An Act for extending to Ireland an Act passed in the last session of Parliament, entitled "An Act for better securing trust funds, and for the relief of trustees"	The whole Act.
12 & 13 Vict. c. 74	An Act for the further relief of trustees	The whole Act.
13 & 14 Vict. c. 60	The Trustee Act, 1850	Sections seven to nineteen, twenty-two to twenty-five, twenty-nine, thirty-two to thirty-six, forty-six, forty-seven, forty-nine, fifty-four and fifty-five; also the residue of the Act except so far as relates to the Court exercising jurisdiction in lunacy in Ireland.
15 & 16 Vict. c. 55	The Trustee Act, 1852	Sections one to five, eight, and nine, also the residue of the Act except so far as relates to the Court exercising jurisdiction in lunacy in Ireland.
17 & 18 Vict. c. 82	The Court of Chancery of Lancaster Act, 1854	Section eleven
18 & 19 Vict. c 91	The Merchant Shipping Act Amendment Act, 1855	Section ten, except so far as relates to the Court exercising jurisdiction in lunacy in Ireland
20 & 21 Vict. c. 60	The Irish Bankrupt and Insolvent Act, 1857	Section three hundred and twenty-one.
22 & 23 Vict. c. 35	The Law of Property Amendment Act, 1859	Sections twenty-six, thirty and thirty-one.
23 & 24 Vict. c. 38	The Law of Property Amendment Act, 1860	Section nine.

Session and Chapter.	Title or Short Title	Extent of Repeal.
25 & 26 Vict. c. 108	An Act to confirm certain sales, exchanges, partitions, and enfranchisements by trustees and others	The whole Act.
26 & 27 Vict. c. 73	An Act to give further facilities to the holders of Indian stock	Section four.
27 & 28 Vict. c. 114	The Improvement of Land Act, 1864	Section sixty so far as it relates to trustees; and section sixty-one.
28 & 29 Vict. c. 78	The Mortgage Debenture Act, 1865	Section forty.
31 & 32 Vict. c. 40	The Partition Act, 1868	Section seven.
33 & 34 Vict. c. 71	The National Debt Act, 1870	Section twenty-nine.
34 & 35 Vict. c. 27	The Debenture Stock Act, 1871	The whole Act.
37 & 38 Vict. c. 78	The Vendor and Purchaser Act, 1874	Sections three and six.
38 & 39 Vict. c. 83	The Local Loans Act, 1875	Sections twenty-one and twenty-seven.
40 & 41 Vict. c. 59	The Colonial Stock Act, 1877	Section twelve.
43 & 44 Vict. c. 8	The Isle of Man Loans Act, 1880	Section seven, so far as it relates to trustees.
44 & 45 Vict. c. 41	The Conveyancing and Law of Property Act, 1881	Sections thirty-one to thirty-eight.
45 & 46 Vict. c. 39	The Conveyancing Act, 1882	Section five.
46 & 47 Vict. c. 52	The Bankruptcy Act, 1883	Section one hundred and forty-seven.
51 & 52 Vict. c. 59	The Trustee Act, 1888	The whole Act, except sections one and eight.
52 & 53 Vict. c. 32	The Trust Investment Act, 1889	The whole Act, except sections one and seven
52 & 53 Vict. c. 47	The Palatine Court of Durham Act, 1889	Section eight.
53 & 54 Vict. c. 5	The Lunacy Act, 1890	Section one hundred and forty.
53 & 54 Vict. c. 69	The Settled Land Act, 1890	Section seventeen
55 & 56 Vict. c. 13	The Conveyancing and Law of Property Act, 1892	Section six.

S

INDEX.

THE END.

PRINTED BY WILLIAM CLOWES AND SONS, LIMITED, LONDON AND BECCLES.

Lightning Source UK Ltd.
Milton Keynes UK
UKHW031913130819
347826UK00023B/890/P

9 781240 113798